UNDERSTANDING THERAPEUTIC ACTION

Psychodynamic Concepts of Cure

Psychoanalytic Inquiry Book Series

Volume 15

Psychoanalytic Inquiry Book Series

UNDERSTANDING

THERAPEUTIC ACTION

Psychodynamic Concepts of Cure

edited by

LAWRENCE E. LIFSON

THE ANALYTIC PRESS

1996   Hillsdale, NJ   London

Published by
The Analytic Press, Inc.
   Editorial Offices: 101 West Street
   Hillsdale, New Jersey 07642

Typeset by AeroType, Inc.

Library of Congress Cataloging-in-Publication Data

Understanding therapeutic action: psychodynamic concepts of cure /
   Lawrence E. Lifson, editor.
       p.   cm. — (Psychoanalytic inquiry book series : v. 15)
       Includes bibliographical references and index.
       ISBN 0-88163-205-8
       1. Psychodynamic psychotherapy.   2. Personality change.   I. Lifson,
   Lawrence E.   II. Series.
       [DNLM: 1. Psychoanalytic Therapy—Methods.   2. Psychoanalytic Theory.
   W 1   PS427F   v. 15   1996 / WM 460.6   U55   1996]
   RC489.P72U53   1996
   616.89′14—dc20
   DNLM/DLC
   for Library of Congress   95-35827
                                                                            CIP

Printed in the United States of America
10 9 8 7 6 5 4 3 2 1

This book is dedicated in loving memory to Davide Limentani, M.D. and James Mann, M.D., who were two of my cherished teachers, colleagues, and friends.

Contents

III.   An Integrative Approach to the Concept of Cure

Contributors

Gerald Adler, M.D., Training and Supervising Analyst, Boston Psychoanalytic Society and Institute; Faculty, Boston Psychoanalytic Institute; President, Boston Psychoanalytic Society and Institute.

Anne Alonso, Ph.D., Associate Clinical Professor of Psychology, Department of Psychiatry, Harvard Medical School/Massachusetts General Hospital; Director, The Center for Psychoanalytic Studies, Massachusetts General Hospital.

George G. Fishman, M.D., Instructor in Psychiatry, Harvard Medical School; Training and Supervising Analyst, Boston Psychoanalytic Society and Institute; Faculty and Supervising Analyst, Massachusetts Institute for Psychoanalysis; Director of Psychotherapy Training, Beth Israel Hospital.

James M. Herzog, M.D., Assistant Professor of Psychiatry, Harvard Medical School; Senior Scholar, Children's Hospital Medical Center; Psychoanalytic Scholar, Beth Israel Hospital; Training and Supervisory Analyst and Child and Adolescent Supervisory Analyst, Boston Psychoanalytic Society and Institute; Faculty, Massachusetts Institute for Psychoanalysis.

Otto F. Kernberg, M.D., Professor of Psychiatry, Cornell University Medical College; Training and Supervising Analyst, Columbia University Center for Psychoanalytic Training and Research; Director, Personality Disorders Institute, The New York Hospital-Cornell Medical Center, Westchester Division.

Joseph D. Lichtenberg, M.D., Clinical Professor of Psychiatry, Georgetown University School of Medicine; Founding Member and Director, Institute of Contemporary Psychotherapy; Editor-in-Chief, *Psychoanalytic Inquiry.*

Lawrence E. Lifson, M.D. (Editor), Lecturer on Psychiatry, Harvard Medical School; Associate Clinical Professor of Psychiatry, Tufts University

ix

School of Medicine; Faculty, Boston Psychoanalytic Institute; Director, Continuing Education Program, Massachusetts Mental Health Center.

William W. Meissner, S.J., M.D., University Professor of Psychoanalysis, Boston College; Training and Supervising Analyst, Boston Psychoanalytic Institute and Society.

Stephen A. Mitchell, Ph.D., Training and Supervising Analyst, William Alanson White Institute; Faculty, New York University Postdoctoral Program; Editor, *Psychoanalytic Dialogues*.

Arnold H. Modell, M.D., Clinical Professor of Psychiatry, Harvard Medical School; Training and Supervising Analyst, Boston Psychoanalytic Society and Institute.

Anna Ornstein, M.D., Professor of Child Psychiatry and Codirector of the International Center for the Study of Psychoanalytic Self Psychology, Department of Psychiatry, University of Cincinnati School of Medicine.

Paul H. Ornstein, M.D., Professor of Psychoanalysis and Codirector of the International Center for the Study of Psychoanalytic Self Psychology, Department of Psychiatry, University of Cincinnati School of Medicine. Editor, *The Search for the Self*.

Paul L. Russell, M.D., Clinical Instructor in Psychiatry, Harvard Medical School; Associate Psychiatrist, Beth Israel Hospital; Faculty, Boston Psychoanalytic Institute; Faculty and Supervising Analyst, Massachusetts Institute for Psychoanalysis.

Martha Stark, M.D., Lecturer on Psychiatry, Harvard Medical School; Faculty, Boston Psychoanalytic Institute; Faculty and Supervising Analyst, Massachusetts Institute for Psychoanalysis.

Judith Guss Teicholz, Ed.D., Clinical Instructor of Psychology, Department of Psychiatry, Harvard Medical School; Faculty and Supervising Analyst, Massachusetts Institute of Psychoanalysis.

Preface

A s Director of the Continuing Education Program at the Massachusetts Mental Health Center and Chairman of Continuing Education at the Boston Psychoanalytic Society and Institute, I have had the good fortune to be associated with many of the leading thinkers and teachers of psychodynamic psychotherapy. These highly respected theoreticians and clinicians represent the spectrum of varying psychodynamic persuasions. Rarely, however, did they present and debate their points of view at the same conference. Martha Stark, M.D., Director of the Continuing Education Program at Three Ripley Street, Newton Centre, Massachusetts, and I decided to collaborate on a conference that would bring together many of these gifted teachers in the hope of elucidating a comprehensive overview and synthesis of the different models of the therapeutic action of psychodynamic psychotherapy. We believed that such an approach needed to take into consideration structural conflict, structural deficit, and relational conflict. In so doing, we would enable psychodynamic psychotherapists to integrate a contemporary model of therapeutic action leading to cure.

It quickly became apparent, however, that such a conference would serve primarily as an exciting catalyst for the exploration of the curative factors in psychodynamic psychotherapy. To provide practicing clinicians with a truly comprehensive and integrative approach to the therapeutic action of psychodynamic psychotherapy, something more would be required. Martha Stark quickly convinced me that each of our speakers should contribute an original chapter to a book that would flow from themes expressed in such a conference. We then invited many of the leading theoreticians and clinicians of different psychodynamic persuasions both to present their ideas of the curative process at our conference and to contribute an original chapter to a book that would represent and elucidate their points of view.

Gerald Adler, M.D., George G. Fishman, M.D., James M. Herzog, M.D., Otto F. Kernberg, M.D., Joseph D. Lichtenberg, M.D., Stephen A. Mitchell, Ph.D., Arnold H. Modell, M.D., Anna Ornstein, M.D., Paul H. Ornstein, M.D., Paul L. Russell, M.D., Judith Guss Teicholz, Ed.D., and Martha Stark, M.D. participated in an electrifying two-day conference moderated by Sheldon Roth, M.D. and James Barron, Ph.D. The presenters expounded on their models of treatment at this conference and contributed original chapters that carefully define and elaborate their understanding of the curative factors in psychodynamic psychotherapy. Anne Alonso, Ph.D. and William W. Meissner, M.D. were unable to participate at the conference but did contribute chapters to this volume.

I wish to extend my heartfelt appreciation to all the contributors to this book. It was a privilege for me to have them participate in this endeavor. I would like especially to mention three of the contributors. Joseph D. Lichtenberg, M.D. provided encouragement and support in the early stages of this book. George G. Fishman, M.D. was always helpful and thoughtful in sharing his wise counsel and suggestions about innumerable aspects of this book. His friendship has remained a treasure to me. In many ways, I regard Martha Stark, M.D. as the inspiration behind this book. Although she was unable to join me as a coeditor, she nevertheless unfailingly gave me the benefit of her advice, assistance, and creative abilities. I would also like to note the help provided by Paul E. Stepansky, Ph.D. and his able staff at The Analytic Press. When I presented the early form of this book to Paul and expressed some doubt about pursuing the project, he softly remarked, "This is a book that should be done." His words of encouragement buoyed me during the more difficult times of bringing this book to press. Jean Fierro, my administrator, effectively aided me in the many matters required to ready a book for publication. Lastly, I wish to acknowledge the constant support and love of my family—my parents, Irving and Eva Lifson, my wife, Marcie, and my children, Deborah and Jennifer. They all have enriched my life and provided me with sustaining love and happiness.

I

Therapeutic Structure and Structural Change

1

Toward a New Understanding of Neutrality

Anne Alonso

Neutrality ranks high among the more challenging concepts in psychoanalysis. The word itself has generated confusion about the analytic stance and has preoccupied thinkers from the beginning of psychoanalysis. For a whole host of reasons, which I will try to address in this chapter, it is timely now to reexamine the concept of neutrality. In particular, I mean to apply the concept of neutrality to psychoanalytic psychotherapy, rather than classical analysis (where the idea began) in the hope that this will shed some light on some of the new thinking that informs our techniques. The past few decades have ushered in some changes in clinical practice that have extended the application of the psychoanalytic model beyond classical dyadic psychoanalysis. In addition to individual psychoanalytic psychotherapy, clinicians are now applying the same dynamic principles to group psychotherapy, family psychotherapy, short-term therapy, inpatient treatment, and partial hospitalizations. Recent attention to the needs of population-specific or symptom-specific patients confounds the goals and methods of the therapeutic endeavor, and threatens to further confuse any understanding of neutrality. The emergence of a variety of theories and therapies calls for a more precise description and rationale for the basic assumptions of psychoanalytic theory, including reliance on neutrality and transference resolution.

The cornerstones of psychoanalysis remain as valuable and effective as they ever were, and neutrality is a prime example of an idea that is fundamental yet ambiguous enough to challenge even the "truest believers" among us. It is incumbent upon those of us who practice psychoanalytic psychotherapy to offer perspectives that reexamine our technique and its rationale—lest we risk throwing out the baby with the bathwater. One way to respond is to be clearer about some of our murkier and more provocative concepts, foremost among which is the relevance of neutrality.

This chapter will focus on what neutrality is, discuss the various meanings of neutrality as we have come to articulate them at the end of the 20th century, and examine some useful forms and applications of neutrality to the theory and technique of psychoanalytic psychotherapy.

Neutrality is a burdened term and one that has historically been the source of mocking and angry diatribes. For example, Wachtel (1986), in decrying the problems of defining neutrality in a useful way, suggests that "the ideas and practices associated with so-called neutrality are deeply flawed and . . . we would do well to relinquish our ties to that particular attempted solution to the hazards of doing psychoanalytic therapy" (p. 60).

Hoffer (1985), in speaking to the difficulty of even arriving at a definition of neutrality, points out that "The word raises a fundamental question for the analyst: 'Are genuine involvement with another person and honest neutrality somehow antithetical?' " (p. 772).

The ambiguity is further seen in attempts to define neutrality by saying what it is *not*. We therapists read that it is not indifference, coldness, remoteness, blandness, an armed truce, or a lack of concern for and devotion to the patient. It is further described as not taking action when abstaining is better; such a response is appropriate, not making judgments—or at least not imposing them on the patient, and not giving advice.

Many of the current challenges to the concept of neutrality echo the historic debates in the psychoanalytic literature. These debates are far ranging, and are implicit in almost any writing on analytic technique. Any consideration of transference and counter-transference has at its roots some assumptions about the neutrality of the analyst, without which the emergence and resolution of the transference neurosis is precluded and the analyst's countertransference becomes a dangerous and out-of-control variable leading to potential damage to the patient. For the purposes of this chapter, I will organize the discussion around three aspects of the literature concerning neutrality:

1. the differences between drive theorists and relational theorists
2. the question of safety
3. the curative factors in psychoanalytic theory and the place of neutrality in them

DRIVE-STRUCTURE VERSUS RELATIONAL-FIELD THEORIES

One group of controversies centers around the differences between a drive-structure model of development and a relational-structure model (Greenberg, 1986, p. 88). Greenberg describes the drive-structure model as a one-person psychology that understands structure as the transformation of original drive energies. These drives seek a target and the repressed conflicts that ensue in the course of development lead to the neurotic symptomatology that brings the patient to treatment. In contrast, the relational-structure model shows development as the sequelae of early interpersonal exchanges. The introjected, partially transformed internalizations of these early exchanges determine how the individual develops in the matrix of his or her future relationships, and the basic assumptions that the patient brings to "current realities are embedded in these part-object representations from a dimly remembered or repressed past" (Greenberg, 1986, p. 92). Greenberg goes on to elaborate that the drive-structure theory has at its roots a Cartesian ideal of impersonal observation from outside the observational field, whereas the relational-structure model is a field structure, and is informed by Heisenberg's uncertainty principle and Einstein's theory of relativity (Greenberg, 1986, p. 94). Each of these models prescribes a direction for the analyst's position vis-à-vis the value and form of neutrality. It follows then that in the drive-structure model, the concepts of "evenly hovering attention" (Freud, 1912), "blank screen," "reflecting mirror," and "surgical detachment" are all appropriate prescriptions for the analyst as external observer. Another theorist from this side of the debate is Anna Freud (1936), who articulated the most commonly accepted definition of neutrality as a position of "equidistance from id, ego, and superego." Glover (1955) expresses his belief that any activity beyond interpretation on the part of the analysts leads to the abandonment of neutrality. Before long, the idea of neutrality was extended to include the analyst's own experience, though always with an eye to keeping him or her from interfering with the analytic field. Fliess (1942) and Hartmann (1954) represent this camp. Eventually Freud moved toward a relational theory, and this move was to be the thrust of the English school of object relations theory (Klein, Fairbairn, Winnicott, Guntrip, and in this country, Sullivan and Havens). From the relational model there emerge concepts such as Sullivan's (1954) "participant observation" and Fairbairn's "analyst as interventionist" (1952). Greenberg and Mitchell (1983) and Greenberg (1986) argue that there is no such thing as invisibility and that one cannot study a phenomenon without participating in it to some extent. More recently, theorists have attempted to bridge the two positions. They focus on the specific aspects of the situation about which the analyst should or should not be neutral. Hoffer (1985) and Sandler (1976) have extended Anna Freud's definitions to include, in Hoffer's words, "neutrality in relation to the analyst's intrapsychic conflict and the interpersonal conflict at any level in the analytic relationship" (p. 777). In summary, Hoffer (1985) states:

> the concept of neutrality with respect to specifiable conflicts is thereby also broadened to include (a) interpersonal conflict within the analytic relationship and (b) conflict within the analyst. With these explicit additions, the concept of neutrality with respect to conflict becomes congruent with the current emphasis on the nonauthoritarian two-person aspects of the psychoanalytic relationship, without detracting from the primary analytic goal of deeper understanding of intra-psychic conflict [p. 793].

I agree with Hoffer that the early meanings of neutrality as they emerged from drive theory have proved to be insufficient, and that over the years, the addition of relational theory to drive theory leads therapists to new and more vital meanings of neutrality in work with our patients.

THE SAFE-ENOUGH CLINICAL ENVIRONMENT

Another major area of concern in the literature on neutrality centers on the question of safety, that is, an atmosphere in which the patient is safe enough to tolerate the uncovering of the hidden self. Milton Viederman (1991) states, "I distinguish between the climate of analysis, which is the prevailing emotional tone of the relationship in part created by the analyst, and the weather which more closely approximates the usual transference vicissitudes" (p. 453). Similar distinctions are made by Schafer (1983), Sandler (1983), Weiss (1982), Myerson (1981), and Greenberg (1986). If we go on to ask what the patient needs to be protected from, we can conclude that the patient needs to be protected from undue shame and intolerable anxiety. This leads to the question of what kinds of neutrality contribute to a safe atmosphere for the patient.

The emergence of theories of shame and its management in the clinical hour speak to the patient's need for safety from humiliation (Kohut, 1971; Morrison, 1983; Nathanson, 1987; Alonso and Rutan, 1988). To be relatively safe from undue shame, the patient must be able to rely on the capacity of the clinician to be nonjudgmental about his or her intrinsic worth, and to remain respectful in the face of the whole panoply of human behavior and motivation that a patient may present. The clinician must be dedicated to the belief that the patient's symptoms represent the patient's best available solutions, and that the underlying threat to the patient's ego will only be uncovered in an atmosphere of minimal shame and humiliation. Kris (1990) claims that owing to "an unrecognized failure of neutrality" (p. 605), analysts have failed to help patients recognize and resolve their persistent self-criticism born of shame. These authors, as a group, tend to agree that the analyst's stance must be affirming, empathic, and kind.

Their stance, however, is at a remove from the position of the analyst as impartial observer outside the experience. To be empathic, the analyst must be willing and able to temporarily merge with some aspects of the patient's experience, to stand near the patient's internal dilemmas and passions, and to recognize some aspect of the self in the patient's fears and ideals. It is precisely the oscillation between standing apart and joining the moment that provides a neutrality that is both challenging and safe for the patient.

Beyond the problem of shame, the management of undue anxiety is also a subject of some debate. Chused (1982) argues that the neutral stance allows the patient to make whatever use of the analyst he or she can tolerate, and expands the range of possibilities for developing the analyst as a safe new object to introject. Expanding on Chused's definition, Greenberg (1986) argues that the analyst needs to "establish an optimal tension between the patient's tendency to see the analyst as an old object and his capacity to experience him as a new one" (p. 97). Presumably, the old object is the dangerously perceived source of conflict that is repressed and will reemerge in the neutral atmosphere, while the new and safe object is experienced in the person of the analyst in the well-developed working alliance. Others (Schafer, 1983; Modell, 1990; Viederman, 1991) also argue that, at times, a departure from anonymity enhances neutrality and promotes safety for the analytic patient and the work in which patient and analyst are engaged.

NEUTRALITY AND THE CURATIVE FACTORS IN PSYCHOANALYTIC THEORY AND PRACTICE

The focus on patients' safety leads us to a consideration of safe from what, and toward what end? The goals of treatment also vary depending on whether one is using a drive model or a relational model. Whereas the classical drive theorist sees the goal as that of making the unconscious conscious, the relational theorist might define the goals of analysis as the internalization of a new relationship that evokes and reorganizes the internalized part-object representations that were conflictual for the patient at the beginning of the treatment. Neutrality remains a valued and central aspect of the work in either case, but is defined differently according to one's understanding of the curative factors in the work. The drive theorist will seek to uncover repressed conflicts in the patient's intrapsychic apparatus, and consequently will seek to provide a blank screen on which the patient will project aspects of the repressed conflict. The relational theorist will tend to rely much more on the process of projective identification between the patient and the analyst, a process eloquently described by Hamilton (1990). He acknowledges a debt to the early writings of Bibring (1937), Glover (1937), Strachey (1937), Bion (1957), and Blatt and Behrends (1987)—all of whom recognized that the patient internalizes aspects of the analyst during the treatment. Hamilton's own summary represents this position well: "The concept of the container and the contained in psychoanalysis describes a process whereby the patient's projective identifications are internalized by the analyst, transformed, given meaning, and returned to the patient in a useful fashion." This understanding of the curative action in psychoanalysis leads to a definition of neutrality that involves a flexible stance that sometimes gratifies and sometimes frustrates, that offers the analyst sometimes as a "real" figure and sometimes as a fantasied one. Representing this position on the continuum of the argument about neutrality, Viederman (1991) states that "on occasion, confirmation by the analyst of the verity of an experience in the patient's early life facilitates the analytic process." Bridging the two positions, Cooper (1987) states that while he, as the analyst, serves as a Proustian madeleine evoking affects from a dimly remembered past, he also "played an equally important role as the necessary background of safety for the patient's experimentation with new self- and object-representations" (pp. 90–91).

To briefly sum up the complex theoretical approaches to neutrality to date, the following aspects emerge:

1. Virtually all the literature emerges from and relates to classical psychoanalysis, and with very few exceptions, neutrality is rarely explored in terms of its place in psychoanalytically informed psychotherapy.

2. With the evolving state of analytic theory, the view of the analyst as a blank screen is but one position. Relational theory has added a view of the analyst as a participant observer. In doing so, analytic theory has come to focus more on the real relationship as well as the transference relationship between patient and analyst. This has led to a demarcation of the concept of neutrality, and added a discourse about the negative as well as positive implications of the neutral position.

3. Concerns about safety lead to an increasing concern about the real relationship, and to a more flexible stance toward abstinence versus gratification of the patient, and toward the clinician's opaqueness vs. transparency in the clinical situation.

4. There has been a gradual shift in what is seen as curative. Strachey (1937) strictly held the belief that the only cure came from the inter-

pretation of the transference, which in turn only emerged from adherence to the basic rule of free association. Since Strachey's time, the field has added a belief in the curative aspects of increasing identifications, which could result from an uncovering and resolution of the patient's projective identifications in the work with the analyst. With this movement toward integrating a drive-instinct theory with a relational field as curative, neutrality then took on new meanings. Now neutrality came to have more to do with concepts such as fair-mindedness, nonjudgmental empathy, nonintrusiveness, nonpossessive caring, and respect for all aspects of the patient's inner life.

CURATIVE FACTORS AND THE PLACE OF NEUTRALITY IN PSYCHOANALYTIC PSYCHOTHERAPY

There is a continuing debate about the differences between psychoanalysis and psychoanalytic psychotherapy that is beyond the scope of this work. For the purposes of this chapter, I rely on Wallerstein's (1986) view of the continuum model, in which these are overlapping treatments. He offers some valuable distinctions: In psychoanalysis, free association is the fundamental *rule,* whereas in psychotherapy, it is a fundamental *permission.* The goal of psychoanalysis is the resolution of infantile repressed conflicts as they emerge in the transference neurosis and are so interpreted; whereas in psychoanalytic psychotherapy, the focus is on the analysis of defense and resistance, that is, on characterological patterns as they are illuminated in the transference, with or without a deepening analysis of their genetic roots. They have a shared goal of conflict resolution and character change. Analysis relies more on insight to generate personality reorganization, whereas psychotherapy relies not only on insight but also on behavior change based on improved reality testing, identification with a "better" new object, an ability to delay impulse discharge, and a broadened range of sublimatory channels, with ensuing gratifications leading to a more fulfilling life. It is obvious that the more the treatment goes in the direction of the latter, the more the definition of neutrality moves away from the "indifferenz" described by Freud (1914) and toward the nonjudgmental and containing presence of the analyst.

The differences in the definitions of and the patient populations served by these models lead logically to differences in technique. Psychoanalysis requires that a patient have a strong capacity to tolerate anxiety and regression, a willingness and ability (financial and otherwise) to invest a number of hours a week to treatment, and a sophisticated capacity for introspection and psychological mindedness. Psychoanalytic psychotherapy, by inference, can and does serve a whole population, the members of which may or may not meet the above criteria, or have such global goals. In addition, recent attention to the dilemmas of character pathology—and the recognition that they are inherent in all human conflict—has challenged the dyadic analytic method as the only and primary arena for the treatment of the healthier patient.

Psychoanalytic psychotherapy differs from psychoanalysis in the timing and structure of the meeting (usually from one to three times a week, usually face to face) and the model, that is, individual, family, or group psychoanalytic psychotherapy, which may involve other interventions, such as psychopharmacology, partial hospitalizations, and so forth. All of these variations continue to rely on the emergence and exploration of transference and countertransference, and place new demands and responsibilities for neutrality on the psychoanalytic psychotherapist. I will proceed now to a discussion of neutrality in psychoanalytic psychotherapy with a focus on the three factors considered earlier in the discussion of psychoanalysis, that is, the drive-structure versus relational-structure debate, the question of safety in psychotherapy, and an exploration of what and how cure is effected in psychoanalytic psychotherapy.

PSYCHOTHERAPY, NEUTRALITY, AND DRIVE VERSUS RELATIONAL PSYCHOLOGY

One of the major changes in the field of analytic therapy came about with the passing of the Community Mental Health Act during Lyndon B. Johnson's War on Poverty in the 1960s. With a stroke of the pen, large numbers of people who had not been perceived as candidates for psychotherapy were now presenting themselves to community clinics, and the pressure was on psychoanalytic thinkers to develop techniques that could appropriately serve this population without abandoning their basic beliefs in the importance of free association, neutrality, and the use of the transferential field as an important arena for emotional exploration and change. At the same time, the categorical nosological systems focused on character disorders as one way of organizing areas of mental distress. In addition to these demographic factors, analytic theory moved further from classical drive theory toward relational theory and the increased possibility it offered for understanding the sicker patient. Kernberg, Kohut, Adler and Buie, and others explored the severe character problems of the borderline and narcissistic patient, many of whom were dubiously served by the methods of classical analysis, and few of whom could sustain the intensity of analysis. These patients increasingly were treated in psychoanalytic psychotherapy, first dyadically, and more and more frequently in systems, such as their families, group therapy, and a variety of milieus that approximated the old inpatient settings, such as the Menninger Clinic and Chestnut Lodge.

The change in direction away from classical drive theory and its emphasis on the fundamental rule led to the need to think anew about the transference, and whether anything *but* the strict adherence to the fundamental rule could be considered an analyzable transference. Could one rely on analytic neutrality where the analyst was visible to the patient physically as well as functionally? Could there be a return of the repressed in once-a-week treatment under the pressure of symptoms that needed to be contained and managed before the patient could begin to remember the past rather than just repeat it? Could the psychoanalytic psychotherapist remain available but noninterventionist, and thus neutral in the patient's life, and did this constitute neutrality or was it irresponsible and dangerous, as implied in cartoons of the patient on the window ledge and the passive analyst commenting on the suicidal wish?

The dilemmas highlighted by the more traditional forms of abstinent neutrality consistent with the drive-structure theory were partly relieved by the addition and integration of relational-structure theory. There were many variables that contributed to this easing of what had begun to seem like an irresolvable set of problems in applying classical analysis to psychotherapy. Whereas classical drive theory focused on the resolution of the Oedipus complex as the fulcrum for development, relational theory paid greater attention to the conflicts and deficits of the first two or three years of life. Given the range of psychotherapy patients, many of whom presented with an array of problems originating in very early development, it is not surprising that many of the theorists writing about the sicker patient emerged from the relational theories. Projective identification came to be understood as equal in importance to Freud's "irrational involvement between two people" as a metaphor for addressing the transferential involvement between patient and therapist. The definition of projective identification, as derived from Klein (1946), Bion (1957), Kernberg (1965), Ogden (1979), and Hamilton (1990), refers to a mental mechanism whereby the subject attributes an aspect of the self and attendant affects to the object, while retaining some of the other parts in an effort to control in the other what cannot be controlled in the self. Ogden (1979) points out that while the patient internally attributes aspects of the self to the object, he or she behaves in such a way as to elicit from the analyst the experience of "pressure to think, feel, and behave in a manner congruent with the projection." Viewed through this lens, neutrality means being available to participate in all dimensions and forms of the patient's projections, to resonate to all aspects of the patient without censoring and selecting, and to remain outside the merger of the projective identification enough to recognize it for what it is. In other words, neutrality here integrates the distant observer model with the participant observer model. To the extent that the analytic therapist can succeed in maintaining this form of neutrality, he or she has the opportunity to create an empathic confrontation with the patient about the disowned aspects of the self that are the sequelae of the early and disturbed object relationships embedded in the patient's unconscious. The patient's eventual ability to bear the confrontation depends on his or her perception of the therapist as neutral in the sense of nonjudgmental and noncondemning of the patient's basest wishes and needs.

CASE EXAMPLE

Ms. A, a 40-year-old woman, entered treatment to deal with a debilitating depression. This took the form of profound passivity on her part, in addition to which she was morbidly obese and had recently been diagnosed as diabetic. She began twice-a-week, individual psychoanalytic psychotherapy, and negotiated a reduced fee based on her inability to manage full-time work. In the hour, she was often inarticulate and would simply weep silently while staring out the window. The therapist struggled with an increasing urgency within herself to rescue the patient by asking questions, or otherwise trying actively to engage the patient in some conversation. Whenever she did so, the patient would weep even more and occasionally tell the therapist how embarrassing it was for her to be so inept. Clearly this patient was unable to obey the fundamental rule required by the drive-structural model, and the treatment threatened to founder. Even viewed from the perspective of relational model's fundamental permission to free associate, the treatment looked seriously compromised. Before long, of course, the therapist began to feel quite inept herself and was at a loss for words to explain the treatment to herself or to her supervisor. In addition, the patient was accumulating a sizable bill that she claimed not to be able to pay, but she assured the therapist that she would pay it as soon as she could. The therapist began to plan to reduce the frequency of the treatment and was only dimly aware of her anger with the patient for "using up" the therapist's precious hours.

When the patient finally announced that she was taking a holiday in a foreign country, the therapist's resentment burgeoned and she was able to recognize the projective identification in which she and her patient were participating. The patient's need to be gratified without challenge were mirrored by the therapist's need for the patient to gratify her by "getting well"—without the therapist having to challenge the patient's entitlement. This recognition allowed the therapist to gently but firmly and persistently present the patient with this reality and eventually move the therapy forward. The patient took a full-time job, paid her bills (although never quite on time), and became much more engaged in the process of the treatment.

In this example, the therapist's neutrality required that she be anything but indifferent. To the contrary, she needed to be willing to temporarily merge with this patient's colossal entitlement, to identify aspects in herself that resonated to this dilemma, to step out of the merger and hand back the patient's projections by interpreting them both in the present and in their genetic origins. It can be said that the therapist had to neutralize her own countertransferential impulses before she could be helpful to her patient. At that point, she could tell the patient about her irritation in hearing the patient plan an expensive trip while owing the therapist a great deal of money, and use the moment to help the patient appreciate the impact of her action on the therapist, whom she in fact cared for a great deal.

It is not clear that this patient profited as much from insight as she did from internalizing a new object, thereby developing a broader range of more acceptable sublimatory channels for some of her impulses. Her obesity remains problematic, and syntonic. Nonetheless, she continues to show improvements in other aspects of her life.

THE SAFE-ENOUGH ENVIRONMENT FOR PSYCHOANALYTIC PSYCHOTHERAPY

Many aspects of the psychotherapy environment contribute to the problem of safety. Here, too, the patient needs to be protected from undue shame and humiliation, as well as from unmanageable anxiety. Although the therapist can be sensitive to the narcissistic assaults that are inherent in the very process of becoming a patient, there are factors external to the dyad that may generate considerable anxiety. For example, the Tarasoff ruling imposes on the therapist the duty to warn those against whom the patient makes believable threats. A litigious climate may pressure the therapist to break neutrality by hospitalizing the patient against his or her will. The limits of confidentiality also threaten the privacy of the therapeutic hour, and may exert for both the therapist and the patient a powerful pull away from a desirable exploration of the patient's darkest fantasies. The participation of third-party payers gives them claim to some aspects of the otherwise confidential therapeutic dialogue, and as part of the treatment environment these systems greatly compromise neutrality, especially as they demand behavioral proofs of the patient's progress.

On a more internal level, both patient and therapist are under the pressure of time limitation and infrequent contact. The problem of managing a balance between an expressive and exploratory therapy on the one hand, and protecting the patient's adaptive capacity on the other hand, is of constant concern.

CASE EXAMPLE

Mr. B, a 30-year-old married man, entered outpatient treatment because he was tormented by an impulse to hurt his wife. He worked part-time, and wrote graphically violent stories as a hobby. He was seen twice weekly in individual sessions. He had read a good deal of psychology and came into treatment with the concern that he had "borderline personality disorder." He claimed that he had a reasonable marriage, and that of late he had cut back on his job so that he could spend more time working to improve his marriage. Mr. B had an active fantasy life, and would often masturbate to pornographic videotapes with sadomaso-chistic themes. He also frequented the "combat zone" (an area frequented by prostitutes and drug dealers), spending most of his time just "watching the action." He would speak proudly about his ability to use people to achieve his goals, and, in the next moment, he would feel badly about this. He had no friends, and wished to make some. He also reported a history of acting impulsively and driving recklessly and getting involved in fights on the highway with other drivers who objected to it. He also had a history of heavy alcohol and drug abuse when he was younger, but claimed to be sober at the time he began treatment.

In the treatment, Mr. B. would become enraged and report his fantasies of hurting his therapist as well as his wife. This would happen during or after a session in which the patient would remember difficulties with his mother, whom he adored but feared in equal measure because she could suddenly turn cold in the midst of a loving and seductive exchange. Mr. B.'s father committed suicide after his business fell apart during the patient's adolescence.

This case was a major challenge to the therapist's neutrality from the many dimensions and meanings of safety. The ability to make a judgment about the duty to warn the patient's spouse or to hospitalize the patient required that the therapist delve deeply into the patient's material and interfered with the clinician's ability to remain as interested in all the patient's productions, such as the patient's interest in work or aims to discuss his or her hope for the long-term goals of the treatment. The more difficult task, however, was that of managing the patient's anxiety and containing the impulses of a patient who was so patently vulnerable and unstable. The balance between inviting the patient's projections to learn from them and contain them and offering support to shore up a fragile defensive structure was a burdensome one, and one that left the therapist grasping for some neutral but safe position in the countertransference. The challenge was to "keep the faith" in the treatment model while avoiding denial of the potential danger to patient, therapist, and others.

This case is not atypical for the patients seen in our clinics and serves well to illuminate the problems with the technique of neutrality when working with the very distressed patient in outpatient psychotherapy. We therapists might all agree with the shibboleth that uncovering and working with the transference requires that the patient have one foot firmly rooted in reality and the other in the transference, but this balance is not so easy to assess or to maintain in the chaotic inner life of the patient and in the ensuing chaotic countertransference of the therapist. In such cases, the maintenance of any stable neutrality would be well supported by consultation with a senior mentor, or with another senior advisor who has expertise in and respect for the possibilities and limits of psychoanalytic psychotherapy.

CURATIVE FACTORS IN PSYCHOANALYTIC PSYCHOTHERAPY

The therapist who uses the drive-structure model will work to develop a transference neurosis that can then be interpreted, providing the patient with insights that will lead to personality reorganization. The fundamental rule that has classically been seen as indispensable for this work is challenged here, given the many successful treatments of patients in once- or twice-a-week psychoanalytic psychotherapy. Although the abstinent and nongratifying individual therapist can elicit a powerful transference with certain patients, this is difficult to do and requires considerable training, experience, and confidence in the value of the method. There is increasing awareness among psychoanalytic thinkers of all types that neutrality must balance an abstinent stance regarding action with a warm and respectful attitude that provides a condition of safety and tolerance (Weiss, 1982; Schafer, 1983; Sandler, 1983). Only then will the patient feel able to associate, expose, and reexperience previously repressed and traumatic conflicts in the transference with the therapist and make them available to interpretation and resolution.

For the therapist who uses the relational-structure model, the change in the therapy is seen as emanating from the patient's ability to engage in a series of evolving projective identifications with the neutral therapist who can be available to the wide range of affects and impulses of his or her patients. When this happens, the patient can then borrow ego strength from the therapy, develop new and higher level defenses, identify with and introject the "new" object as represented by the therapist, and like the drive-structural therapist's patient, find ego where there was id.

CASE EXAMPLE

Mr. C entered twice-a-week psychoanalytic psychotherapy with a therapist using a drive-structural model when his academic tenure was denied. He claimed that he had sought help only because his wife threatened to leave him if he didn't do something to relieve his depression and anger. The patient had lost all interest in sex and was a virtual recluse, avoiding all of his former friends, whose pity he feared. He had become even "more sarcastic and hostile than usual," by his own admission, and threatened regularly to throw in the towel—to leave the state and abandon his wife and children so that they could be unencumbered by his professional failures and black moods. He was very psychologically sophisticated, and had a great deal of intellectual awareness of the genetic causes of his present state. He spoke of the toxic household in which he grew up, with alcoholic parents and two younger sisters, one of whom eventually became psychotic and now lives as a street person. Prior to this crisis, the patient had never felt he needed professional help, and managed to pull himself through bad times by playing music with friends, skiing with his wife, and working at his profession. However, his equilibrium rested on a somewhat precarious early development, and he found himself anxious and despairing and very, very angry. At the beginning of and throughout the treatment, the patient felt comforted by the rather abstinent neutrality practiced by his therapist. He feared invasion and reacted negatively whenever the therapist expressed empathy or made any other efforts to encourage him. The patient developed a profound transference in the course of the twice-a-week therapy. He tended to free associate readily, and responded well to interpretation along classical lines. Deeply repressed conflicts of a genetic nature emerged in the transference, and were dealt with. The patient's father had jettisoned a promising career as a lawyer by drinking and taking drugs, and the patient felt himself doomed to repeat the pattern in his own life, just when he felt he had "the golden apple in his hand.'' His mother had scorned his father in the patient's presence, and told the patient that he was, after all, the only real man in the family. His easy victory over his father left him all too available for his mother's adulation, which he attempted to repel by failing in his own life. He became aware that his professional inhibitions led to his failure to achieve tenure, and he knew that he was threatening his marriage by his sexual coldness. Virtually all the analytic work centered on the emergence and interpretation of the transference with his formal male therapist. The latter, despite his strict formality and abstinence in the work, was in fact a warm and dedicated clinician, and this undoubtedly allowed the patient to tolerate and thrive in the neutrality of the doctor's clinical technique. Ultimately, the patient's libidinal and aggressive life was reinvigorated, and he proceeded to a more successful marriage and a new and thriving career.

In conclusion, neutrality, when applied to psychoanalytic psychotherapy and perhaps to many psychoanalyses as well, may need to be redefined in ways that take into account the complexity of the healing process. De facto, this has happened, and most writers, even among the most orthodox classicists, would now agree that the stance of ''indifferenz'' is not enough to sustain an optimal treatment. It is neither necessary nor helpful to abandon what we have learned in the past. Instead, the history of ideas is one of increasing, deepening, and integrating new learning as it becomes available to us. So it is with the concept of neutrality. Freud's attempts at scientific objectivity are still very valid reminders that therapists need to attend to patients from as bias free a position as they can summon. At the same time, observation alone will not do. The internal world of the patient is evoked and engaged in the relationship with the clinician. Similarly, the clinician's evoked transference toward the patient becomes a critical source of data about the therapeutic endeavor. In addition to remaining objective, the clinician needs to find a way to engage the patient's archaic internal object representations as they appear in the transferences created between them. Winnicott (1965) proposed that the child needs to learn how to be ''alone as in the presence of a mother,'' suggesting the possibility that the patient will thrive in an atmosphere with a warm presence and a hovering but nonintrusive analytic ''mother'' of whatever gender. The unfolding of the patient's repressed psychic conflicts, whether perceived from a drive or relational theory, can surface only if the atmosphere of vigorous curiosity seen in the unimpeded young child is encouraged in the analytic situation. The interpretation of the unconscious problems of the patient remain the primary goal of the analytic endeavor. Such a balanced exploration is supported by a receptive, warm, challenging, and respectful stance of genuine neutrality.

REFERENCES

Alonso, A. & Rutan, J. S. (1988), The treatment of shame and the restoration of self respect in groups. *Internat. J. Group Psychother.*, 38:3–14.

Bibring, E. (1937), Symposium on the theory of the therapeutic results of psychoanalysis. *Internat. J. Psycho-Anal.*, 18:170–189.

Bion, W. (1957), Differentiation of the psychotic from the non-psychotic personalities. *Internat. J. Psycho-Anal.*, 38:266–275.

Blatt, S. J. & Behrends, R. S. (1987), Internalization, separation-individuation, and the nature of therapeutic action. *Internat. J. Psycho-Anal.*, 68:279–297.

Chused, J. (1982), The role of analytic neutrality in the use of the child analyst as a new object. *J. Amer. Psychoanal. Assn.*, 30:3–28.

Cooper, A. (1987), Changes in psychoanalytic ideas. *J. Amer. Psychoanal. Assn.*, 35:77–98.

Fairbairn, R. (1952), *Psychoanalytic Studies of the Personality.* London: Tavistock.

Fliess, R. (1942), The metapsychology of the analyst. *Psychoanal. Quart.*, 11:211–227.

Freud, A. (1936), *The Ego and Mechanisms of Defense.* New York: International Universities Press.

Freud, S. (1912), Recommendations to physicians practicing psycho-analysis. *Standard Edition*, 12:109–120. London: Hogarth Press, 1958.

—— (1915), Observations on transference love. *Standard Edition*, 12:157–168. London: Hogarth Press, 1958.

Glover, E. (1937), Symposium on the theory of the therapeutic results of psychoanalysis. *Internat. J. Psycho-Anal.*, 18:125–132.

—— (1955), *The Technique of Psycho-Analysis.* New York: International Universities Press.

Greenberg, J. (1986), Theoretical models and the analyst's neutrality. *Contemp. Psychoanal.*, 22:87–106.

—— & Mitchell, S. (1983), *Object Relations and Psychoanalytic Psychotherapy.* Cambridge, MA: Harvard University Press.

Hamilton, N. G. (1990), The containing function and the analyst's projective identification. *Internat. J. Psycho-Anal.*, 71:445–453.

Hartmann, H. (1954), Technical implications of ego psychology. In: *Essays on Ego Psychology.* New York: International Universities Press, pp. 31–43.

Hoffer, A. (1985), Toward a definition of psychoanalytic neutrality. *J. Amer. Psychoanal. Assn.*, 33:771–795.

—— (1991), The Freud–Ferenczi controversy—A living legacy. *Internat. Rev. Psychoanal.*, 18:465–472.

Kernberg, O. F. (1965), Notes on countertransference. *J. Amer. Psychoanal. Assn.*, 13:38–56.

Klein, M. (1946), Notes on some schizoid mechanisms. *Internat. J. Psycho-Anal.*, 27:99–110.

Kohut, H. (1971), *The Analysis of the Self.* New York: International Universities Press.

Kris, A. (1990), Helping patients by analyzing self-criticism. *J. Amer. Psychoanal. Assn.*, 38:605–636.

Modell, A. H. (1990), *Other Times, Other Realities.* Cambridge, MA: Harvard University Press.

Morrison, A. P. (1983), Shame, the ideal self, and narcissism. *Contemp. Psychoanal.*, 19:295–318.

Myerson, P. (1981), The nature of the transactions that occur in other than classical analysis. *Internat. J. Psycho-Anal.*, 8:173–189.

Nathanson, D., ed. (1987), *The Many Faces of Shame*. New York: Guilford.

Ogden, T. (1979), On projective identification. *Internat. J. Psycho-Anal.*, 60:357–373.

Sandler, J. (1976), Countertransference and role-responsiveness. *Internat. Rev. Psychoanal.*, 3:43–47.

—— (1983), Reflections on some relations between psychoanalytic concepts and psychoanalytic practice. *Internat. J. Psycho-Anal.*, 64:35–45.

Schafer, R. (1983), *The Analytic Attitude*. New York: Basic Books.

Strachey, J. (1937), Symposium on the theory of therapeutic results of psychoanalysis. *Internat. J. Psycho-Anal.*, 18:139–145.

Sullivan, H. S. (1954), *The Psychiatric Interview*, ed. H. S. Perry & M. L. Gawel. New York: Norton.

Viederman, M. (1991), The real person of the analyst and his role in the process of psychoanalytic cure. *J. Amer. Psychoanal. Assn.*, 39:451–489.

Wachtel, P. (1986), On the limits of therapeutic neutrality. *Contemp. Psychoanal.*, 22:60–70.

Wallerstein, R. S. (1986), *Forty-Two Lives in Treatment*. New York: Guilford.

Weiss, J. (1982), *Psychotherapy Research: Theory and Findings, Theoretical Introduction*. Psychotherapy Research Group, Department of Psychiatry, Mount Zion Hospital & Medical Center, Bulletin 5.

Winnicott, D. W. (1965), *Maturational Processes and the Facilitating Environment*. London: Hogarth Press.

2

The Therapeutic Alliance and the Real Relationship in the Analytic Process

W. W. Meissner

My effort in this chapter stems from a longstanding concern that the therapeutic alliance has been a poorly articulated, poorly understood, and inadequately implemented dimension of the therapeutic relationship. My concern has led me, in my article "The Concept of the Therapeutic Alliance," to try to discern more clearly what the therapeutic alliance means and what it involves (Meissner, 1992). For a more encompassing impression of my view of what the therapeutic alliance entails I would encourage the reader to consult that article, especially since the implications and connotations of the therapeutic alliance (and its congener, the working alliance) have suffered from a good deal of confusion and a lack of clarity (Gutheil and Havens, 1979).

An important element in that discussion was the distinction between the therapeutic alliance and the real relationship, a distinction that is little acknowledged and less utilized. As a rule, the preoccupation in the analytic literature has fallen on the distinction between transference and the real relationship. Consequently, insofar as the therapeutic alliance is also distinguished from transference, it is lumped together with the real relationship as though they were synonymous or whatever differences there might be between them were of no consequence. In my view, this is the sort of misunderstanding that allows Thomä and Kächele (1987), in their comprehensive discussion, to write:

> It is said that if the negative transferences gain the upper hand, they can completely paralyze the analytic situation. The basic prerequisite for cure, namely the realistic relationship, is then undermined. Here Freud introduced an apparently objective or external truth—patient and analyst are based in the real external world (1940, p. 173)—which, examined more closely, is in fact no less subjective than the truth which comes from

transference. The introduction of the real person, the subject, into the working alliance does not prevent verification of the truth; on the contrary, it makes the subjectivity of our theories manifest [p. 63].

In terms of the present discussion, I would maintain that the basic prerequisite for cure in analysis lies in the therapeutic alliance rather than in the real relationship, and correspondingly it is not the real person who engages in the alliance but the analyst in his role as therapeutic agent. It is this issue that I address in this discussion. I emphasize the distinction between the therapeutic alliance and the real relationship and I will argue that the locus of effective therapeutic intervention lies in the therapeutic alliance and not in the real relationship. The real relationship is itself worthy of more extensive investigation, but my focus here is on its distinction from the therapeutic alliance. I will attempt to make a clear distinction between these intertwined aspects of the analytic process, then review some of the history of this problem, and, finally, offer some considerations regarding the application of this distinction in the therapeutic setting.

ALLIANCE VERSUS REAL RELATIONSHIP

Previous discussions of the therapeutic alliance have suffered from the necessity to distinguish it from transference. The therapeutic relationship includes both transference and nontransference components, but little effort has been expended in drawing a line between the alliance and the real relationship, both of which are nontransferential. In Viederman's (1991) excellent clinical discussion of the reality of the analyst in the analytic process, for example, he does not distinguish between the real relationship and the therapeutic alliance. The failure to establish and maintain such a distinction between alliance and reality has led to some problematical misunderstandings. However, the failure to draw these distinctions is perhaps understandable, insofar as these factors intermingle and interact in the actuality of the therapeutic relationship—a fact that tends to obscure the distinctions between them and the different ways in which they contribute to the overall relationship.

A recent article clarifies the basis for this reflection (de Jonghe, Rijnierse, and Janssen, 1991). The authors argue that the classic psychoanalytic view divided the analytic relationship into three components— transference, working relationship (alliance), and real relationship. (A postclassical view, however, adds the primary relationship to the list as a fourth dimension.) De Jonghe and colleagues define the primary relationship as "the reliving or re-experiencing of early infantile modes of functioning: affects, needs and wishes dating from the pre-oedipal, even the earliest pre-verbal period. It is essentially a recapitulation of the very early relationship between mother and infant, the experience of the undifferentiated self–object representation of the mother–child symbiotic phase and the separation-individuation phase (Mahler, 1975). It is a tie or bond of a pre-oedipal nature, not a relationship between separate individuals'' (p. 699). Thus the real relationship and the alliance derive from mature object relations based predominantly on object cathexis. Transference derivatives are also object related, but the objects are more infantile. By contrast, the primary relationship is derived from involvement with an infantile object, but the relationship is rooted in narcissism rather than object cathexis. These distinctions are helpful in locating concepts like primary love (Balint, 1965) and selfobject transferences (Kohut, 1984), or even Stone's (1961) "primary maternal transference" in the transference paradigm.

The "realistic relationship" in this approach is described as referring "to mature, realistic and healthy aspects of the relationship other than the working relationship. These aspects relate to the other person in his own right, not as a parent substitute nor as a working partner. It is the relationship between the patient and the analyst as real persons, not in their functions of analyst and analysand" (de Jonghe et al., 1991, p. 696). This formulation clearly distinguishes the real relationship from transference on the one hand and alliance on the other. The distinction from transference is valid, even though transference and reality can fall into conjunction—for example, a fat analyst may stimulate associations to a fat parent and thus offer support to transference displacements.

This point is brought into focus by Thomä and Kächele's (1987) emphasis on the dependence of transference and transference resistance on the shaping of the analytic situation by the analyst, and, more recently, by Langs's (1992) advocacy of an interactional perspective on transference: Transference is not simply determined by unconscious drive-derivative displacements on the part of the patient but may also involve responses of the patient to stimuli coming from the experience of the encounter with the real analyst. Baudry (1991) reinforces this understanding when he comments: "I believe that the analyst's real character traits serve as hooks on which patients can hang their transference reactions and give them a measure of plausibility. It is important for the analyst to be in touch with his characteristic responses so as to be able to monitor his own contributions and see how the patient uses them" (p. 928). The same phenomenon can involve any real attribute of the analyst, or, conversely, the patient (Bernal y del Rio, 1984). A somewhat more operational description is offered by Baudry (1991),

"By real relationship I mean one in which the analyst interacts with the patient outside the boundaries of what is commonly defined as the therapeutic role—for example, gives advice, acts as a friend, socializes with the patient, tells him about himself and his own life, freely responds directly to questions" (p. 921).

The "mature, realistic and healthy" (de Jonghe et al., 1991, p. 696) part of the real relationship may be open to question. The reality of the patient, as well as the analyst, may be somewhat less than mature, realistic, or healthy. If so, these qualities enter the analytic relationship as characteristics of the here-and-now personality of the person, whether analyst or patient. For Viederman (1992), the "real person" of the analyst refers "not only to his outward traits, but to his unique characteristics as a person and to his behavior in the analytic situation which goes beyond interpretation and clarification. The analyst's presence is rooted in the revelation of his personality and at times certain aspects of his experience, and in the idiosyncratic ways that two people develop a relationship and establish a dialogue with characteristics unique to that dyad" (pp. 452–453).

The qualities that enter into the alliance, however, are dictated not immediately by the personality of either participant but by the analytic situation, the work, and the engagement capacity of each of them. Winnicott (1949), for example, wrote about an "objective and justified hatred" toward a patient that was merely a natural reaction of the analyst to disagreeable aspects of the patient's personality rather than any form of transference. Clearly such a reaction may stem from the real relationship and not pertain to the therapeutic alliance—in fact may act in contradiction to it.

REALITY IN THE ANALYTIC RELATIONSHIP

Reality pervades the analytic relationship. There are the realities of time, place, and circumstance. The realities of the location of the analyst's office, the physical surroundings, the furniture and decorations in the room, the geographic location itself, and even how the analyst dresses, have their effects in the analytic situation and influence how the patient experiences the person of the analyst. The surrounding circumstances that create the framework for the analytic effort—the patient's financial situation, job demands, arrangements for payment of the fee, whether the patient has insurance or not and what kind, what kinds of pressures are pushing the patient into treatment—are reality factors that are extrinsic to the analysis but exercise significant influence on the analytic relationship and how it is established and maintained.

The most important and central reality for the patient is the person of the analyst. Every analyst has his or her own constellation of personal characteristics, including mannerisms, style of behavior and speech, habits of dress, gender (Lester, 1990), way of going about the task of managing the therapeutic situation, attitudes toward the patient as another human being, prejudices, moral and political views, and personal beliefs and values. These are all relevant aspects of his or her existence and personality as a human being. They are realities that play a role in and condition the therapeutic relationship. They are entirely exclusive of and distinct from transference and countertransference. In terms of the analytic process, none of this is lost on the patient who is comprehensively observant of and sensitive to the smallest details of the analyst's real person.

A similar set of realities is operative in the therapist's view of the patient. The patient has certain determinate real qualities and characteristics that stamp him or her as a unique individual. They involve the same elements and qualities as those possessed by the therapist but carry the stamp of his or her own individuality. Central to this configuration of reality elements are aspects of the patient's personality and behavioral style. The patient may have certain mannerisms or forms of behavior that elicit a reaction from the analyst. A female patient may be beautiful and behave in a sexually seductive manner—aspects of her usual style of behavior and mode of interaction with men. These are real aspects of the patient's person that cannot be reduced to transferential components. They may elicit a response from the therapist, especially if the therapist is male, that may even be affective in tone, but this has nothing to do with countertransference. The therapist is simply responding to the reality of an attractive woman.

Similarly, from both sides of the analytic relationship, the objective qualities of the participants come into play continually to shape the quality and course of the interaction between them. The analyst may be authoritarian and directive in his style of intervention and interpretation. His approach to the analytic situation and interaction may be simply an expression of the analyst's habitual manner of interacting, or it may to some degree be dictated by defensive needs and even derived from underlying unresolved conflicts, and still not necessarily constitute an expression of countertransference. It may simply be a facet of the analyst's personal style and his habitual mannerisms in approaching and dealing with this particular patient (Kantrowitz, 1992).

In addition, strict adherence to norms of abstinence and neutrality may in certain cases create a situation of deprivation for the patient and result in an angry counterattack or submissive avoidance (Viederman, 1992). Emotional distance or studied indifference on the part of the analyst may be experienced as sadistic by many masochistic patients. Although the distinction between these real aspects of the therapeutic interaction and elements of transference is more familiar and accepted in the analytic purview, the related distinction between such real factors and the therapeutic alliance is less familiar and more difficult. The alliance concerns itself with the specific negotiations and forms of interaction between the therapist and patient that are required for effective and meaningful therapeutic interaction.

The element of basic trust, for example, is not part of the real relationship, even though it arises between real people and reflects aspects of their real functioning and interacting. The ability to trust entails a quality of interaction within the object relationship that must be engendered by specific behaviors that aim at the establishing and sustaining of such trust. The capacity for trust may be a part of the reality of the patient's personality structure and functioning. But this capacity must be realized in the ongoing interaction between analyst and patient as a functional part of the specifically therapeutic context and interaction, and in this sense becomes a contributing element in the therapeutic alliance. Trust, then, as it enters the therapeutic alliance is quite different from a form of trusting disposition that the patient may have toward any significant figure in his or her environment. Trust in the alliance is specifically focused in the analytic setting as a contributing element of the analytic process and directed to mutual involvement and collaboration with the analyst in the work of the process. In analysis, authentic trust would allow a patient to reveal his deepest and most shameful secrets and perverted fantasies, but he would not give the analyst the key to his safe deposit box. Trust in the alliance is specific to the analysis, and is invested in the analytic object for purposes of the analytic process.

Also, a patient may have a real capacity for autonomous functioning, but that capacity must be implemented and allowed to emerge as a functional aspect of the analytic relationship and interaction in order to be regarded as a factor in the therapeutic alliance. Moreover, the alliance is specific to the therapeutic situation and relationship, whereas the reality of the patient's personality structure pervades his whole life experience and relationships. Insofar as these same qualities become involved in the analytic process and contribute to the mutually reinforcing collaboration of analyst and patient in the work of the analysis, they are part of the therapeutic alliance. Outside the analysis they belong to the patient's real personality.

THE REAL RELATIONSHIP AS RESISTANCE

We are usually disposed to think of resistance as the specific defensive maneuvers used by the patient to divert or frustrate the analytic process and the analytic effort of the analyst. However, if we accept a more broadly conceived notion of resistance as anything impeding the analytic process, then reality and the real relationship between the analyst and patient can under certain circumstances serve that function. Not only can reality serve as resistance for the patient, but I would assert that it can be utilized for the same purpose by the analyst—however repugnant the idea might be that the analyst might introduce resistances into the analytic process. My major point here is that reality and the real relationship are not always positive or promotional factors in the performance of the analytic task.

In analytic material there is always the tension between factual data and the patient's recounting of events, between fact and fantasy, between historical and narrative truth (Spence, 1982), between factual events and the patient's remembered imaginative recall. Patients' adherence to their version of their own life history as unquestionably factual can become a resistance to the extent that it obscures exploration of the psychodynamic factors that determine the form the history takes. Along the same vein, if the analyst were to accept the account of the patient as veridical, he would short-circuit the exploration of the dynamic determinants that enter into the telling and the story—a form of analyst resistance.

To take this a step further, the real relationship can also become the vehicle of resistance. For some patients, adherence to the real relationship provides a way of avoiding transference, with its associated affects. For other patients, some real characteristics of the analyst may stimulate transference reactions in the patient—a circumstance that not only abets the analytic process but can lead to further exploration and clarification of transference dynamics. But for some of these patients, the resemblance of the transference object to real objects, whether erotically stimulating or traumatically damaging, can serve as the basis for a resistance to the transference that takes the form of failure to recognize or acknowledge the transference and any differences that may occur in the transference object along with the similarities. For some of these patients the difference between transference and reality is obliterated so that the transference is experienced as an intolerable repetition of previous traumatic experience. In such cases, if an adequate footing cannot be gained in the alliance to allow for exploration of both the reality and the transference, therapeutic progress may be frustrated and the prospects for resolution doomed to failure.

By the same token, were the analyst to take the patient's transference for something real, he would introduce a distortion into the analytic process. Just as taking the patient's account of himself or herself as reflecting a veridical reality can become a resistance to analytic exploration, so the acceptance of transference manifestations as real undermines analytic investigation and understanding. Analogously, if the analyst introduces a real factor into the analytic interaction with his patient, it can distort the analytic process and serve as a focus of resistance. To take a benign example, an analyst who had been seeing his patient for a reduced fee, which on further reflection seemed inappropriate, informed his patient that he wanted to raise the fee and opened a negotiation to determine what a reasonable fee would be. The reality of payment of a fee for services rendered was thus brought into the analytic process. The analyst's approach to the question was cast in terms of the alliance with due respect for the patient's autonomy and freedom to decide. This led to a further exploration with the patient of the meaning of the fee, the issues of entitlement and expectation that it brought to the surface, and a consolidation and deepening of the alliance. The same proposal could have been tendered to the patient in declarative and authoritarian terms that would have imposed the new fee on the patient and demanded his submissive acceptance. The expectable resentment and anger of a patient to such authoritarian treatment could easily plant the seeds of discontent and rebellion—to the detriment of the treatment. The troublesome question as to when the introduction of real factors into the analysis serves to facilitate or impede the analytic process pervades the rest of this discussion.

SOME RELEVANT HISTORY

From the perspective of this discussion, we can argue that the place of the real relationship and its association with alliance was at issue in the differences between Freud and Ferenczi, as was expressed in their correspondence (Ferenczi, 1949; Grubrich-Simitis, 1986) and in Ferenczi's (1932) clinical diary. At issue were Ferenczi's experiments with his active technique, which included displays of affection—even hugging and kissing—and other realistic intrusions into the patient's life, and, later in the twenties, his relaxation technique. This later approach was a reaction to the earlier active technique and emphasized empathic acceptance and security in the analytic relation, reminiscent of more current advocates of the holding environment, containment, and empathy. Hoffer (1990) puts Ferenczi's approach in these terms:

In keeping with the consistent portrayal of the patient as child and victim of the insensitive parent and analyst, overwhelming trauma to the ego serves as the paradigm for Ferenczi's understanding of his disturbed patients. Psychological surrender in the service of psychological survival is vividly described as the basis for a group of defence mechanisms. The analyst's task, repeatedly articulated by Ferenczi, is to provide a safe, accepting, loving, empathic, relaxed setting where the trauma necessitating these disruptive defences can be re-experienced, remembered and thereby ultimately resolved [p. 725].

Freud disapproved of such developments as deviations from the work of analysis. For Freud (1912), the analytic field was defined by the transference: "This struggle between the doctor and the patient, between intellect and instinctual life, between understanding and seeking to act, is played out almost exclusively in the phenomena of transference. It is on that field that the victory must be won—the victory whose expression is the permanent cure of the neurosis" (p. 108). And as far as the analytic relationship was concerned, Freud (1915) wrote succinctly: "It is, therefore, just as disastrous for the analysis if the patient's craving for love is gratified as if it is suppressed. The course the analyst must pursue is neither of these; it is one for which there is no model in real life" (p. 167).

The active technique was a direct challenge to and refutation of Freud's principle of abstinence. But, as Hoffer (1991) has pointed out, criticisms of his approach made Ferenczi more aware that the active technique could be harsh, abusive of patients, and excessively authoritarian. It resulted at times in patients who became compliant out of fear, thus reproducing earlier infantile traumata. In retreat from this tendency and from Freud's advice, Ferenczi advocated a more positive approach. As Hoffer (1991) comments, "By this time, Ferenczi had come to view Freud's technical recommendations as essentially negative ones. He took it upon himself to enrich psychoanalytic technique by including the 'positives' which he felt Freud omitted, including 'tact', 'empathy' (*Einfühlung*), elasticity, indulgence, warmth, candour and responsiveness, in an egalitarian rather than in an authoritarian atmosphere" (p. 467).

The difference between Freud and Ferenczi lies in their conceptions of the analytic relationship. For Freud, the analysis was encapsulated, removed from the patient's real life, and focused in the confines of the analytic hours. This allowed him to analyze his own daughter, as well as Ferenczi, a close and valued colleague. For Ferenczi, the analysis could not be corralled within designated hours, but embraced the whole of his relationship with Freud. Ferenczi believed that there was no distinction between the analytic relationship and the real relationship: The analytic relationship was the only relationship, so that inclusion of the reality of the patient—his or her life and personality—and the reality of the analyst was made on the same terms. The extreme manifestation of this belief occurred in his practice of mutual analysis, in which patient and analyst took turns analyzing each other. Ferenczi had to abandon the experiment because of his fear of violating the confidentiality of his other patients in the course of free associating (Hoffer, 1991).

From a historical perspective, I would conclude that in Ferenczi's technique the analytic relationship was absorbed into the real relationship in such a way that the effects of transference were obscured. Many of the recommendations of his positive technique would fall within the alliance. For Freud, who had no concept of therapeutic alliance, there was no basis for accepting any of Ferenczi's modifications of analytic technique without casting them as intrusions of reality that violated the essential transference experience. I would like to think that a distinction between the therapeutic alliance and the real relationship may have offered a middle ground on which Freud and Ferenczi might have reached agreement. Without a concept of alliance, Freud had no way to come to terms with Ferenczi's insistence on the demands of reality, and Ferenczi had no basis for dealing with the nontransferential aspects of the patient in a manner that would respect Freud's principle of neutrality and abstinence.

In any case, the issues embedded in their controversy have not disappeared. They can be found in analytic views that debate the relative therapeutic merits of interpretation versus the interpersonal and interactional aspects of the relationship between analyst and patient. Where does the curative power of analysis lie? In mutative interpretations? In the quality of personal relationship between the participants in the process? In both? In what degree? The balance may differ from patient to patient—we can presume that Ferenczi was dealing with patients somewhat lower on the scale of character pathology. His emphasis on relational aspects may come closer to the view of many contemporary theorists concerning the broadening scope of psychoanalysis. It certainly has its reverberations in the self psychology of Kohut.

THE CHARACTERS OF THE ANALYST AND THE PATIENT

The character or personality of the analyst impinges on the analytic process in a variety of ways. It represents a major contributing factor in the real relationship and contributes significantly to the therapeutic alliance. It may also influence transference by providing characteristics congruent with transference determinants. Nonetheless, the character of the analyst is one of the real factors that frame the analytic process. A useful inquiry into the role of the analyst's character in the analytic process comes from Baudry (1991); I will utilize and comment on his discussion, as well as broaden it to include the question of the character of the patient and its influence on the analytic process as another salient component of the real relationship.

The personality of the analyst is an unavoidable dimension of the analytic interaction but tends to be numbered among "those subtle, unfathomable, intuitive aspects of the professional behavior of an analyst that provide much of the frame and background of the analytic relationship" (Baudry, 1991, p. 917). It may be expressed in aspects of the analyst's individual style, although the links between style and character may be somewhat loose. The personality attributes that impinge on the analytic process may include the analyst's competence as an analyst, commitment to the process, values, ideals, training and education, use of language, habits, interests, physique, and life experience (Ticho, 1966). The same list of characteristics is applicable mutatis mutandis to the patient. Each party may react to the personality characteristics of the other in ways that are outside the alliance and transference.

Baudry (1991) raises the question of whether and how the analyst's character might influence his or her technique. He offers three possibilities:

(1) general self-syntonic beliefs and attitudes which permeate all aspects of the analyst's functioning both personal and professional: pessimism/optimism, degree of permissiveness, activity vs. passivity, degree of warmth vs. distance, rigidity/flexibility, authoritarian tendencies, and so forth; (2) aspects of the style of the given analyst—tone, manner, verbosity, use of humor, degree of irony; (3) the analyst's characteristic reactions to various affects of the patient or to problems in the treatment, such as stalemated situations [p. 922].

Although any or all of these possibilities can influence the interaction between the analyst and the patient, it is important to note that these are not necessarily aspects of countertransference. There is always the possibility that countertransference dynamics may enter the picture, but the qualities we are discussing belong to the analyst's personality exclusive of transference. For the purpose of clarity, I would favor a specific definition of countertransference here, namely, one that bases the countertransference in the analyst's neurotic transference to the patient, whether that reaction is conscious or unconscious, is affective or cognitive, or facilitates or impedes the analytic process. Thus, the analyst's tendency to assume a relatively authoritarian position may not reflect countertransference at all, but may be merely a personality characteristic. At the same time, the patient's response—whether rebellious or compliant—may or may not reflect transference, but may represent no more than a characteristic of his or her adaptive style. And once again, I would underline the fact that similar characteristics of the analysand are not necessarily aspects of transference or resistance, but may be merely characteristics of the patient's personality and style. Attribution of such forms of behavior and/or interaction to transference or countertransference are more reliably made when there is evidence to support such a claim.

CLINICAL RELEVANCE

To the extent that reality factors enter into the analytic process, they raise the question as to how much and in what manner they might contribute to or interfere with the therapeutic effort. Does the impingement of reality erode the analytic abstinence and neutrality that Freud thought was so important to analytic work? Must reality factors always be taken as a form of resistance to the analytic process? Baudry (1991) takes an unequivocal position on this question: "I do not believe I am overstating the case in seeing the purpose of technique and its structure as an effort to tame the personality of the analyst so as to allow psychoanalytic work to be done. That is, the rule of abstinence limits the development of a real relationship between the patient and the analyst" (p. 920).

Certainly, the effects of the real relationship on the patient cannot be excluded from the process. Commenting on the changes in the patient's relationship to the analyst, Balint (1965) observes:

> [A]ll these changes appear to point into one direction, which is accepting the analyst as a "real" person. That means that the patient tries to find out his analyst's wishes and desires, interests, needs and sensitivities and then is at pains to adapt his behaviour and associations, even his use of phrases and forms of speech, to the image formed of his analyst, in order to find pleasure in the analyst's eyes [p. 132].

But this need also evolves; presumably reacting to Ferenczi's stress on mutuality, he continues:

> The patient gradually realizes, understands and accepts his analyst's shortcomings, especially in relation to himself (the patient). Parallel with this process he renounces bit by bit his wish to change the analyst into a co-

operative partner, i.e. to establish a harmonious relation in which the two partners—patient and analyst—will desire the same satisfaction in the same *mutual* act, and turning towards the world of reality tries to find someone else there, better suited for such a purpose [p. 133].

In other words, according to Balint, the patient would seek to draw the reality of the analyst into the transference. The analyst's abstinence and resistance to the transference pull would then set the stage for transference analysis and surrender of the transference desire. I would argue that an essential part of this process occurs in the alliance sector, because the patient will only surrender his wishes to the extent that he can join the analyst in the therapeutic effort and intent. The gradual shift in accepting the characteristics and limitations of the analyst reflects a greater focusing of the analytic effort in the alliance. The point of abstinence, it seems to me, is to maintain the alliance in the face of both transferential pressures and the patient's desire to erode the alliance by putting the relationship on a realistic basis. This is a salient component of every analytic process and forms one of its most significant resistances. The distinction between the reality of the analyst in the analytic process and the intrusion of personal influence outside of the accepted channels of the analytic interaction is central; the former is unavoidable and a natural component of the interaction, whereas the latter is a violation of abstinence in the analyst and a form of resistance in the patient.

A THERAPEUTIC MISMATCH

It seems likely that many of these reality factors play a significant role in the problem of matching between analyst and patient. It can be safely asserted that no analyst is equipped to deal equally effectively and competently with every sort of patient. We all do better with some sorts of cases than with others. By the same token, it seems reasonable to presume that most patients will do better with one kind of analyst rather than with another. The mesh of personal characteristics and styles that make for successful analysis is not well understood, but in the practice of analysis we need to keep the possibility of a mismatch between analyst and patient in perspective.

Prediction in this area is pitifully weak. Usually we can only sense the dimensions of a mismatch after it has been experienced. If an analyst senses dislike, irritation, impatience, or perhaps even lack of sympathy with a given patient, the better choice might be to refer the patient rather than to venture into an analysis. But these are paltry and highly subjective criteria that bear little weight. More often the analyst does not know that a mismatch exists and only finds out in the course of the analytic effort. Unfortunately, the patient's criteria of judgment are no better. For the patient, a feeling of comfort and security, and a sense that this analyst can understand and be helpful, are as much as can be hoped for. Entering analysis always involves an element of risk.

THE DEMAND FOR REALITY

I think that the most problematic area in which the role of reality in the analytic process comes into play consists of those rare instances in which the patient forces the issue and demands some intrusion of reality into the analytic process. This, of course, was the bone of contention in the debate between Freud and Ferenczi—Ferenczi did not hesitate to introduce such reality factors, probably responding to the demand, explicit or implicit, of more primitive character disordered patients (Hoffer, 1991). One striking example of an explicit demand was recorded by Casement (1982). The episode has been commented on by several authors, and I will add my own observations since the material lends itself so well to this discussion. The point is in no way to pass judgment on Casement's solution to the dilemma, but to focus the issues pertaining to the role of alliance versus reality in the analytic process.

Casement's patient was a young woman who had suffered a severe scalding as a child of 10 months. Later, when she was 17 months old, the scar tissue was operated on under local anesthesia. Her mother, who was holding her hand, fainted, so she could no longer hold the child's hand to comfort her. Regardless, the surgeon continued the procedure. The experience of facing the surgeon alone without the support of her mother was traumatic for the patient. In recalling and reexperiencing the terror of this trauma, the patient begged Casement to hold her hand so that she could tolerate the anxiety. She even threatened to leave the analysis if he did not comply. Casement judiciously explained that many analysts would not permit such a thing, but that he also appreciated that the patient's need was so great that holding his hand might be the only way for her to tolerate reliving the experience. He told the patient that he would think about it and let her know after the intervening weekend.

The rationalization for holding the patient's hand would be to provide a corrective experience—the reliving of the trauma, this time with the support of a protective mother figure. Realizing that he was excessively influenced by his fear of losing the patient, Casement decided not to hold the patient's hand, feeling that it would not have helped her that much; no doubt Ferenczi would have acceded to the request with little hesitation. Hoffer (1991) summarizes the dilemma: ''Does the analyst, by acceding to the demand, provide a corrective emotional experience which then *precludes* a genuine resolution of the affects originating in the traumatic event? Or, by not acceding to the expressed need, does the analyst anti-therapeutically *re-traumatize* the patient?'' (pp. 469–470).

Casement's dilemma was either to offer a corrective emotional experience and try to provide the patient with a better mother or to be withholding and become the unempathic surgeon in a persecutory delusion (Fox, 1984). Fox comments: ''[T]he principle of abstinence must be viewed in terms of the management of the clinical situation in order to create the conditions for the development of an interpretable transference. In this case, too great a frustration (or absence) seemed to precipitate a delusional transference. Optimal frustration-distance, however, enabled the transference illusion of the mother who failed to emerge and to be worked through'' (pp. 231–232). And further:

> In his [Casement's] carefully articulated description, he shows the critical need for an optimal presence–absence in a patient who was struggling to maintain an analysable relationship with him. He demonstrated how he was able to substitute an on-going empathic attitude for her request for physical contact so that she was able to work through a critical separation in her early development. As is perhaps most clear in this case, a degree of gratification is necessary to maintain an analytic presence. Some of the recent work of Kohut and his followers may be viewed in the light of this reformulation of the principle of abstinence [p. 234].

Hoffer (1991) supports Fox's (1984) view that abstinence serves as a guiding principle for managing the dimensions of frustration–gratification and isolation–involvement in the analytic situation. He then adds a further consideration:

> In my view, the crucial point is that the analyst be free to 'consider such a possibility', and be willing to do the active work of re-thinking the technical 'principles' in each clinical situation. The analyst must tolerate the tension and the 'essential ambiguity' (Adler, 1989) of the analytic situation in order to maintain the genuineness of the analytic relationship. Rigid adherence to any 'absolute rule' of treatment can remove the immediacy required for a genuine analytic relationship. Analysands will deal with questions and the associated feelings and fantasies in an 'as-if' way if they know the analyst's thinking is foreclosed by strict adherence to any preformed doctrine [p. 470].

I would like at this point to review Casement's experience in terms of the tension between the therapeutic alliance and the real relationship.

There are a number of indications in the case material to suggest that Casement was dealing with a patient whose personality structure was pitched at a more or less borderline level—I would consider the intense vulnerability to regression, the tendency to act out tensions, the relative intolerance of anxiety or other dysphoric affects, the relatively poor capacity for delay of gratification, the demand for immediate gratification, the tendency to relate to significant objects on a need-satisfying basis, and the poor capacity to maintain the discrimination between fantasy and reality, as indices of relatively poor structure and as consistent with a diagnosis of primitive character disorder (Meissner, 1984). This is part of the context for the dilemma posed by the patient's acute need.

If we pose the issue in terms of the tension between reality and the therapeutic alliance, the patient is seeking relief of intolerable anxiety by appealing for a disruption of the alliance. Casement had to make a judgment—which need was primary in the patient in terms of the facilitation of the analysis? Was the infantile need for physical contact and support she experienced in the intensity of reliving the event uppermost? Or was the more important kind of support the support offered in the analysis, which would help sustain her capacity to tolerate the affects and work them through? Was the first a necessary prologue to the second? Or, in other terms, was the introduction of a real element necessary to preserve or reestablish the alliance?

Casement's resolution of the difficulty was admirable, but why? Was it because he at least offered the possibility of real gratification? Would the real gratification have served this purpose better, as Ferenczi might argue? I would urge that the essential element was his restitution of the alliance in the face of the patient's transference demand. The elements that contributed to this resolution were his empathy with the patient's need and terror, his understanding of the traumatic roots of it, his avoidance of any rigid or authoritarian stance, his willingness to leave the question of whether or not to gratify the patient's wish open to consideration, and his openness to discuss the various sides of the dilemma with her. These are all stances that I would regard as aspects of the therapeutic alliance. One might view the dynamics of the situation in terms of the patient's feelings of victimization and vulnerability in the analytic situation and her attempt to turn the analytic tables and victimize the analyst by demanding that he abandon his analytic stance and accede to her wishes. Casement found a way to avoid the Scylla of gratification and violation of analytic boundaries and the Charybdis of unempathic distance. These tensions can be resolved, I contend, only within the therapeutic alliance.

The issue in large measure is whether to support the infantile need of the patient or the patient's more mature capacities to tolerate the anxiety and to work through the traumatic experience in an analytically useful way. The approach through the alliance would direct itself to the latter prospect. The analytic situation offers ample gratification and support to the patient without the violation of physical boundaries. But these supportive elements, which in some degree are required for all patients, are dependent on the therapeutic alliance. The analyst's willingness to consider options and to discuss them openly and nondefensively with the patient are integral parts of the alliance-based interaction.

In this sense, one can draw the strong conclusion that the intrusion of reality factors in the analytic process is substantially a form of resistance that counters and erodes the alliance; the correction of the intrusion of reality lies in the reconstitution and confirmation of the therapeutic alliance. Even so, there are occasions when analysts appeal to the introduction of reality as a means of confirming or reestablishing the alliance. Fields (1985), for example, cites the case of a man who stoutly resisted his transference interpretations and demanded that Fields advise him about what to do about his wife's suspected infidelities. Fields's effort to explain his reasons for not gratifying the patient's wish went nowhere. In the face of this impasse, Fields decided to offer advice in order to regain the alliance. Rather than seeing this approach as building the alliance, I would see it as undermining it. Over and above the potentially paranoid quality of the patient's outlook, a cautious analyst would have to consider the possibility of a transferential trap in which he could be held accountable and blamed for any unfortunate consequences of his or her advice. Giving advice crosses the boundary between alliance and reality and undermines the alliance. In contrast, an approach through the alliance would have some empathy for the patient's anxiety, and would find a way to explore the patient's wish for advice and the potential consequences of either gratifying or denying the wish.

From another perspective, the conclusion may not be quite so strong. Here a clearer sense of the distinction between reality and the alliance plays a significant role. The analyst's intervention lies not in absolute abstinence and interpretation in such cases, but in approaching the patient in terms of the alliance, whereby the involvement and presence of the analyst is cast in nontransferential terms. The analyst's presence in the interaction is not in these terms reality based, but alliance based. The alliance demands some degree of personal involvement and give-and-take in the analytic relationship—but the give-and-take is cast within the framework of the consistent and firm boundaries of the therapeutic alliance. Any principle of genuine abstinence and analytic neutrality must take into consideration and allow room for the essential role of the therapeutic alliance in all analytic work. When the foundation of the analytic process in the therapeutic alliance is not possible or becomes so distorted that it is beyond redemption, analytic work is no longer possible.

REFERENCES

Adler, G. (1989), Transitional phenomena, projective identification, and the essential ambiguity of the psychoanalytic situation. *Psychoanal. Quart.*, 58:81–104.

Balint, M. (1965), *Primary Love and Psycho-Analytic Technique.* New York: Liveright.

Baudry, F. (1991), The relevance of the analyst's character and attitudes to his work. *J. Amer. Psychoanal. Assn.*, 39:917–938.

Bernal y del Rio, V. (1984), The "real" similarities and differences in the psychoanalytic dyad. *J. Amer. Acad. Psychoanal.*, 12:31–41.

Casement, P. J. (1982), Some pressures on the analyst for physical contact during the reliving of an early trauma. *Internat. Rev. Psychoanal.*, 9:279–286.

de Jonghe, F., Rijnierse, P. & Janssen, R. (1991), Aspects of the analytic relationship. *Internat. J. Psycho-Anal.*, 72:693–707.

Ferenczi, S. (1932), *The Clinical Diary of Sandor Ferenczi,* ed. J. Dupont. Cambridge, MA: Harvard University Press, 1988.

—— (1949), Ten letters to Freud. *Internat. J. Psycho-Anal.*, 30:243–250.

Fields, M. (1985), Parameters and the analytic process: A contribution to the theory of the "mature transference." *J. Amer. Acad. Psychoanal.*, 13:15–33.

Fox, R. P. (1984), The principle of abstinence reconsidered. *Internat. Rev. Psychoanal.*, 11:227–236.

Freud, S. (1912), The dynamics of transference. *Standard Edition*, 12:97–108. London: Hogarth Press, 1958.

—— (1915), Observations on transference love. *Standard Edition*, 12:157–171. London: Hogarth Press, 1958.

Grubrich-Simitis, I. (1986), Six letters of Sigmund Freud and Sandor Ferenczi on the interrelationship of psychoanalytic theory and technique. *Internat. Rev. Psychoanal.*, 13:259–277.

Gutheil, T. G. & Havens, L. L. (1979), The therapeutic alliance: Contemporary meanings and confusions. *Internat. Rev. Psychoanal.*, 6:467–481.

Hoffer, A. (1990), Review of *The Clinical Diary of Sandor Ferenczi. Internat. J. Psycho-Anal.*, 71:723–727.

—— (1991), The Freud–Ferenczi controversy—A living legacy. *Internat. Rev. Psychoanal.*, 18:465–472.

Kantrowitz, J. L. (1992), The analyst's style and its impact on the analytic process: Overcoming a patient–analyst stalemate. *J. Amer. Psychoanal. Assn.*, 40:169–194.

Kohut, H. (1977), *The Restoration of the Self.* New York: International Universities Press.

—— (1984), *How Does Analysis Cure?* ed. A. Goldberg & P. Stepansky. Chicago: University of Chicago Press.

Langs, R. (1992), *Science, Systems, and Psychoanalysis.* New York: Karnac.

Lester, E. P. (1990), Gender and identity issues in the analytic process. *Internat. J. Psycho-Anal.*, 71:435–444.

Mahler, M. S., Pine, F. & Bergman, A. (1975), *The Psychological Birth of the Human Infant.* New York: Basic Books.

Meissner, W. W. (1984), *The Borderline Spectrum: Differential Diagnosis and Developmental Issues.* New York: Aronson.

—— (1992), The concept of the therapeutic alliance. *J. Amer. Psychoanal. Assn.,* 40:1059–1087.

Spence, D. P. (1982), *Narrative Truth and Historical Truth.* New York: Norton.

Stone, L. (1961), *The Psychoanalytic Situation.* New York: International Universities Press.

Thomä, H. & Kächele, H. (1987), *Psychoanalytic Practice, Vol. 1: Principles.* Berlin: Springer Verlag.

Ticho, E. (1966), The effect of the analyst's personality on psychoanalytic treatment. *Psychoanal. Forum,* 4:135–172.

Viederman, M. (1991), The real person of the analyst and his role in the process of psychoanalytic cure. *J. Amer. Psychoanal. Assn.,* 39:451–489.

Winnicott, D. W. (1949), Hate in the countertransference. *Internat. J. Psychoanal.,* 30:69–75.

3

Trauma, Memory, and the Therapeutic Setting

Arnold H. Modell

The enormous complexity of the therapeutic process is further complicated by the fact that every patient makes use of the therapeutic process in his or her own distinctive fashion. The therapist may have hopes and expectations regarding the use the patient will make of the treatment, but it is always the patient who decides. The implication here is that there is a "wisdom of the mind" that parallels the "wisdom of the body." The person who suffered from traumas and deprivation or parental absence will of necessity make use of the treatment in a different fashion from the so called "classical neurotic" patient. As treatment works differently for each individual, there can be no standardized explanations. Yet even with this disclaimer in mind I believe it is possible to make some generalizations concerning the therapeutic action in cases of developmental trauma.

Therapists' concept of developmental trauma has been enlarged to include not only gross acts of physical violence or sexual seductions but also the more subtle chronic traumatic interactions between the caregiver and the child, such as a deficiency or developmental absence when there should have been a presence. We therapists believe that patterns of early interaction between mother and child become engrafted within the self even prior to the stage of language acquisition (Trevarthen, 1979).

When we therapists consider traumatic cases we must recognize the uniqueness of the individual and the fact that for reasons that we need to investigate, some individuals can transcend childhood traumatic experiences and some, of course, cannot.

But what is new in our thinking about the therapeutic process? The basic elements of the therapeutic process, such as transference, resistance, interpretation, and the therapeutic setting, were all described by

Freud before World War I. What is new is that since Freud's time all of these concepts have undergone a continuous evolution leading to their redefinition. For example, Freud essentially invented the therapeutic set-up that is the conventional arrangement regarding time and space in therapy. Although Freud devised this basic set-up, he minimized the significance of the patient's actual relationship with the therapist (Modell, 1990). Many therapists believe that the therapeutic setting that is conjoined with the highly individualized relationship between patient and therapist in current time is the foundation on which the treatment rests. In this respect I have often quoted Rycroft (1985), who has expressed this as well as anyone:

> Psychoanalytic treatment is not so much a matter of making the unconscious conscious, or of widening and strengthening the ego, as of providing a setting in which healing can occur and connections with previously repressed, split-off and lost aspects of the self can be re-established. And the ability of the analyst to provide such a setting depends not only on his skill in making "correct" interpretations but also on his capacity to maintain a sustained interest in, and relationship with, his patients [p. 123].

To most of you this is hardly news, but not very long ago this would have been considered a controversial assertion and still is so considered by some ultraconservative analysts.

Winnicott's (1954) well-known comment on this Freudian set-up assumes the conjointness of the setting and the patient's relationship with the therapist. He said: "At a stated time the analyst would be reliably there, on time, alive, breathing. For the limited period of time prearranged (about an hour) the analyst would keep awake and become preoccupied with the patient. The analyst expressed love by the positive interest taken, and hate in the strict start and finish and in the matter of fees and so forth" (p. 285).

Although Freud (1912) recognized the existence of a therapeutic relationship in current time (p. 105), which he called the un-objectionable positive transference, he considered this relationship to be no different from any other healing relationship, like that which occurs between physician and patient. It was a necessary ingredient in the treatment, but it was something that could essentially be taken for granted. Freud did not consider it to be a part of technique and for this reason he felt free to invite his patient, the Rat Man, to partake in the Freud family meal.

As I have said, thought about the basic elements of the therapeutic process has undergone a gradual evolution. The concept of transference has become more egalitarian. There is widespread recognition that transference is not the patient's creation alone but represents an intersubjective process involving both patient and therapist. The therapist is not the only one who is knowledgeable and the patient's criticism of the therapist can no longer be easily dismissed as a resistance. This can be described as a relational or two-person view of the therapeutic process. But I would also caution that a relational view of the transference can be overdone. Therapists must still allow for the possibility that the transference is a projection in the old-fashioned sense; what the therapist does or the personality of the therapist may provide a convenient target for a projection. This may be especially true in cases of trauma in which there is a splitting of the self and portions of the unwanted self are projected outward, as in the process of projective identification.

In my book, *Other Times, Other Realities* (Modell, 1990), I described two kinds of transference—the dependent/containing and the iconic. The dependent/containing transference is another way of considering the therapeutic setting. It is nonspecific in that it occurs in every treatment and I believe that without this form of transference there can be no significant therapeutic action. Conversely, the iconic transference is highly individualized and may or may not be present and therapeutic progress can occur in its absence through the use of the holding environment. But it is difficult for me to imagine that in cases of trauma a significant cure can result without the activation of specific affective memories in the transference.

When we therapists think about therapeutic action in traumatic cases, we must consider the process of memory. When Freud believed, as he did originally, that the neuroses were of traumatic origin, he was especially interested in the role of memory. Freud understood that hysteria represented a disturbance of memory. The somatic conversion symptom represented the detached affective component of an unassimilated traumatic experience. Freud believed that psychopathology resulted when something interfered with the process of retranscription of memory. He described this as a failure of translation of the memory (for discussion of this concept, see Modell, 1990). Indeed, this was Freud's original understanding of what constitutes repression: Repression is evidence of a failure in the translation of memory. He initially thought that a surplus of sexual energy prevented normal translation (Freud, 1896, p. 230). What did Freud mean by translation? What is it that is translated in memory that is analogous to the translation from one language to another? Freud believed that the stages of psychological development were analogous to foreign languages. Experiences held in memory are repeatedly retranscribed by subsequent development. In health, the memory of a traumatic event in childhood occurring at age x

is modified when that chid enters age y and is modified again at age *z* and so forth. Freud's deep insight was that memory is continually modified by subsequent experience, that the past changes the present and the present can also modify the past and change our expectations regarding the future.

Freud therefore understood memory to be a highly dynamic and plastic process. There is not a fixed record of experience that is engraved on our minds for all time. Instead, Freud proposed that memory consists of a retranscription, the process of which he referred to as *nachträglichkeit*. Freud outlined his highly original theory of memory in a letter to his colleague Fliess on December 6, 1896 (Masson, 1985). It is of sufficient importance that I will quote from this letter.

> As you know, I am working on the assumption that our psychic mechanism has come into being by a process of stratification: the present in the form of memory traces being subjected from time to time to a *rearrangement* in accordance with fresh circumstances—to a *retranscription*. Thus what is essentially new about my theory is the thesis that memory is present not once but several times over, that it is laid down in various kinds of indications. . . . I should like to emphasize the fact that the successive registrations represent the psychic achievement of successive epochs of life. At the boundary between two such epochs a translation of the psychic material must take place. I explain the peculiarities of the psychoneuroses by supposing that this translation has not taken place in the case of some of the material which has certain consequences . . . [p. 287].

Freud's 1896 theory of memory as a retranscription has recently been given new life because an analogous theory has been proposed by the Nobel prize–winning neurobiologist Gerald Edelman, who was not aware of Freud's theory of *nachträglichkeit*. He had arrived at similar ideas independently in the course of proposing a global theory of the relation between the mind and the brain. His basic idea is that memory consists not of a static record in the brain, but of a dynamic reconstruction, that is, context bound and established by means of *categories*. According to Edelman's theory (Edelman, 1992) long-term memory consists of categories of experiences awaiting activation. Although as yet there is no firm scientific evidence of how long-term memories are stored in the brain, Edelman suggests that what is stored in the brain is not something that has a precise correspondence with the original experience, but rather, a potentiality awaiting activation. What is stored in memory is not a replica of the event but the *potential* to generalize or refind the category or class of which the event is a member.

The idea of categories has special relevance for trauma. Edelman believes that the formation of perceptual categories is a characteristic of the function of the brain in lower animals as well as in humans. The capacity to perceive the world in terms of categories does not require an advanced brain with linguistic abilities: The capacity to form perceptual categories can be demonstrated in animals as lowly as pigeons. Pigeons can be taught to differentiate images of women from images of fish, neither of which form part of their natural environment.

The perceptual and motor apparatus serve memory by means of a scanning process in which there is an attempt to match current experience with old memory categories. Long-term memories and affective memories are both pleasurable and painful, so that from an evolutionary perspective there is an adaptive advantage for the individual in refinding categories of pleasurable experience as well as in anticipating danger by identifying categorical memories of painful experiences. I have suggested in *Other Times, Other Realities* that the repetition compulsion that Freud attributed to the death instinct might be more properly understood as a quality of memory. Individuals actively repeat painful experiences when such experiences remain unassimilated, in Freud's terms, untranslated—that is, when trauma remains unmodified by subsequent experience. We therapists observe memories of unassimilated affective experiences in our patients. I believe that one aspect of Edelman's theory can be confirmed in that these memories are categorical; I have described them as *affect categories.* In referring to affect categories, I have essentially revived the old idea of *complexes,* which can now be placed in a neurobiological context.

What is meant by an affect category? A psychological category can be thought of as a gestalt that in a metaphorical sense represents a class of experiences. This can be best illustrated by a clinical example. A patient related the following incident: Because the airline on which he had booked a flight went out on strike, my patient was stranded in a distant city and unable to return home. He did everything possible to obtain passage on another airline, cajoling and pleading with the functionaries of other airlines, all to no avail. Although my patient was usually not unduly anxious, and was in fact a highly experienced traveler who in the past had remained calm under circumstances that would frighten many people, in this particular situation he experienced an overwhelming and generalized panic. He felt as if the unyielding airline representatives were like Nazis and that the underground passages of the airline terminal resembled a concentration camp. The helplessness of his not being able to return home, combined with the institutional intransigence of the authorities, evoked an old affect category in my patient. When this man was 3 years old he and his parents were residents of a central European country and, as Jews, were desperately attempting to escape from the Nazis. They did in fact manage to obtain an airline passage to freedom, but until that point the outcome was very much in doubt. Although my patient did not recall his affective state at that time, his parents reported that he seemed cheerful and unaffected by their great anxiety. In this example, his helpless inability to leave a foreign city combined with the intransigence of the authorities evoked a specific affect category that remained as a potential memory of an unassimilated past experience.

In this example a specific old affect category was evoked because of its metaphoric correspondence to a current life experience. In cases of trauma, specific affect categories are evoked within the transference, which is, of course, not the same as the evocation of a specific affect category by a comparable life experience. When these ideas are applied to cases of trauma, I find it necessary to cite Fairbairn's (1952) theory of splitting of the self. Fairbairn observed that in cases of traumatic relationships, both actors—the self and the other—are internalized within the self. Although Fairbairn did not originally describe the affective component, it has since been discovered that these split-off aspects of the self are centered on specific affective memories of the traumatic interaction between the self and the other. Each of these specific affectively charged memories corresponds to an affect category. The incoherence of these two conflicting aspects of the self leads to a dissociative splitting of the self, which in turn seriously impedes the recategorization of memory. Both the self as victim and the self as aggressor are internalized as split-off aspects of the self. During the process of projective identification these dissociated aspects of the self are activated within the transference and, if unrecognized by the therapist, may lead to a therapeutic stalemate.

We therapists have learned that the patient may unconsciously assume the role of the stage director who assigns us roles that may conflict with our therapeutic ideals and we may thus find ourselves acting in unexpected ways. In cases of developmental trauma the affect categories that come into play are split-off aspects of the patient's self. At times the therapist is the aggressor, at other times he or she is the victim, and perhaps most confusing, the therapist may be simultaneously both victim and aggressor.

Freud had a deep insight, which he expressed in his letter to Fliess, namely, that psychopathology results if there is a failure of retranscription of memory in subsequent stages of development. When there is a dissociative splitting of the self, such a retranscription cannot take place. This is evident in cases of severe trauma in which the present appears to be "telescoped" into the past and everything in current time is interpreted as a confirmation of the traumatic past. Such individuals may find it almost impossible to experience novelty. If this is the case, if novelty cannot be experienced, how then can such an individual change?

It is important to keep in mind the centrality of the therapeutic setting and the therapeutic relationship. It has long been recognized that one element in the therapeutic action of psychotherapy is the contrast between an old relationship and the new relationship with the therapist. This is implicit in the much maligned expression "corrective emotional experience." Therapists are now better able to specify what this difference consists of. I would suggest that a major difference between the past and the present is that an effective therapeutic setting provides the patient with a background of safety or a holding environment. There is a further difference between the traumatic past and the current therapeutic relationship in that the therapeutic setting takes on a reality that is different from that of ordinary life. This is implicit in the concept of the *therapeutic frame*. This term has been used in many different contexts, but here would suggest an analogy to the frame that functions like the frame on a painting—it encloses a separate reality. The reality that is enclosed within the therapeutic setting is different from that of ordinary life. The metaphor of the frame is consistent with yet another metaphor—that of the therapeutic setting as a playing space and the rules of the therapeutic relationship as analogous to the rules of a game. For when one enters a game one also enters a reality separate from that of ordinary life. This idea is also implicit in Winnicott's notion that treatment takes place in a potential space, an area in which illusions are generated. He also referred to this potential space, this shared reality, as a playful or illusionary intermingling of the inner world of the two participants. Winnicott (1971) said:

> Psychotherapy takes place in the overlap of two areas of playing, that of the patient and that of the therapist. Psychotherapy has to do with two people playing together. The corollary of this is that where playing is not possible then the work done by the therapist is directed towards bringing the patient from a state of not being able to play into a state of being able to play [p. 38].

It should be clear that the term *game* need not imply something that is frivolous; play is not necessarily contrasted to serious things in life. Games, in order to take place, require certain conditions of safety. I have suggested that what the therapist does as part of ordinary, "good enough" technique contribute to this sense of safety. I have in mind the therapist's reliability and punctuality—that he or she is there primarily to meet the patient's needs and not vice-versa, that the therapist is constantly attentive and listening, that the therapist attempts not to retaliate, and so forth. All of this differentiates the therapist from people in the patient's ordinary life. In a sense, what I have described is part of the rules of the game, the rules that maintain the frame. Gregory Bateson (1971) pondered the implications of his observations of animals at play. He observed animals at mock fighting in a zoo and reasoned that some sort of communication must exist that would tell the participants: "This is only play." Similarly, there must exist a set of signals between the two participants to inform each other that "This is not ordinary life." And so it is in the therapeutic setting.

All of this is background to the question I raised earlier: How is novelty introduced in traumatic cases? I am suggesting that a key element of the therapeutic action in cases of trauma consists of the reactivation of specific affect categories within the safety of the play space of the therapeutic setting. This environment, within the frame, an environment that is separate from that of ordinary life, permits a recategorization of memory that would not occur in ordinary life. But there is a paradox here, for if the therapist always remained within the frame, the recategorization of traumatic memories would not be facilitated.

I earlier used the hypothetical example of a traumatized patient who unconsciously communicates two disparate affect categories—that of the victim and that of the aggressor. Affects are contagious, if we therapists are emotionally open to our patients, we will respond internally in a fashion complementary to theirs. At times this response will be controlled by the therapist, but there are also times when the therapist may be swept up in an uncontrolled emotional response, as occurs in cases of projective identification. It is customary these days to refer to such instances as the therapist's "enactments." If the therapist behaves as someone in ordinary life would, it may be experienced by the patient as a disruption of the frame. But as I indicated, this may prove—paradoxically—to be therapeutic, provided that the frame is restored. I believe that at certain times in the treatment a level of authenticity is therapeutic, but I must add that I do not recommend that we continuously respond to our patients as one would do in ordinary life. I believe that it is the shift between ordinary life and the illusion contained within the frame that facilitates the recontextualization of traumatic memories. The shift from ordinary life back into the frame is usually accomplished by means of interpretation. Simply the act of interpretation signifies the therapist's assumption of a role within the frame. It has long been thought that the therapeutic effect of transference interpretations resides in the fact that they are made at the point of affective urgency. Specific affect categories are evoked within the transference but are then recontextualized.

There is first a repetition of the past, then the same affective experience is placed within a new and different context. It is this contrast between the old affect category and this new experience in current time that facilitates the recategorization of the affective component of memory that I believe is at the heart of the therapeutic process. The memory of the traumatic experience itself may, of course, remain unaltered.

However, we therapists know that, despite our best efforts, in some cases this therapeutic action does not occur. On the negative side, therapists refer to this as resistance, but in a positive sense, we can observe something that enables some individuals to transcend traumatic relationships, at times without the help of psychotherapy. We recognize that those individuals who can find sources of sustenance within the private self tend to be resilient to the blows of fate. Children who survive intensely traumatic environments have been systematically observed (Anthony and Cohler, 1987). One such child, who was subjected to the psychotic outbursts of a manic-depressive mother, remained composed in the midst of her mother's attacks and thrived both scholastically and interpersonally. She was asked to make a cardboard construction of what it felt like to live with her sick mother. She constructed a "castle," which she described as the little space that she arranged for herself in the household and into which she could retreat when things got rough.

Freud spoke of a necessary translation of traumatic experiences. I would interpret this to mean that in order to transcend trauma one must be able to actively transform the experience, that is to say, to bring it into the domain of the private self. I can best illustrate this process by turning to the biography of a great artist, Charlie Chaplin (Robinson, 1985). Charlie Chaplin's alcoholic father deserted the family and Chaplin and his brother were left in the care of their mother, who was described as schizophrenic. She was reportedly a loving mother, but when she became acutely ill she had to be periodically hospitalized. At these times, Chaplin and his older brother were domiciled in public institutions for the poor. When their mother recovered, there would be a joyous family reunion. There is a famous scene in *City Lights* in which Chaplin meets a millionaire who when drunk is his best friend. This man brings Chaplin home and entertains him lavishly, but when he becomes sober he does not know Chaplin and throws him out of his house. This scene suggests a parody of Chaplin's relationship to his mother, who was by turns totally loving and totally absent. In fact, Chaplin's debut involved another transformation of the trauma of his mother's illness. The story is told that Charlie's mother was a vaudeville singer whose voice cracked during a performance, which caused her to become confused and leave the stage in complete humiliation. Charlie, then aged 5 or 6, took her place on the stage and gave a comic imitation of his mother's performance, for which he was roundly applauded.

What I am suggesting is that the transformation of traumatic affective memories through recontextualization may depend on the capacity to generate new meanings, which is, of course, the ultimate aim of all of psychotherapeutic endeavors.

REFERENCES

Anthony, J. & Cohler, B. (1987), *The Invulnerable Child.* New York: Guilford.
Bateson, G. (1971), A theory of play and fantasy. In: *Steps to an Ecology of Mind.* New York: Ballantine, pp. 177–193.
Edelman, G. (1992), *Bright Air, Brilliant Fire.* New York: Basic Books.
Fairbairn, W. R. D. (1952), *Psychoanalytic Studies of the Personality.* London: Tavistock.
Freud S. (1896), Letter to Fliess May 30, 1896. In: Extracts from the Fliess papers (1892–1899). *Standard Edition,* 1:229–232. London: Hogarth Press, 1966.
——— (1912), The dynamics of transference. *Standard Edition,* 12:97–108. London: Hogarth Press, 1958.
Masson, J., ed. & trans. (1985), *The Complete Letters of Sigmund Freud to Wilhelm Fliess.* Cambridge, MA: Harvard University Press.
Modell, A. (1990), *Other Times, Other Realities.* Cambridge, MA: Harvard University Press.
Robinson, D. (1985), *Chaplin.* New York: McGraw-Hill.
Rycroft, C. (1985), *Psychoanalysis and Beyond.* London: Chatto & Nindus.
Trevarthen, C. (1979), Communication and cooperation in early infancy: A description of primary intersubjectivity. In: *Before Speech: The Beginning of Interpersonal Communication,* ed. M. Bullova. Cambridge: Cambridge University Press, pp. 321–347.
Winnicott, D. W. (1954), Metapsychological and clinical aspects of regression within the psycho-analytic set-up. In: *Collected Papers.* New York: Basic Books, 1958, pp. 278–294.
——— (1971), *Playing and Reality.* New York: Basic Books.

4

The Importance of Diagnosis in Facilitating the Therapeutic Action of Psychodynamic Psychotherapy of an Adolescent

Otto F. Kernberg

The effectiveness of psychodynamic psychotherapy is guided by an appropriate assessment of the indications, contraindications, and prognosis for psychotherapeutic interventions, and a specific frame for psychotherapy. Adequate theoretical understanding of any individual case is predicated on establishing an accurate diagnosis of the patient. Such a diagnosis is especially important in evaluating the severity of any character pathology in an adolescent, given the difficulty in differentiating varying degrees of emotional turmoil as part of a neurosis or an adjustment reaction in adolescence from more severe character pathology that makes its first appearance at this time of life. This chapter elaborates on establishing the diagnosis of narcissistic pathology as the initial step in the treatment of a troubled adolescent with character pathology.

THE DIAGNOSIS OF IDENTITY DIFFUSION AND REALITY TESTING

The narcissistic personality disorder is one of the most prevalent severe personality disorders, presenting the syndrome of identity diffusion typical for borderline personality organization. Therefore, the diagnosis of identity diffusion is an essential aspect of the diagnosis of pathological narcissism. It is the first step in the evaluation of the severity of any character pathology in an adolescent.

The most important task for the psychiatrist examining a troubled adolescent is to establish a reliable diagnosis regarding the severity of the psychopathology. Varying degrees of anxiety and depression, emotional outbursts and temper tantrums, excessive rebelliousness and/or dependency, sexual inhibition and polymorphous perverse sexual impulses and activities may present both in adolescents without severe character pathology and in those with very severe characterological disturbances.

The key anchoring point of the differential diagnosis between milder types of character pathology and neurotic personality organization, on one hand, and severe character pathology and borderline personality organization, on the other, is the presence of normal identity integration as opposed to the syndrome of identity diffusion. This differential diagnosis should not present many difficulties to the experienced clinician. It is important to differentiate normal identity crises in adolescence from their severe counterpart, the syndrome of identity diffusion. Identity crises reflect the impact of the relatively rapid physical and psychological growth in these years including the changes that emerge with puberty, the adolescent's confusion regarding the emergence of strong sexual impulses and the contradictory pressures regarding how to deal with them, and the widening gap between the perception of the adolescent on the part of his or her family and the adolescent's self-perception.

Adolescent identity crisis, in short, refers to the significant discrepancy between the adolescent's rapidly shifting self-concept and others' unchanging perceptions of the adolescent as the adolescent experiences them (Erikson, 1956). Identity diffusion, in contrast, refers to a severe lack of integration of the concept of the self and of the concept of significant others, and usually has its roots in early childhood, related to a lack of normal resolution of the stage of separation-individuation (Mahler, Pine, and Bergman, 1975). The syndrome of identity diffusion may have already made its appearance throughout a patient's childhood, but, given the protective functions of the structured environment of an ordinary childhood experience, the symptoms derived from identity diffusion, except in the most severe cases, usually become evident only when the structure of the parental home environment diminishes in the course of a patient's adolescent development.

Adolescents with symptoms of identity diffusion may present either a completely chaotic and contradictory view of themselves (without their being aware of the contradictory or chaotic nature of the description of self that they convey) or a rigid adherence to social norms, the overidentification with traditional norms or adolescent group formations that is reflected in what has been called the "quiet borderline patient," who impresses the therapist as relatively affectless, indecisive, undefined, and pseudosubmissive (Sherwood and Cohen, 1994). In response to the diagnostician's request of the adolescent to describe himself or herself briefly, to provide a picture that would permit the diagnostician to differentiate him or her from all other persons, the adolescent's self-description in the case of identity diffusion is usually contradictory and chaotic, except when the flatness and overly compliant attitude toward family demands and cultural clichés predominate. This is usually in sharp contrast to the rich and highly personalized image an adolescent with normal identity integration may give of himself or herself. In addition, adolescents with an integrated self-concept describes themselves in ways that are harmonious with their interactions with the diagnostician, in contrast to the sharp discrepancies that exist between the description of the self-concept and the interactions in the diagnostic interviews in the case of adolescents with identity diffusion.

The question complementary to that of the self-concept to be raised when evaluating an adolescent's ego identity is that of the integration of the representations of significant others. This aspect of ego identity is even more important than the integration of the self because, in the special case of the narcissistic personality that I shall examine below, a pathological grandiose self contributes to an integration of sorts of the adolescent's self-concept, while the integration of the concept of significant others remains glaringly absent. Lack of integration of the concept of significant others shows in the adolescent patient's incapacity to convey to the diagnostician a live and integrated picture of the most important persons in the patient's life.

In this regard, as I pointed out in earlier work (1984), an adolescent with a neurotic personality organization, severe conflicts at home and/or at school, and a rebellious and affectively unstable style of interpersonal interactions, may be highly critical of the adults who surround him or her, particularly parents and teachers, may be involved in intense conflicts of loyalties and group formation, and yet may be able to describe with remarkable depth the personalities of all of those with whom he or she has intense personal conflicts. In contrast, the adolescent with identity diffusion shows a remarkable incapacity to convey a live picture of those who are closest to him or her and with whom conflicts, dependency, submission, and/or rebellion are most intense. Therefore, a consistent request to the adolescent to convey a live picture of the persons who are most important in his or her life—regardless of whether the adolescent likes or dislikes them—provides crucial information regarding the adolescent's capacity for integration of the concept of significant others. Naturally, in cases where the personalities of the patient's significant others are objectively chaotic and contradictory, the adolescent with normal identity formation should be able to describe such chaos, but to do it critically, accompanied by an internal need and an active attempt to sort out these chaotic contradictions in his or her significant others.

While the combination of a lack of integration of the self-concept and a lack of integration of the concept of significant others defines an adolescent's identity diffusion and, by itself, determines the diagnosis of borderline personality organization, the certainty of this diagnosis can be reinforced by the evaluation of an adolescent's superego functioning. One central consequence of normal ego identity integration is the facilitation of the integration of the superego, that is, the completion of the process by which the earliest layer of persecutory superego precursors; the later layer of idealized superego precursors; the still later layer of realistic superego precursors of the oedipal period; and the final processes of depersonification, abstraction, and individualization of the superego have been integrated. The absence of normal identity integration in the ego interferes with this integration and brings about various degrees of lack of maturation of the superego.

In fact, the degree of superego integration or lack of such integration is one of the two most crucial prognostic factors for all types of psychotherapeutic intervention, the other factor being the quality of the adolescent's object relations. Here the issues to be evaluated are an adolescent's capacity to invest in values beyond narrow self-interest and direct narcissistic gratification: an adolescent's interest in work, art, and culture; his or her commitments to ideology; and the maturity of his or her value judgments related to such investments. Obviously, the cultural background of the adolescent will crucially codetermine his or her orientation toward value systems, but within any particular socioeconomic and cultural background, adolescents with normal identity integration have the capacity to invest in values such as commitment to friends; loyalty; honesty; interest in sports, music, or politics; the success of a group they belong to, or the history of their particular social group. Under conditions of adolescent identity diffusion, there is a remarkable poverty of such investment in value systems, even in the absence of antisocial behavior. Naturally, the more severe the lack of maturation of the superego, the more prevalent may be antisocial behavior that, in turn, has to be evaluated as the adolescent's adaptation to a particular social subgroup rather than as a high degree of individualized antisocial behavior.

An additional indicator of a normally integrated adolescent superego is the capacity for romantic idealization and falling in love. While not having falling in love in early or middle adolescence may not yet be diagnosable as an indication of superego pathology, the presence of intense love experiences, of having fallen in love, are positive indicators of good superego integration; this capacity emerges normally very fully since the latency years, and there has been a conventional underestimation of the importance of such love experiences in early childhood development (P. Kernberg and Richards, 1994).

In contrast to these key indicators of ego identity and the derived maturation of the superego, the following characteristics that usually indicate severe character pathology in adults are less meaningful in adolescents. To begin, the presence or even dominance of primitive defensive operations, typical for borderline personality organization in adults, has much less diagnostic meaning in adolescents. Given the significant regression in the adolescent's early adaptation to the upsurge of sexual impulses; his or her efforts to reduce the dependency on parents and to transfer early conflicts within the home into the school, the social group formation, and the relations to authorities outside the home; and given, particularly, the normal reactivation of intense oedipal conflicts and preoedipal defenses against them, a broad spectrum of defensive operations—from the mature ones centering around repression to the primitive ones centering around splitting—may be activated in the adolescent patient's interpersonal interactions. Splitting, primitive idealization, devaluation, projection and projective identification, denial, omnipotence, and omnipotence control may coexist with an increased tendency toward repression, reaction formations, displacement, intellectualization, and various inhibitions—all of which manifest themselves in the early diagnostic interviews.

Typically, however, in the case of neurotic personality organization, once the initial anxiety of the adolescent in the diagnostic interviews decreases, primitive defensive operations tend to decrease as well, but may continue unabated in the present areas of conflict outside the treatment situation. By the same token, the severity of neurotic symptoms, affective crises, polymorphous perverse activities, or sexual inhibition do not, by themselves, indicate severity of pathology, except in the case of a patient's consolidated perversion with significant and dangerous sadistic and masochistic components. In these latter cases, the extent to which superego controls protect against excessive activation of aggression become an important aspect of the diagnostic assessment.

All the criteria examined so far serve the purpose of differentiating neurotic personality organization from borderline personality organization. The criterion of reality testing, in contrast, permits the differentiation of borderline personality organization from psychotic personality organization, in other words, the most severe character pathologies from incipient or atypical psychotic developments. The diagnosis of present or absent reality testing is, therefore, crucial. Reality testing, as I have pointed out in earlier work (Kernberg, 1975, 1984), consists in the capacity to differentiate self from non-self and the intrapsychic from the external origin of stimuli, and in the capacity to maintain empathy with ordinary social criteria of reality.

In practice, reality testing may be tested first by exploring whether the adolescent presents hallucinations and/or delusions, that is, "productive symptoms" of psychosis—obviously, the presence of psychotic symptoms indicates loss of reality testing. Second, in cases where there is no overt evidence of hallucinations or delusions, but where abnormal sensory perceptions or ideation are present—such as pseudohallucinations, hallucinosis, illusions, or overvalued ideas—it is very helpful to evaluate the adolescent patient's evaluation of his or her symptom and capacity to empathize with the therapist's evaluation of such a symptom.

More generally, a very helpful method to clarify reality testing is to evaluate what in the patient's behavior, affect, thought content, and/or formal organization of thought processes, impresses the diagnostician as most strange, bizarre, peculiar, or inappropriate in their interaction. At some point in the interview, the diagnostician should tactfully confront the patient with puzzlement over what seems most inappropriate in the patient's behavior, affect, or thought, in order to evaluate to what extent the adolescent may be able to empathize with the diagnostician's observation and provide an explanation that reduces the discrepancy between the observed behavior and the diagnostician's subjective experience of the strangeness of that behavior. When such an explanation on the part of the patient in effect reduces the discrepancy, and indicates that the patient is perfectly able to resonate with the reality testing of the therapist, reality testing is considered to be maintained. When, in contrast, the adolescent patient would seem to disorganize further under the impact of this confrontation, reality testing is probably lost. This is a relatively simple procedure in the hands of an experienced clinician, and of enormous value, as mentioned before, in the differential diagnosis of atypical psychosis.

For example, one adolescent became depressed because, after having been the best student in mathematics throughout elementary school and high school, he only came out second in a mathematics test in his senior year of high school. On further exploration of why this had produced such a depressive reaction, the adolescent insisted that he was convinced he was "the best mathematician of the world," and this was an unforgivable failure. On tactful inquiry, however—how could he be sure that he was the best mathematician of the world if, for example, another young man of his age in a country totally unbeknownst to this patient might be even better in mathematics?—the patient became very angry.

He told the examining psychiatrist that he was "completely idiotic" and then exploded in a rage attack! Subsequent exploration of this breakdown in communication confirmed the impression in the diagnostician that this young man's grandiose idea had delusional qualities and was not an overvalued idea that was part of a pathological grandiose self, that is, a narcissistic personality structure. The diagnosis of a schizophrenic illness was confirmed by further developments later on.

The diagnosis of reality testing by the method described above usually solves the problem of the differential diagnosis between borderline personality organization and psychotic personality organization, in one or several interviews, in the large majority of cases. There are, however, some conditions that make this diagnosis particularly difficult. First, in cases where there is a severe, chronic withdrawal from reality, where, even without any pathological sensory perception or delusion formation, the patient's severe social withdrawal, breakdown in studies and family life, and incapacity for intimate relations represent a dramatic development to outsiders, while the adolescent patient appears to present a strange indifference to his or her plight. In these cases, a careful confrontation of the patient with this discrepancy over a period of time usually permits the differential diagnosis between a severe schizoid or schizotypal personality disorder and a simple form of schizophrenic development.

Second, in cases of paranoid psychosis, often the adolescent patient still knows well enough what might be considered psychotic by the diagnostician and withholds the corresponding information. The diagnosis in such cases is that of an extremely paranoid development in the diagnostic interviews, and the differential diagnosis may take much longer than in most other cases, although it may be strengthened by independent information from projective psychological testing, observations derived from the patient's life outside the diagnostic situation, family interviews, and psychiatric social work.

A third, frequent, difficult diagnostic situation is that presented by patients with a severely defiant, negativistic reaction in the diagnostic interviews, so that not even reality testing regarding this striking behavior may be successfully attempted. Here again, a careful assessment of the patient's functioning at home and in school, his or her social environment, psychological testing, psychiatric social work evaluation, together with a series of diagnostic interviews, may gradually facilitate the diagnosis. Nonpsychotic negativism usually tends to decrease over a period of time throughout the diagnostic interviews, whereas a truly psychotic negativism is much more resistant to the relatively brief period of diagnostic evaluation.

A final, relatively rare type of case where the testing of reality testing proves to be very difficult is that of patients who relate the presence of hallucinatory or delusional experiences of many years' duration, predating by many years the present symptomatology that has brought them to the attention of a psychiatrist—for example, patients who harbor the delusions over many years, sometimes from childhood on, that they will die at a certain early age or who have had chronic hallucinatory experiences over many years without other indications of emotional illness. Once again, repeated testing of reality testing, projective diagnostic testing, and the effort to test reality testing in all other areas except that of this one long-lasting symptom, will eventually provide an adequate diagnostic judgment. Some of these cases with chronic hallucinatory and/or delusional symptoms, particularly if they have a depressive tone, reflect an atypical major affective illness, and the search for other symptoms confirming chronic depression imbedded in the personality structure may facilitate the establishment of this diagnosis.

THE DIAGNOSIS OF NARCISSISTIC PATHOLOGY

The more severe the narcissistic character pathology, the earlier its presence becomes noticeable. Children with narcissistic personality disorder during the school years may present severe problems in their relationships at home and in school; they may replace ordinary friendships with a tendency toward exclusive relationships of dominance and submission, the enactment of grandiose fantasies, the exercise of omnipotent control at home, and/or the intolerance of any relationship in which they are not dominant or the center of attention. The lack of the capacity for mutuality, gratitude, and nonnarcissistically gratifying object investments differentiate pathological narcissism in childhood from normal infantile narcissistic attitudes.

The cases that make their first appearance during adolescence are less severe than those diagnosed in childhood, yet usually more severe than those whose pathology first emerges in early adulthood, reflected in the incapacity to establish intimate love relations and in the breakdown in studies and work. This relationship between the severity and age of emergence of narcissistic psychopathology parallels that for borderline personality organization in general, but the narcissistic personality disorder has some particular features that permit its differentiation within the broader range of patients with borderline personality organization.

First, the syndrome of identity diffusion in the narcissistic personality shows the particularity of an apparent good integration of the self-concept—except that it is a pathological grandiose self-concept—while the representations of significant others usually show severe lack of integration. In fact, it is characteristic of those with narcissistic personality disorders that they have very little capacity for empathy with others. Their relationships with others are dominated by conscious and unconscious envy; they evince a combination of devaluation of others, symbolic spoiling of what they receive from others, exploitativeness, greediness, entitlement, incapacity to truly depend on others, and a lack of capacity for commitment and loyalty in friendships. Regarding the pathological, grandiose self, these adolescents show an exaggerated self-reference and self-centeredness, a tendency toward grandiose fantasies that are very often expressed in exhibitionistic traits, an attitude of superiority, recklessness, and a discrepancy between high ambitions and limited capacities. They are overly dependent on the admiration of others, which may be misinterpreted as their being dependent, but they evince a lack of capacity for gratitude toward those whom they depend on and a shallowness of their emotional life and self-experience that is often reflected in a sense of emptiness, boredom, and stimulus hunger.

Frequently, a dominant symptom of narcissistic adolescents is a significant failure at school. As I have described in earlier work (1984), they show great difficulties in learning from others, from books, in contrast to their fantasy that all knowledge stems from themselves or from their automatic absorption or effortless incorporation of what they come in contact with. If narcissistic adolescents are very bright, they may be excellent students as long as they do not have to make any effort—and often these adolescents show a combination of excellent functioning in subject matters where they are at the top and total breakdown in subject matters where they are not at the top, where they would have to make an effort, where such an effort—and the unconscious envy stirred up by it—is experienced as an insult to their self-esteem. Secondary devaluation of the subjects in which they do not succeed then leads to a vicious cycle of school failure. One patient, who was able to swim since he was a small child and excelled in swimming, never was able to learn to ski because his experience of the first lesson, the comparison with his older siblings who were much better skiers than he was, interfered with his willingness to learn.

The experience of grandiosity and entitlement and of inordinate envy and devaluation, as well as the limitations in empathy and commitment, are cardinal symptoms of the narcissistic personality and easily observable in narcissistic adolescent patients. The surface behavior of these patients, however, may be quite variable. In the typical case, an attitude of superiority and self-assurance and a charming, engaging, seductive friendliness may characterize the patient's early contacts, reflecting the underlying pathological grandiose self. In atypical cases, however, the adolescent's surface behavior may include anxiety, tension, insecurity, and timidity and where fear over nonrecognition of the patient's superiority or of a lesion to his or her narcissistic demands predominate. These adolescents experience bouts of insecurity, in sharp contrast with the usual sense of self-reliance and superiority that characterize most narcissistic patients, and the severity of such bouts of insecurity may bring about the secondary defense of a timid surface behavior that protects them from the actual disappointment of their narcissistic aspirations. Sometimes what dominates in better functioning patients is a certain conventional rigidity, the replacement of the normal capacity for in-depth relationships with significant others, with ideas and values, by a rigid adherence to conventional clichés.

The lack of superego integration of borderline personality organization is accentuated in the case of narcissistic pathology because of the absorption of the idealizing layer of superego precursors—in other words, the ego ideal—into the pathological grandiose self. This condensation between the pathological grandiose self and the ego ideal brings about a kind of false identity integration and facilitates the nonspecific manifestations of ego strength (anxiety tolerance, impulse control, some capacity for sublimatory functioning) that make these patients appear to function much better than the ordinary borderline patient.

The main price, however, for this absorption of the ego ideal into the self—in addition to the deterioration of the world of internalized object relations and of the capacity for nonnarcissistic object investment—is a significant weakening of the maturation of the normal superego. In relatively mild cases, this deterioration shows itself in the persistence of childish values, such as the search for external admiration by physical attractiveness, clothing, possessions, and/or some conventionally determined personal decor, the surface manifestations of which depend on the cultural background of the narcissistic adolescent patient. In addition, the lack of superego integration is reflected in an incapacity to experience normal, mournful grief reactions, and a tendency toward self-regulation by severe mood swings rather than by differentiated self-criticism—the dominance of "shame" culture over "guilt" culture.

In more severe cases, the lack of superego integration is reflected directly in antisocial behavior, the tolerance of aggression infiltrated into the pathological grandiose self and manifest in forms of ego-syntonic sadistic or self-aggressive, self-mutilating, suicidal behavior, and strong paranoid characterological features derived from the reprojection of the earliest layer of persecutory superego precursors onto the external environment. Because of the absorption of the ego ideal into the pathological grandiose self, the persecutory superego precursors cannot easily be absorbed into an overall integrated superego and are reprojected as paranoid traits. The combination, in these severe cases, of narcissistic personality disorder, antisocial behavior, ego-syntonic aggression, and paranoid orientation constitutes the syndrome of malignant narcissism, the most severe—although still psychotherapeutically treatable—form of narcissistic personality disorder. Cases in which superego deterioration proceeds further—to the extent of a total deterioration or absence of superego functions—constitute the antisocial personality disorder (in a strict sense, as opposed to the less precise definition of this personality structure in the DSM classification system).

THE ANTISOCIAL PERSONALITY DISORDER IN ADOLESCENCE

I need to stress that the antisocial personality disorder is the most severe form of narcissistic character pathology; it may be defined as a narcissistic personality disorder with extreme deterioration or absence of superego functions. Clinically, the antisocial personality disorder may be divided into an aggressive type and a passive-parasitic type (Henderson, 1939; Henderson and Gillespie, 1969).

Although practically all patients with antisocial personality disorders, on careful exploration, have a history of symptoms of this disorder reaching back into early childhood, the tendency, in the DSM-III and DSM-IV nomenclature, to separate "conduct disorder" in childhood from the antisocial personality disorder in adulthood (with an artificial limit set at age 18 before the diagnosis of an antisocial personality may be established) ignores this continuity (Hare, 1970; Hare and Shalling, 1978; Kernberg, 1989). The distinction between these two disorders (conduct disorder and antisocial personality disorder) seems absurd from a psychopathological and clinical viewpoint. Given the grave implications of an antisocial personality disorder at any age, it is important that the clinician examining an adolescent with significant antisocial behavior be prepared to diagnose this disorder. I have explored the differential diagnosis between the antisocial personality disorder, the syndrome of malignant narcissism, and the narcissistic personality disorder in earlier work (Kernberg, 1989) and shall summarize briefly the main characteristics of the antisocial personality disorder proper that permit a differential diagnosis with the syndrome of malignant narcissism and the less severe narcissistic personalities with antisocial behavior.

It is important to keep in mind that the passive-parasitic type of antisocial personality is less frequently noticed during early childhood, particularly if antisocial features of the patient's family and social background "submerge" the patient's antisocial behavior into culturally tolerated patterns. Thus, for example, early cheating in school, stealing, and habitual lying may appear less severe in an ambience of social disorganization and severe family pathology than would be the case when such a pathology emerges in a relatively stable and healthy social and family environment. The parents' antisocial tendencies or severe narcissistic pathology may provide convenient "cover-ups" for a child's passive-parasitic antisocial behavior, characterized by manipulativeness, exploitativeness, lying, stealing, and cheating at school.

The predominantly aggressive type of antisocial personality disorder usually becomes apparent because of the impact this pathology exerts over the immediate social environment of the child. As Paulina Kernberg (1989) has pointed out, the aggressive type of antisocial personality disorder in children is characterized by extreme aggression from early childhood on, to the extent that violent and dangerous behavior may be expressed toward siblings, toward animals, and in the destruction of property, and their parents are usually afraid of these children. These children show an "affectless" expression of aggression, chronic manipulativeness and paranoid tendencies, a marked incapacity to keep friends, and sometimes a true reign of terror at home or in their immediate social circle at school. Often the parents are unable to convince mental health professionals of the gravity of the situation. In early adolescence, this aggression extends beyond the family circle and may include frankly criminal behavior.

From a diagnostic viewpoint, the essential characteristics of the antisocial personality proper are, first, the presence of a narcissistic personality disorder as described before. Second, in the case of the antisocial personality of a predominantly aggressive type, the symptoms of malignant narcissism. In the case of the predominantly passive-parasitic type, there is no violence, only passive-exploitative behavior, such as lying, cheating, stealing, and ruthless exploitation. Third, the corresponding antisocial behavior from early childhood on, knowledge of which is provided by a careful evaluation of the past history of the patient.

Fourth, and very fundamentally, these patients present an absence of the capacity for feeling guilt and remorse for their antisocial behavior. They may express remorse for behavior that has been discovered, but not for behavior that they believe is still secret or unknown to anybody else. It is also striking that they are unable to identify with the moral dimension in the mind of the diagnostician, to the extent that, while they may be very skilled in assessing other people's motivations and behavior, the possibility of an ethical motivation is so foreign to them that the exploration of this issue—for example, in wondering how they believe the therapist may be reacting to the patient's antisocial behavior—often reveals their striking incapacity to imagine the therapist's sadness and concern, and even moral shock, regarding their acts of cruelty or exploitation.

Fifth, these adolescents show a total incapacity for any nonexploitative investment in others, an indifference and callousness that extends also to pets, which they may mistreat or abandon without any feelings. Sixth, they show a lack of concern for themselves, as well as for any other person, and present a lack of sense of time and of future and an inability to plan. Often, while a concrete antisocial behavior may be carried out with the perfect sense of a short-term plan, the long-term effects of cumulative antisocial behavior are totally ignored and emotionally insignificant to these patients: a sense of future is a superego function, in addition to an ego function, and glaringly absent in these cases. Seventh, the lack of an affective investment in significant others is matched by a lack of normal love for the self in such patients, expressed in defiant, fearless, potentially self-destructive behavior; a proneness to impulsive acts of suicide when they experience themselves driven into a corner; and, of course, under the impact of intense rage, they present the risk of severely aggressive and homicidal behavior toward others.

Eighth, these patients show a remarkable incapacity for depressive mourning and grief, and an incapacity for the tolerance of anxiety, which shows up in their immediately developing additional symptoms or antisocial behavior when they feel threatened or controlled by external structure. Ninth, these patients show a remarkable lack of learning from experience, which sometimes shows dramatically in their incapacity to really absorb anything provided by the therapist—behind this symptom is a radical devaluation of all value systems, a sense that life is an ongoing struggle either among wolves, or between wolves and sheep, with many wolves disguised as sheep.

Finally, these patients are incapable of falling in love, of experiencing an integration of tenderness and sexuality, and their sexual involvements have a mechanical quality that, in revenge, is eternally unsatisfactory to them. When antisocial personalities suffer from a sadistic perversion, they may become extremely dangerous to others. The combination of severe aggression, the absence of any capacity for compassion, and the lack of superego development is the basis for the psychopathology of mass murder as well as murder in the context of sexual involvements.

In the diagnostic interviews with these patients, their manipulativeness, pathological lying, and shifting rationalizations create what Paulina Kernberg (personal communication) has called "holographic man"—these patients are able to evoke flimsy, rapidly changing, completely contradictory images of themselves, their lives, and their interactions. The diagnostic evaluation of these cases requires taking a complete history from them, to compare shifts in the references to their past communicated at different occasions, to observe their interactions with the therapist as well as with significant others, and to obtain a very full social history in order to compare external observations and information with the patient's communication.

The exploration of the lives of these patients should include tactful questions of why they did not engage in what would seem, under some specific circumstances, expectable antisocial behaviors in their case, which often reveals the lack of the capacity to identify with ethical systems even while the patient is trying to portray a picture of himself or herself as an honest and reliable individual. Naturally, the patient who lies to the diagnostician should be confronted with that in nonpunitive ways, mostly to assess the extent to which the capacity for guilt, remorse, or shame are still available. The antisocial personality disorder patient with passive-parasitic tendencies will show the same general characteristics mentioned for the aggressive type, except direct aggressive attacks on others, on property, on animals, and on the self. Patients with the syndrome of malignant narcissism but without an antisocial personality proper, will present the capacity for guilt, concern for self, some nonexploitive relations, some remnants of authentic superego functions, some capacity for dependency, and their prognosis is significantly better.

Antisocial behavior may present in patients who do not have a narcissistic personality disorder, that is, who do not belong on the continuum I have described, which includes the range of disorders from the narcissistic personality disorder to the syndrome of malignant narcissism to the antisocial personality proper. There are patients with borderline personality organization and other than narcissistic types of personality disorders who may show antisocial behavior, as well as some patients with neurotic personality organization and good ego identity integration. In addition, antisocial behavior may, at times, reflect a neurosis with strong rebellious features in an adolescent, and even a "normal" adaptation to a pathological social subgroup (the "dyssocial" reaction). In all these cases, the antisocial behavior has a much better prognosis, in fact, an excellent prognosis with the psychotherapeutic treatment of the underlying character pathology or neurotic syndrome. Therefore, in all adolescent patients with antisocial behavior, it is essential to evaluate the presence or absence of the syndrome of identity diffusion, of a narcissistic personality disorder, of the syndrome of malignant narcissism, and of an antisocial personality proper.

GENERAL CONSIDERATIONS ABOUT THE DIAGNOSTIC EVALUATION OF CHARACTER PATHOLOGY IN ADOLESCENCE

In general, it is very important to obtain, first of all, a full picture of all the existing symptoms and their respective severity—symptom severity, for example, regarding suicidal tendencies, self-mutilating tendencies, alcohol or drug abuse or dependence, severe depression, or severe eating disturbances—all of which may require immediate interventions that may overshadow a careful evaluation of the patient's character structure. Emergencies have to be taken care of first, and the evaluation of the personality structure may have to wait until the adolescent is in a stable, safe, protected environment.

In all cases, the study of the personality functioning in all areas of the patient's present life takes precedence over taking a past history, and the past history needs to be evaluated in the light of the present functioning of the patient's personality. The comparative analysis of the information provided by the patient, his or her family, and other sources of information—from the school or by psychiatric social work—also needs to be matched with a careful analysis of the interactional features of the relationship between the diagnostician and the patient. This requires an honest communication from the therapist to the patient regarding the information that he or she is obtaining, and a careful discussion of the issue of confidentiality in their interactions.

If an adolescent shows up first with his or her family, there may be an advantage in seeing all of them jointly before seeing the patient alone, and in not seeing family members without the patient first, even if they insist on doing that. By the same token, should the therapist receive information about the patient before seeing him or her, it is important that the therapist share this information with the patient. In families where there exists a culture of keeping secrets from one another, an important part of the diagnostic evaluation should be in opening all channels of communication tactfully but decisively.

Experience in the long-term treatment of patients with severe personality disorders as part of our psychotherapy research project (Kernberg et al., 1989) has taught us that there are some early priorities that require immediate attention: the existence of danger to the physical survival of the patient or of others, the danger of acute disruption of the diagnostic or therapeutic process, the danger of severe interference with the diagnostic process by the patient's and/or other family member's lack of honesty, and the danger of the rapid breakdown of the support system that would otherwise permit carrying out the diagnostic process and that threatens it with premature disruption.

If severely regressive developments occur during the diagnostic process, such as a strong negative reaction toward the diagnostician, it is important to temporarily abandon the pursuit of other information and focus on the adolescent's experience of the immediate situation. Here, psychoanalytic principles of evaluating the acting out of severe negative transferences enter into play, and the experienced clinician may have to spend quite some time in ventilating such negative transference developments without losing sight of the fact that he or she is still in the middle of a diagnostic process. It should be clearly understood that the definitive treatment will have to wait for the availability of complete information regarding the nature of the difficulties. Primitive mechanisms of projective identification, omnipotent control, and severe denial color such early difficulties and may be used to evaluate the existence of identity diffusion, narcissistic pathology, and antisocial behavior.

If the adolescent patient refuses to come to the sessions, work with the family may facilitate the creation of an immediate social structure that will bring the patient back into the diagnostic sessions. For example, the diagnostician may discuss with the family, over a period of time, what measures they can take to bring the patient back to consultations, and may help them to deal with the patient under these circumstances. Should the patient come back to the diagnostic sessions, all these preliminary discussions will have to be shared with him or her. If an acute danger exists to the patient or to the family's physical survival, or if a differential diagnosis with a psychotic process proves to be impossible to achieve in outpatient diagnostic evaluation, a brief period of hospitalization may be indicated to carry out such evaluation in a controlled, supportive environment.

It is always helpful to study the family situation of adolescents who are being evaluated for character pathology. The severity of pathology in the social structure of the family and of the patient's character pathology interact, and family assessment should be part of a routine evaluation of severe psychopathology. The assessment of the extent to which the patient's pathology represents a relatively nonspecific reaction to severe family pathology as opposed to the presence of severe character pathology in the patient—regardless of how severely family pathology interacts with it—is an important aspect of this diagnostic process. Treatment strategies will vary according to the extent to which pathological character structure in the adolescent patient and pathological structure of the family are present.

The careful evaluation of the adolescent patient's social life outside the family structure will provide invaluable data to relate family pathology and character pathology to each other. For example, an adolescent who shows severe behavior disturbances at home, and, initially, in the diagnostic interviews, may have a very active, intense, involved, indepth life of relationships with significant friends and/or admired adults outside the family setting and may gradually "normalize" the interaction in the diagnostic setting as he or she begins to differentiate the diagnostician from family authorities. To the contrary, the family's denial of severe character pathology in their child may be exposed by the adolescent patient's information about the restriction and poverty of his or her emotional investment in significant others and severe conflicts and failure in school. In all cases of significant school failure, intelligence testing, and, when indicated, testing for learning disabilities will clarify further the extent to which character pathology, particularly a narcissistic personality disorder, contributes to the school failure.

The evaluation of the adolescent patient's sexual life provides very important data regarding the capacity for development of object relations in depth, the existence of severe disturbances in sexual functions regardless of the severity of character pathology, and the existence of potentially destructive and self-destructive behaviors in that area that put the adolescent at immediate risk. The tendency toward sexual promiscuity in the age of AIDS may signify active, urgent danger situations that may require rapid therapeutic intervention. At the same time, as mentioned before, the capacity for romantic idealization and falling in love, and, particularly, the capacity to integrate sexual and tender feelings and involvement indicate significant maturation in the area of object relations.

The adolescent's adaptation to group processes also provides important information regarding his character structure. A complete absorption in the group process, the uncritical acceptance of group mores (without personal reflection and differentiation of self within the group), may protect an adolescent from behavioral manifestations of severe identity diffusion, such as potentially severe conflicts in intimacy, by a conventional adaptation to group mores (Kernberg, 1988). The adolescent's capacity for subtle and critical evaluation of the individual members of his or her group will reveal identity integration versus identity diffusion regardless of the adolescent's surface adaptation to the group process.

An adolescent's orientation to a predominant ideology of his or her particular group, be it a general political ideology or an ad hoc ideology of a particular gang, also will provide important information regarding superego development—there is a significant difference between a primitive identification with an idealized group while splitting off of severely hostile evaluations of outgroups, and an awareness that the world is not simply divided between "all good" and "all bad" people. Most political ideologies exist on a spectrum from very paranoid at one extreme to a trivialized and flat conventionalism at the other, with a "humanistic" differentiated middle zone that respects individual differences, sexual intimacy and privacy, and the autonomy of the individual. Where the adolescent patient fits within such an ideological continuum will also reveal important information about his or her superego maturation.

REFERENCES

Erikson, E. (1956), The problem of ego identity. In: *Identity and the Life Cycle*. New York: International Universities Press, 1959, pp. 104–164.

Hare, R. D. (1970), *Psychopathy: Theory and Research*. New York: Wiley.

—— & Shalling, E. (1978), *Psychopathic Behavior: Approaches to Research*. New York: Wiley.

Henderson, D. K. (1939), *Psychopathic States*. London: Chapman and Hall.

—— & Gillespie, R. D. (1969), *Textbook of Psychiatry: For Students and Practitioners*, 10th ed., rev. I. R. C. Batchelor. London: Oxford University Press.

Kernberg, O. F. (1975), *Borderline Conditions and Pathological Narcissism*. New York: Aronson.

—— (1984), *Severe Personality Disorders: Psychotherapeutic Strategies*. New Haven, CT: Yale University Press.

—— (1988), Identity, Alienation, and Ideology in Adolescent Group Processes. In: *Fantasy, Myth, and Reality*. Madison, CT: International Universities Press, pp. 381–399.

—— (1989), The narcissistic personality disorder and the differential diagnosis of antisocial behavior. In: *Psychiatric Clinics of North America*. New York: Saunders, pp. 553–570.

—— Selzer, M. A., Koeningsberg, H. W., Carr, A. C. & Appelbaum, A. H. (1989), *Psychodynamic Psychotherapy of Borderline Patients*. New York: Basic Books.

Kernberg, P. F. (1989), Narcissistic personality disorder in childhood. In: *The Psychiatric Clinics of North America*. New York: Saunders, pp. 671–694.

—— & Richards, A. K. (1994), Love in preadolescence as seen through children's letters. In: *The Spectrum of Psychoanalysis: Essays in Honor of Martin Bergmann*, ed. A. K. Richards & A. D. Richards. Madison, CT: International Universities Press, pp. 199–218.

Mahler, M. S., Pine, F. & Bergman, A. (1975), *The Psychological Birth of the Human Infant*. New York: Basic Books.

Sherwood, V. R. & Cohen, C. P. (1994), *Psychotherapy of the Quiet Borderline Patient*. Northvale, NJ: Aronson.

5

Transitional Objects, Selfobjects, Real Objects, and the Process of Change in Psychodynamic Psychotherapy

Gerald Adler

My interest in the process of change in psychotherapy and psychoanalysis derives from my work with patients with various pathologies, from severe borderline personality disorders through a continuum of psychopathology to neurotic character disorders. In working with these patients, I am not always clear about the determinants that lead to change, or to seeming or real stalemates. Sometimes, my experiences as a consultant to colleagues' treatment dilemmas have illuminated my understanding both of their work and of my own. In this chapter I shall present a framework that has helped me to understand the process of change in psychodynamic psychotherapy (including psychoanalysis). Although it derives from my work with many different types of patients, it emphasizes what I have learned from my colleagues' and my own treatment of patients with borderline and narcissistic personality disorders. These are the patients most likely to get into difficulties with their therapists that feel like or can be impasses, causing both parties the most pain and also providing the most opportunity to learn about the resolution of these anticipated and inevitable "impasses." Although I shall emphasize an object relations formulation, which I feel is most useful in work with these patients, a framework that examines conflict and the resolution of conflict also applies and is necessary for successful treatment. All patients, regardless of their pathology, exhibit conflicts in psychotherapy and need to work with them. However, the treatment of borderline and narcissistic patients has the most to teach therapists about the deficits and pathological internal object relations in their patients, how they become manifest in the treatment, and the complex ways they can be understood and lead to change.

In describing an object relations framework, I shall utilize more than one model, derived from different workers with differences in their perspectives. Thus I shall describe transitional objects, selfobjects, real objects, and pseudotransitional objects, which are all confusing if not defined carefully. I feel that these concepts from different object relations theorists can help to enrich our understanding of the process of change. Although aspects of these frameworks are theoretically incompatible, their clinical utility by far outweighs their inconsistencies and occasional contradictions. I shall first define transitional objects and selfobjects, and describe their origins in the contributions of Winnicott and Kohut. I shall also discuss real objects and the real relationship with the therapist, and the therapist's capacity to work with these patients' intense affects, as manifested in their primitive defenses, including denial, splitting, projective identification, and idealization. I shall emphasize the importance of understanding projective identification in the treatment of these patients (whether the experiences with projective identification are creative or destructive and whether they help establish a safe transitional space or lead to permanent impasses in the treatment) and the importance of the real relationship with the therapist in working with intense experiences and weathering the inevitable impasses. As part of the study of these patients' use of their therapists and other real or inanimate objects in pathological ways, I shall describe pseudotransitional objects and my understanding of their origins. Finally, I shall attempt to integrate all these concepts into an understanding of the process of change in borderline and narcissistic patients.

Because this group of patients uses people in their environment in very complex ways, we have an opportunity to clarify our understanding of "real" versus illusory uses of an object. In addition, the ways in which the object is used, whether as a transitional object, selfobject, or real object, can either be an aspect of the process of change or a manifestation of a stalemated treatment. I shall now begin an exploration of the creative and pathological uses these patients make of the objects around them, both inanimate and living, and relate them to relevant child development issues.

TRANSITIONAL OBJECTS

Cooper and Adler (1990) have compared and contrasted the transitional object and selfobject concepts. They emphasized the multiple functions of the transitional object for the infant's development, including the prevention of catastrophic anxiety secondary to separation, its assistance in maintaining an evocative memory of the object until neuropsychological capacities for evocative memory exist, its use in maintaining an idealized representation of a maternal object, and its ability to help the infant to accept reality through the slow task of ultimately distinguishing a real object from the illusory use of objects.

A transitional object can be either an inanimate object chosen by the infant or small child or a living object (e.g., the infant's mother). The distinction between the object as a transitional object or another kind of object depends on the way the infant or small child uses it. As I shall elaborate shortly, when the object is used entirely as an illusory object by the small child, requiring no activity by the object, then the object can be said to be most likely a transitional object.

Winnicott (1953) noted the importance of the infant's own choice of the transitional object (i.e., it cannot be imposed on the child by another person). He also emphasized that the mother is not to question whether she gave it to the child or whether the child created it. In fact, Winnicott stated that the question was not even to be asked. Also important in our understanding of the transitional object concept is Winnicott's observation that the transitional object can only be used by the infant if the holding environment is adequate. When it fails, the infant loses the capacity to utilize transitional objects. The Robertsons (Robertson and Robertson, 1969) illustrate this phenomenon in their poignant film of John, age 17 months, who is separated from his mother for nine days with an inadequate substitute holding environment. They show that toward the end of this period John can no longer use his teddy bear to comfort himself, in contrast to his behavior several days earlier, before the deprivation became too prolonged.

Relevant both to child development issues and to the treatment of adult patients, which will be discussed later, is an understanding of the fate of the transitional object, which is not mourned in normal development. Winnicott (1953) stated that the transitional object becomes part of cultural experience, although other aspects of his work (1958) imply the internalization of the transitional object as part of the child's developing structure. Marion Tolpin's (1971) contributions to the literature made this internalization clear.

SELFOBJECTS

Kohut's (1971, 1977) use of the selfobject concept defines the functions that others perform for a person who is in need of specific functions because they are not present in that person either transiently or permanently. Although these selfobject functions are provided by the other person, they are simultaneously experienced as part of the self by the person needing that function. Kohut utilized the selfobject concept to define the self-esteem–regulating deficits of those with narcissistic personality disorder and their formation of mirroring and idealizing selfobject transferences in the area of their self-worth deficiencies. His later work clarified the use of selfobjects by all people, the needs for selfobjects throughout life, and the process of change in psychoanalysis, through transmuting internalization, which allows patients to choose more mature selfobjects as deficits are addressed and resolved. The concept of transmuting internalization defined the process of introjects being broken down into their component functions and then internalized.

In my attempt to understand the distinctions between the transitional object and the selfobject, I would like to clarify the following: Kohut describes the idealized selfobject as, for example, the father with whom the child merges and by whose omnipotent power the child is comforted. In my understanding, if the child uses the presence of the father to feel these feelings, without the father performing any active function, then the father is being utilized as a transitional object to evoke previous selfobject experiences with the father. However, if, for example, the father actually talks to the child in a soothing voice and holds the child on his lap, telling him a story about himself that the child experiences as the father being strong and powerful, then the father is the idealized selfobject performing a selfobject function at that moment.

Both transitional objects and selfobjects are important to the developing small child. The child's creative use of an alive object can make it a transitional object, requiring no activity on the object's part at that moment. However, that object may at other times have been a selfobject who had played an important role in developing a sufficient holding environment for the child so that the child could develop the capacity to use transitional objects. In the object's role as selfobject, it would have performed active functions at such times, instead of its existence as a transitional object at other times.

It is clear that in my description of transitional objects and selfobjects I am mixing the concepts of Winnicott and Kohut. However, though derived from different frameworks, they are related and both are relevant to understanding the child's development of an internal world, and, therefore, also to therapeutic work with adult patients.

REAL OBJECTS

The concept of the real object has to be confusing because of the very nature of our awareness of the complexity of psychological processes.

In theory, I am using the concept to refer to something that does not exist in the pure form that I am describing. By "real object" I mean the perception of the object as it really is, without illusion, merger fantasies, or projection. Because one perceptual and psychological being cannot observe another without aspects of the self influencing how that person sees the other, people are limited in their ability to be "objective." The same constraints apply to the capacity of the "real object" to perceive the other person. Therapists are increasingly comfortable with the idea of ambiguity in their ability to know the other person "objectively" and accept such ambiguity and uncertainty as an important aspect of their everyday clinical work when they are functioning optimally (Adler, 1989). Yet they also know that their patients develop an increasing capacity to see the other person as he or she "really is," even though, paradoxically, therapists have to acknowledge their uncertainty about defining the other so "objectively." Experiences with projection, and projective identification, as I shall describe, play an important role in the treatment of narcissistic and borderline patients. Resolution of these experiences can lead to increasing the relative separateness of the two people involved as self and other become more differentiated, including the utilization of higher level defenses that have less projection, projective identification, and primitive merger, therefore allowing the patient a relatively more "objective" view of the other.

The concept of the real object is often related to and confused with the concept of the real relationship, which is also complex and sometimes misunderstood. When I speak of the real relationship between patient and therapist, I am referring to a personal or realistic relationship between them. This relationship includes the personality characteristics of both parties, and the ways in which they relate to each other. The personal or realistic relationship is not to be confused with the therapist's revealing specific details of his or her life. Patients who state that they know little about their therapists are ignoring the vast data they have about their therapists' capacities to bear painful affects; contain provocative experiences; and relate with concern, interest, and caring through a variety of encounters in the therapy. They also know much about the problematic aspects of their therapists through their many interactions with them.

Even at the beginning of therapy, borderline or narcissistic personality disorder patients have an intuitive and partly unconscious sense of the real qualities of their therapists. They also can probably sense whether their therapists have the potential capacities, as part of these real qualities, to provide the ultimate safe environment for the future regressive experiences that are inevitable and necessary for change to occur.

Paradoxically, even though these patients probably cannot define these qualities in detail early in therapy, these qualities are unconsciously noted by them. As I shall discuss later, these personal qualities of the therapist that the patient may need for his or her own development can ultimately be internalized through the complex series of events that occurs in successful treatment.

BORDERLINE AND NARCISSISTIC PERSONALITY DISORDER PSYCHOPATHOLOGY

How do these concepts relate to the treatment of borderline and narcissistic patients and the process of change that occurs in successful therapeutic work with them? I shall now briefly present a psychodynamic view of these patients, and then turn to the process of change that occurs in work with them.

Borderline personality disorder patients can be defined psychodynamically as patients with three areas of difficulties: (1) aloneness, (2) the need–fear dilemma, and (3) primitive guilt (Adler and Buie, 1979; Buie and Adler, 1982; Adler, 1985). Borderline patients' aloneness issues relate to their inability to maintain a reliable evocative memory of important people when faced with the stress of separation. Using an object relations framework, I can state that they cannot depend on their holding and soothing introjects when their anger emerges in the face of an anticipated or actual separation. The needed introjects are primarily holding and soothing, based on the patients' wishes and needs to feel held and to have skin-to-skin contact with the person who is important to them. These patients' own internal resources cannot help them reliably at moments of separation and rage, leading to a regression in which they may experience an annihilatory panic, feel totally abandoned and alone, and have a desperate, empty feeling that no one is there.

The need–fear dilemma issues of borderline patients are related to Burnham, Gladstone, and Gibson's descriptions (1969) of schizophrenic patients. However, borderline patients fear and defend against the experiences of schizophrenics. While schizophrenics lose the distinction between self and other through the fusion of self and object representations, borderlines *fear* this occurrence. Thus, borderline patients will flee from situations or act out in ways to keep themselves from the danger of this loss of boundaries, which indeed can occur transiently in them. Both the aloneness and the need–fear dilemma issues make it difficult for borderline patients to remain reliably in the office with their therapists, as they fear a regression to annihilatory panic and the possibility of loss of self and other boundaries. Because borderline patients have many higher level defenses, their wish to avoid situations in which regressive experiences can overwhelm these defenses is understandable. Paradoxically, these regressive experiences, when contained in a successful treatment setting, are necessary for change to occur.

The guilt of borderline patients is "primitive" for two reasons: It has an all-or-nothing quality, and it is easily projected. These patients may feel horribly bad and evil, or rapidly feel that their therapists see them that way. The back-and-forth flow from grandiosity to total badness is related to Kernberg's (1975) concept of splitting. In addition, the relationship of these superego issues to the interactive aspects of projective identification complicate this experience of guilt and therapists' participation in it. Freud's (1923) description of the negative therapeutic reaction is best illustrated in working with these issues in borderline patients.

Borderline personality disorder psychopathology, with its annihilatory anxiety (experienced as a life and death panic), can be contrasted with the narcissistic personality disorder issues of self-worth. Using Kohut's framework, the narcissistic personality disorder patient can be defined as someone who forms selfobject transferences in psychotherapy or psychoanalysis in the area of self-worth. Kernberg's (1975) framework emphasizes the pathological internal object relations of these patients, most of whom he defines as having a borderline personality organization. Kernberg stresses the self-sufficiency of these patients, who envy, and both devalue and idealize defensively. Kohut relates their vulnerabilities to the experiences that rupture the selfobject bond, and the relationship between these ruptures in treatment and failures of such patients' selfobjects in their childhoods.

My work as therapist (including my treatment of borderline and narcissistic patients), as supervisor, and as consultant involving colleagues has led me to the formulation that there is a continuum of psychopathology to consider in working with these patients (Adler, 1985). When the aloneness and need–fear dilemma issues of borderline patients are largely resolved, these patients look more and more like narcissistic personality disorder patients, in that the primary focus becomes their tenuous self-worth. Although borderline patients form selfobject transferences and initially can appear to be similar to narcissistic patients, the regression that accompanies their emerging separation issues results in a much more tenuous capacity to maintain relatively stable selfobject transferences as they return over and over to aloneness problems. The resolution of the issues around borderline patients' tenuous holding and soothing introjects allows them to have a new stability, which is manifested by selfobject transferences that are more resilient to rupture. Gradually, the regressions that occur with these ruptures are less related to aloneness and need–fear dilemma problems, and more focused on self-worth problems.

The tasks and requirements for a psychotherapeutic situation that allows for emotional growth include many aspects. Among them are: (1) the establishment of safety, (2) the work of mourning, (3) the modification of the internal world of the patient through the complex interaction of the new experiences with the therapist and the reliving of old experiences, and (4) conflict resolution.

I have begun to address some of the issues about the establishment of safety in discussing transitional objects and the holding environment necessary for the small child to use them, and shall describe these issues further. As I have noted earlier, although conflict resolution is crucial in all treatment, I shall not pursue its exploration in this brief chapter.

All successful psychodynamic psychotherapy includes significant aspects of mourning work. In patients who have had especially painful childhood experiences, the emotional pain, sadness, and anger resulting from relative or actual loss is particularly relevant, and the mourning that is part of successful treatment ultimately has to occur. However, in the aspects of the process of change that I am addressing at this time, the significant capacity to mourn is something that develops later in therapy as new structure is established. Borderline patients, with their aloneness, need–fear dilemma, and primitive guilt issues, have a very limited capacity to mourn in any consistent way relatively early in treatment. They have a fragility and regressive potential that allows only some sadness before it becomes brittle and overwhelms them, and have little capacity to bear disappointment and anger before it turns into self-hatred. Although the precursors of a capacity to mourn are present early in treatment, it requires the relatively successful resolution of the aloneness issues before these patients can reliably bear sadness. In order to mourn, a person has to have solid introjects of important people, which include affective memories of experiences with them in the context of that person's ambivalence. In addition, the reliable capacity to remain affectively connected to the therapist must exist in the face of current ambivalence, that is, libidinal object constancy must have been achieved. When borderline patients resolve aloneness issues, they move from an incapacity to maintain these introjects to an ability to remember important people with feelings present, that is, they move from a state of aloneness to one of loneliness, in which they can miss people and long for them, all manifestations of libidinal object constancy. It is only then that a solid capacity to mourn is present. Simultaneously, borderline patients have modified their primitive guilt sufficiently to experience anger without destructive self-punishment.

I shall now address the complex interaction of the establishment of safety, its relationship to destructive or creative projective identification, and the development of a transitional space.

PROJECTIVE IDENTIFICATION

The projective identification concept was first defined by Melanie Klein (1946) and used to describe aspects of a person placed into another person in complex ways. This concept, without an interpersonal component, can seem magical or unclear (Malin and Grotstein, 1966; Bion, 1967; Shapiro, 1982). In elaborating the complexity of projective identification I shall use the model described by Ogden (1979), and then relate it to some of my thoughts (Adler, 1989) about its creative or destructive aspects.

In projective identification, the projector places aspects of himself or herself, which either are intolerable or are to be preserved, into another person. These aspects are old experiences involving self and object representations and affects, and, in essence, fantasies. In addition, the projector, through his or her actions, unconsciously attempts to get the recipient to respond in a way consistent with the parts projected. What fuels this sequence is the fact that most people have unresolved aspects of themselves that are similar to those in others. Thus, the recipient can be expected to have unconscious parts that can respond to an unconscious interpersonal provocation by the projector. In the psychotherapeutic situation, it is hoped that the therapist's unresolved difficulties are less problematic than those of the patient, who is projecting and interpersonally provoking. To paraphrase Semrad (Rako and Mazer, 1980), who captured the essence of the dangers and potential in projective identification in his descriptions of psychotherapy: Psychotherapy is a situation in which one mess is attempting to help a greater mess.

The recipient's response to the projection and provocation determines whether a creative or destructive experience occurs. If the recipient "contains" the projection (Bion, 1967), there is the possibility that the projection can be modified. In the psychotherapeutic situation, containment is often relative. For example, a patient's projection and provocation of an old experience involving a rageful interaction with a parent is in theory ideally empathically interpreted by the therapist who feels rage in the projective identification experience, conceptualized either as the rage of the parent or that of the child. However, it is likely that the interpretation under such charged circumstances will be less than ideal, perhaps conveying some irritation. Yet, the containment will have been relatively successful if the therapist did not respond with a riddance anger.

The creative movement that can lead to structural change in the patient is related to the therapist's relative containment and the patient's capacity to internalize a modification of the original projection, which has been modified through this containment experience with the therapist. Conversely, the projective identification experience can be destructive if the therapist's containment is inadequate, leading therapist and patient to enact too destructively the old experiences that have been recreated. Whether projective identification is creative or destructive depends both on the therapist's capacity for relative containment and on the intensity and "primitive" nature of the patient's projections and provocations; the latter is referred to as "excessive projective identification" by Bion (1967).

The use of the projective identification model to explain structural change, I believe, is more accurate than the related model that defines the importance of patient and therapist both surviving the borderline patient's rage as well as the therapist's own rage in the first phases of the psychotherapy with these patients (Frosch, 1964; Winnicott, 1969; Kernberg, 1975; Adler, 1985). Projective identification describes the specific processes involved, and helps clarify the slow, incremental gains made in the psychotherapy of, for example, borderline patients.

THE RELATIONSHIP OF PROJECTIVE IDENTIFICATION TO TRANSITIONAL PHENOMENA

As I have already discussed, the child's use of the transitional object requires illusion, which can only occur in an adequate holding environment. Comparably, in successful psychotherapy a holding environment gets established that allows for experiences of illusion, and an environment that permits transitional object formation and use. When the experience is present in the psychotherapeutic situation, it can be said that an intermediate or transitional space has been developed that allows for illusion, "play," and relatively safe fantasy. Such a transitional space permits the evolution of the transference, and transference neurosis, which ideally allows for an ambiguity, leaving unclear what is from the past or present and what is really from the therapist or what is from the patient's projections and displacements onto the therapist. This experience of play and illusion is often at the heart of successful psychotherapy and psychoanalysis, and is related to the ambiguity that is an essential ingredient both in the psychoanalytic setting and psychoanalytic technique (Adler, 1989). When these experiences occur in treatment, conceptually there is little difference between the patient's use of this transitional space in relation to the therapist and creative projective identification.

However, it is important to note that borderline patients are often incapable of tolerating the ambiguity of a psychoanalytic or psychoanalytic psychotherapy situation in the early phases of treatment. For them, a setting and technique that encourages ambiguity is akin to the experiences of neglect and abandonment that permeated their childhood. They may at times require interactions that they can experience as protective, which are also related to aspects of their real relationship with their therapists.

TRANSITIONAL OBJECTS AND PSEUDOTRANSITIONAL OBJECTS

In discussing the process of change in psychotherapy, it can be puzzling to try to understand situations in which the therapist thinks that change should occur, but, instead, the treatment appears to be stalemated. There are many possible explanations for these impasses or seeming impasses, based on the complex interactions between patient and therapist, and the old issues evoked in each during the treatment. I want to discuss one common and important contribution to this state of affairs: a situation when a supposed transitional object is not really being used as a transitional object at all. Instead, it is or has become what I shall call a "pseudotransitional object." My discussion also relates to Freud's (1927) description of fetishes.

Freud's amplification of the fetish concept focused on the child's use of the fetish to deny the absence of the penis in a woman. Renik (1992), in his paper describing the patient's use of the analyst as a fetish, clarifies how patients who use others as fetishes blur the distinction between fantasy and reality, maintaining both beliefs split off and existing side by side. They can thus continue the blurry connection between fantasy and reality in a way that allows them to take a "maybe" position rather than one of a firm "yes" or "no."

In Freud's (1927) paper on fetishes, he broadens his discussion to include the distinction between psychosis and neurosis and demonstrates how two of his patients, whose father died when they were children, could do something similar to that of patients with a fetish.

Freud stated that "[T]he attitude which fitted in with the wish and the attitude which fitted in with reality existed side by side. . . . The patient oscillated in every situation in life between two assumptions: the one, that his father was still alive and was hindering his activities; the other, opposite one, that he was entitled to regard himself as his father's successor" (p. 156).

Clearly Freud's and Renik's discussions relate to Winnicott and his work on illusion, transitional phenomena, and transitional objects. Winnicott, himself, in his first paper on transitional objects and illusion (1953) was very aware of the literature on fetishes. He attempted to distinguish between, for example, "delusion of a maternal phallus," which would be pathological and a fetish, and "illusion of a maternal phallus, that is to say, an idea that is universal and not pathological" (p. 241). However, as Freud and Renik have described, the use of the fetish is not delusional, which would be psychotic, but an attempt to maintain an ambiguity about whether something is really "real" or an illusion.

I prefer thinking about transitional objects in the context of the therapeutic situation and the patient's creative use of them, for example, in order to help evoke the inadequately internalized holding and soothing qualities of the therapist and to tolerate separations. It is therefore important to attempt to understand when it is that the patient can use an inanimate object or the therapist as a transitional object, and when that process fails, and, instead, the inanimate object or therapist becomes a fetish or a pseudotransitional object. I use this new term, *pseudotransitional object,* to name the patient's unsuccessful attempts to use the object as a creative transitional object. What may seem to have begun as a transitional object either becomes a pseudotransitional object or was a pseudotransitional object from the beginning. What is or has become a pseudotransitional object may have been chosen initially with a creative, dilemma-solving wish; however the patient failed in this creative attempt because of failures of the holding environment in the past, which are often recreated in his or her current life and psychotherapy.

As previously noted, Winnicott emphasizes that the child's use of the transitional object depends on the establishment and maintenance of a good-enough holding environment. When that holding environment fails, the child's capacity to use the transitional object also fails. This childhood paradigm can be cautiously translated to situations involving adult patients. Those patients who fall within the spectrum of borderline and more severe narcissistic disorders often have a very delicate balance of experiences throughout childhood and adolescence that demonstrate the historical and/or narrative evidence that their negative earlier experiences outweighed the positive, which they and their therapists inevitably tend to recreate in their treatment. In their histories, much evidence can be found for significant failures of parental holding, soothing, mirroring, and self-worth–enhancing experiences. Evidence can also be found for their attempts to find new selfobjects or to use transitional objects creatively. And it can be demonstrated that pseudo-transitional objects, such as alcohol, drugs, and people (involving relationships that were stuck and often repeated negative past experiences), were often used by these patients.

Although the use of pseudotransitional objects originates in the person's wish for something creative to occur, it is accompanied by a feeling of being desperately stuck and dead inside. Alcohol, drugs, or a person, used as a pseudotransitional object, may initially excite the patient but ultimately functions to deaden an unbearable pain. Aliveness requires that the patient have a background of earlier and current safety with the possibility of healthy illusion, rather than a need to defend against unbearable disappointment, sadness, and rage.

I have been defining how patients with significant failures of their childhood holding environments will ultimately form pseudotransitional objects and use their therapists in this way, leading to stalemate, despair, and self-destructive hopelessness. These patients re-create the stalemated hopeless situations of their past in their current treatment. I feel that therapists, as a countertransference response to these situations, often do not recognize this re-creation—with its attendant despair—and the rage that is often hidden within their patients' self-punishing, punishing, and often dead and stalemated interactions with their therapists. The child's inability to bear the enormous rage and disappointments of childhood can now be present in the adult's stalemated, often dead interactions with a therapist who can find no way out of the dilemma.

THE HOLDING ENVIRONMENT, THE REAL RELATIONSHIP, AND
INTERNALIZATION

The complex and yet easy ways that borderline and narcissistic patients repeatedly re-create the seeming or real stalemates of the past within their therapies can now be addressed more clearly in integrating some of the concepts I have been defining. Because their childhood holding environments were tenuous and problematic, it is inevitable that these patients come to treatment with vulnerabilities that will become evident as old issues are re-created. For example, borderline patients' aloneness, need–fear dilemma, primitive guilt, and self-worth vulnerabilities will quickly or slowly stress the therapeutic dyad. Transitional space will both variably and invariably disappear, and projective identification, which can be creative, will occasionally or often become potentially destructive. These patients' experiences with their therapists, which at first can have creative transitional object or selfobject transference aspects, can deteriorate into situations in which the therapist is being used as a pseudotransitional object or selfobject transferences break down into episodes of defensive aloofness, fragmentation, or empty, annihilatory panic as the patients' rage begins to emerge in the therapy.

There is a therapeutic paradox in the fact that in order for creative projective identification to occur, the holding environment has to be adequately in place, and yet, that holding environment in these patients is readily vulnerable to the inevitable regressions I have been describing. The importance of the therapist's person and personality and the formulation he or she uses that allows for aspects of these personal qualities to be used in the treatment, often determine whether the holding environment can endure and be reestablished sufficiently so that significant creative projective identification experiences occur.

Borderline and more severe narcissistic personality disorder patients have often had childhood experiences that result in their misperceiving silence and passivity in their therapists, which reminds them of parental indifference, abandonment, and criticism, and is of course complicated by the projective mechanisms they use. In addition, their earlier experiences often include interactions with important people in which they did not feel genuinely cared about or valued for themselves; these relationships often were inauthentic or were felt to be so. They therefore expect experiences with their therapists to be similar. An approach that works well with the neurotic patients I have treated can be felt by this group of patients to confirm the basic childhood hopelessness and despair that they bring to every new aspect of their lives. The modification of technique used with these patients is still within a psychodynamic framework that emphasizes empathic understanding, clarification, and interpretation, but it simultaneously uses a formulation that addresses their vulnerabilities related to the formation and maintenance of a holding environment.

The careful, repeated analysis of projective identification experiences, with its containment and slow modification of projected aspects that are reinternalized; the analysis of selfobject, dyadic, and triadic transferences; the understanding and analysis of the ways the patient may use the therapist, inanimate objects, or substances as a pseudotransitional object, and the old rage and disappointments and sadness related to these experiences; and the patient's greater capacity to mourn ultimately and slowly permit the modification of structure leading to the resolution of the borderline and narcissistic issues that brought the patient to treatment. Simultaneously, the patient has the opportunity to internalize aspects of the therapist that he or she needs, as part of the new experience that has occurred between them—a part of the real relationship that was present from the beginning and gradually solidified as transference issues were resolved.

REFERENCES

Adler, G. (1985), *Borderline Psychopathology and Its Treatment.* Northvale, NJ: Aronson.
—— (1989), Transitional phenomena, projective identification, and the essential ambiguity of the psychoanalytic situation. *Psychoanal. Quart., 58:*81–104.
—— & Buie, D. H. (1979), Aloneness and borderline psychopathology: The possible relevance of child development issues. *Internat. J. Psycho-Anal., 60:*83–96.
Bion, W. R. (1967), A theory of thinking. In: *Second Thoughts.* New York: International Universities Press, pp. 110–119.
Buie, D. H. & Adler, G. (1982), Definitive treatment of the borderline patient. *Internat. J. Psychoanal. Psychother., 9:*51–87.
Burnham, D. G., Gladstone, A. I. & Gibson, R. W. (1969), *Schizophrenia and the Need-Fear Dilemma.* New York: International Universities Press.
Cooper, S. H. & Adler, G. (1990), Toward a clarification of the transitional object and selfobject concepts in the treatment of the borderline patient. *The Annual of Psychoanalysis, 18:*133–152. Hillsdale, NJ: The Analytic Press.
Freud, S. (1923), The ego and the id. *Standard Edition, 19:*12–59. London: Hogarth Press, 1961.
—— (1927), Fetishism. *Standard Edition, 21:*149–157. London: Hogarth Press, 1961.
Frosch, J. (1964), The psychotic character: Clinical psychiatric considerations. *Psychiat. Quart., 38:*81–96.
Kernberg, O. (1975), *Borderline Conditions and Pathological Narcissism.* New York: Aronson.
Klein, M. (1946), Notes on some schizoid mechanisms. In: *Developments in Psychoanalysis,* ed. J. Riviere. London: Hogarth Press, 1952, pp. 292–320.
Kohut, H. (1971), *The Analysis of the Self.* New York: International Universities Press.
—— (1977), *The Restoration of the Self.* New York: International Universities Press.
Malin, A. & Grotstein, J. (1966), Projective identification in the therapeutic process. *Internat. J. Psycho-Anal., 47:*26–31.
Ogden, T. H. (1979), On projective identification. *Internat. J. Psycho-Anal., 60:*357–373.
Rako, S. & Mazer, H., eds. (1980), *Semrad: The Heart of a Therapist.* New York: Aronson.
Renik, O. (1992), Use of the analyst as a fetish. *Psychoanal. Quart., 61:*542–563.
Robertson, J. & Robertson, J. (1969), *John, Seventeen Months: For Nine Days in a Residential Nursery* [film]. New York: New York University Films.
Shapiro, E. R. (1982), On curiosity: Intrapsychic and interpersonal boundary formation in family life. *Internat. J. Fam. Psychiat., 3:*209–232.
Tolpin, M. (1971), On the beginnings of a cohesive self: An application of the concept of transmuting internalization to the study of the transitional object and signal anxiety. *The Psychoanalytic Study of the Child, 26:*316–352. New Haven, CT: Yale University Press.

Winnicott, D. W. (1953), Transitional objects and transitional phenomena. In: *Collected Papers*. London: Tavistock, 1958, pp. 229–242.

—— (1958), The capacity to be alone. In: *The Maturational Processes and the Facilitating Environment*. New York: International Universities Press, 1965, pp. 29–36.

—— (1969), The use of an object. *Internat. J. Psycho-Anal.*, 50:711–716.

II

*The Self as the Focus
of Therapeutic Action*

6

I. Some General Principles of Psychoanalytic Psychotherapy

A Self-Psychological Perspective

Paul H. Ornstein and Anna Ornstein

In order to present some general principles of psychoanalytic psychotherapy from the perspective of self psychology, we shall summarize those features of the theory that we consider to be central to the conduct of the treatment process.

Self psychology is in its essence beautifully simple, even if the comprehensive theory to which it gave rise is quite complex and still not fully articulated. Kohut (1971), in attempting to close the ever-widening gap between theory and practice in psychoanalysis, struggled with the shortcomings of an oedipal and preoedipal, drive-defense analysis. Using that approach consistently, within the dominant ego psychology paradigm, he missed the mark with patients who clamored for his mirroring, affirming, and echoing responses or who needed to attach themselves to him as they idealized his power, omniscience, and omnipotence. These patients did not struggle primarily with their sexual and aggressive urges, even when these phenomena entered the clinical picture prominently. Listening to his patients empathically (that is, from within their own perspectives), led him to the discovery of the selfobject transferences—transferences that become established in relation to the patients' mirroring, idealizing, and twinship or alter-ego needs. He placed these needs, and the analyst's interpretive responses to them, into the center of the treatment process. This had turned the existing theory upside down: the need for self-cohesion had become primary and conflicts related to the sexual and aggressive drives secondary. These discoveries in relation to the transferences led to the reformulation of the theory of development in health and illness. The freeing of psychoanalysis from its bondage to drive theory and thereby defining the field as a pure psychology—with empathy (vicarious introspection) as the key observational method of the psychoanalyst—constitutes the foundation of self psychology. Empathy as a mode of observation and the selfobject concept are the foundational constructs, and all the rest of self psychology essentially derives from them. The importance of the concept of the selfobject is further enhanced by the fact that, in addition to being at once a developmental and clinical concept, it is also a bridge between the external and the internal worlds: it brings "external reality" into the patient's inner world—it focuses on how a person experiences the surround.

Two additional brief remarks should complete this thumbnail sketch: One has to do with the implication of the self–selfobject matrix for Kohut's view of the nature of psychopathology and of the treatment process; and the other has to do with Kohut's "Image of Man [and Woman]" as this informs his theory and also clearly and explicitly emerges from it.

(1) The idea of the self–selfobject matrix clearly establishes the reciprocal influence between infant and caregiver and recognizes that both the development of the self and the future maintenance of its cohesion, integrity, and vitality will depend on the nature of its connectedness to others—the mature selfobjects, in our parlance—needed throughout the life span. This focus on interconnectedness (initially for structure building and later on for its maintenance) and the reciprocal influence of self and selfobject has drastically altered our view of the treatment process— we can no longer consider the patient a self-contained, closed system in which his or her psychopathology is entirely the patient's fixed attribute. Once patient and therapist establish the treatment situation, their impact on each other will become a significant factor in the nature of their experiences (including the transference) and the manifestations of the patient's psychopathology. Neither diagnosis, nor prognosis, nor outcome, is wholly independent of this reciprocal influence.

(2) Underlying Kohut's theories is his "Image of Man [and Woman]," which, he felt, ultimately set his psychology far apart from all theories that might in some fashion be similar to his and would make efforts at integrating his theories with those of others, or other theories with his, an impossible enterprise (P. H. Ornstein, in press). Kohut's view sees the infant as essentially born strong rather than helpless, on account of its innate, hard-wired capacity to elicit the needed responses from the surround, and as fitting harmoniously into the empathic selfobject milieu into which it is born. The infant is not a bundle of drives, in need of being tamed and socialized, which he or she violently resists, and full of

potentially pathogenic conflicts, which are built into the psyche from the outset. It is the underlying weakness or fragmentation-proneness of the self that makes these conflicts pathogenic and prevents their resolution. Resistance in self psychology is considered to be an expression of the individual's fear of being retraumatized; a protective measure of a vulnerable self.

We shall now embark on an overview of the nature of psychopathology and of some key elements of the psychotherapeutic process, along with its curative factors as we conceive of them today.

THE NATURE OF PSYCHOPATHOLOGY

Without detailing the long and instructive history of the changes in understanding the nature of psychopathology in psychoanalysis, we shall sketch the prevailing views as a background against which we consider the treatment process and the multiple curative factors present in various combinations in each therapeutic experience.

1. According to contemporary *ego psychology* it is the admixture of innate, constitutional factors and the developmental vicissitudes of the basic drives of incestuous sexuality and aggression that lead to the central (oedipal) conflicts and compromises in the psyche that will become the building blocks of either health or illness. Ordinary life experiences in infancy and childhood and the vicissitudes of growing up alone were once considered to be responsible for the development of psychopathology. Trauma was considered pathogenic only insofar as it "validated" the patient's unconscious fantasy. For example, a father's repeated beatings of a boy child would be traumatic because they confirmed the boy's murderous wishes as punishable. Thus, the traumatic origin of the neuroses has been underplayed by modern ego psychology in favor of drive-related, innate, unconscious fantasies as inevitable accompaniments of human psychosexual development and maturation. Once the seduction theory, and with it the traumatic impact of the environment, was discarded in favor of oedipal fantasies and the ego's defenses against them as the core pathogenic agents, the role of actual experience became somewhat fuzzy in the theory, although clinically it was often fully appreciated. In keeping with this theoretical view, unresolved oedipal conflicts (and their consequences) prevented the unhindered unfolding of the ego's innate and acquired capacities and the development of a well-consolidated, well-functioning superego.

Succinctly put, within this context, it is the uncovering of the unconscious conflicts at the root of the patient's psychopathology that was considered to lead to its ultimate cure through insight.

2. The nature of psychopathology according to *object relations theory* is more difficult to describe in brief, simple terms, because there are a variety of object relations theories—some of which have retained drive theory (albeit in a modified form) while others have abandoned it. Drive theory (even within modern ego psychology) underplayed the specific role of early caretakers and later significant others—called "drive-objects" or "love-objects" in psychoanalytic parlance. It was this problem of assigning the proper weight and position to significant caretakers and others in the development of the personality that object relations theories set out to rectify. All of the various object relations theories gave the relations with caretakers a more pervasive and central developmental significance in the acquisition of health or illness. Such significant relations could be traumatic and interrupt the process of internalization of the qualities of key persons (usually the parents) in a child's life—leading to inadequate consolidation of ego and superego structures. This, then, leaves the psyche populated with unintegrated "bad and good experiences" and their internalized precipitates: "bad and good object representations." The result is a lack of reliably integrated and well-functioning internalized structures and unsuccessful defenses built up around them, which are responsible for the unpredictable ups and downs in the lives of people who were traumatized in their early relations to key caretakers. Or, under optimum conditions, such relations would enhance the phase-appropriate integration of bad and good experiences (leading to a fusion of bad and good object representations), safeguarding a well-functioning, integrated ego and superego.

In this context, it is the belated integration, the coming together of these split bad and good memories of the early caretakers, that is considered to be at the root of patients' psychopathology. Here, too, just as in ego psychology, it is insight that is expected to lead to cure.

3. *Self psychology* introduced a very different view of the nature of psychopathology from those of ego psychology and object relations theory (Kohut, 1971, 1977, 1984, and others). Self psychology maintains that it is a combination of endowment and the availability of an optimally responsive emotional environment in infancy and childhood that leads to the acquisition of those psychic structures that enable us— within a very broad latitude—to regulate affect, to establish and maintain self-esteem, and to maintain connectedness to others throughout the life span. The success of these achievements enables human beings to struggle successfully for the attainment of the life goals that emanate from their needs, wishes, desires, and expectations, in keeping with their innate skills and talents.

Psychopathology, from this perspective, is reflected in the many ways in which there is a failure to achieve a structuralization of the self for optimal functioning. Such defects in the structure of the self make it mandatory to find substitute ways (generally unsuccessful or only partially and temporarily successful) to establish self-cohesion—to keep one from being overwhelmed and disorganized by intolerable affects and to try to regain lost self-esteem and maintain connectedness to others. Thus, each patient has a unique constellation of problems and attempted but essentially failed solutions that constitute the essence of psychopathology. These problems and their failed solutions have to become actualized in the transference in order to be understood and interpretively worked through, in keeping with the goals of the particular treatment setting.

A brief elaboration of these ideas is a necessary prelude to the discussion of treatment. Self psychology first recognized new forms of transference—mirror-transference, idealizing transference, and alter-ego or twinship transference—that reflect unique configurations of psychopathology as well as the patient's efforts to heal them. Self psychology then postulated that normal human personality development (a) required the caretakers' phase-appropriate mirroring responses (the acceptance, echoing, admiration, affirmation, and validation of the infant's budding activities and personality features); (b) required the presence of others like oneself as a matrix for the successful unfolding of the child's innate skills and talents; and (c) required the availability of others who could be idealized, looked up to, and felt to be a source of comfort, soothing, and empowerment, for the acquisition of internalized values and ideals. The reliable availability of such "selfobject functions"—as Kohut called them—are a sine qua non for the attainment of emotional health. The various forms of psychopathology, then, are the consequences of individuals' innate predispositions combined with the absence of one or more of these functions, especially early in life. But such predispositions and an absence or faulty availability of selfobject responses even at a later time in life could affect the structural and functional integrity of the self—it could lead to a serious drop in self-esteem, resulting in a temporary or sustained decrease in vitality, and other, varied clinical consequences.

Thus, psychopathology in this view is first and foremost explained as a deficit in the structure of the psyche. Developmentally, such a deficit is based on the absence, or unreliable availability, of the emotional nutrients necessary for the individual's attainment of mental health. Structurally, such a deficit is based on an inadequate consolidation of the various structures of the self that maintain self-esteem and its other manifold functions. Pathogenic conflict in this context is viewed as arising secondarily from the matrix of an enfeebled or fragmentation-prone self. This is the answer self psychology offers as to why ubiquitous, normal conflicts and normal compromises turn pathogenic and often cannot be resolved without treatment: It is the fundamental structural and functional deficiency of the self that precludes the resolution of the ubiquitous, normal conflicts. Thus, there is always a prior self-disorder present, engendering the conflicts and defenses patients bring to us.

As Kohut amplified and extended these ideas about psychopathology throughout his work, he made a startling claim: Kohut (1978) said that we all lived—and needed to live—in a matrix of selfobjects from birth to death. We needed the emotional nutrients available in these relationships. Early on the need is for structure building; later on it is for the maintenance of the integrity of these inner structures. Once the self is formed, the nuclear self strives for the optimal fulfillment of its inner design or life plan. This inner design, or life plan, derives from an individual's combination of innate talents and skills and their appropriate validation by his or her caretakers during the earliest, formative years of development. The unfolding and optimal fulfillment of this life plan (embodied in the nuclear self) needs the empathic milieu of mature selfobjects throughout life.

AN OUTLINE OF THE CONDUCT AND PROCESS OF PSYCHOTHERAPY

What sort of a therapeutic process do we envision with this view of the nature of psychopathology? Let us now turn to an examination of the conduct and process of treatment in order to identify those component factors of the psychotherapeutic process that are responsible for the amelioration or cure of psychopathology.

Our interest in the treatment process in the psychoanalytic psychotherapies began in the framework of ego psychology and continued in the expanded framework of Michael Balint's object relations theory and his special sensitivity to the therapist–patient relationship as the matrix for the therapeutic process. It was at this stage in our professional development that Kohut's work and our supervisory experiences with him decisively altered and gave an entirely new direction to our therapeutic efforts and their conceptualization. It is in relation to these therapeutic efforts and their conceptualization under the heading of "the interpretive process in the psychoanalytic psychotherapies" that we have tried to consolidate and advance Kohut's self psychology (e. g., A. Ornstein and P. H. Ornstein, 1975, 1977; P. H. Ornstein and A. Ornstein, 1980, 1985).

In this chapter we shall present the fundamentals of a psychotherapy based on the demands of clinical practice and the insights of self psychology. We shall focus on the *general principles* of treatment—regardless of the nature of the patients' specific psychopathology—knowing full well that in different clinical conditions the basic elements of treatment will have to be adjusted according to the nature of the specific psychopathology of the patient and of the relationship that will develop between patient and therapist.

There is a reason for our focus on general principles. The demand these days—and perhaps rightly so from a particular perspective—is for the treatment of *specific* clinical conditions. Everyone wishes to be an expert—in the treatment of sexual abuse, phobias, anxiety disorders, marital problems and sexual dysfunction, narcissistic and borderline states, and others—so assiduously that people no longer seem to value the general principles that guide us to the inner life of those who suffer from these conditions. Treating diseases, rather than the people who suffer from them, had become a technicized undertaking even in psychotherapy; each condition supposedly necessitated a special "technique." In sharp contrast, we shall present an approach that holds onto certain values inherent in psychoanalysis since its inception—values that became more clearly anchored within the entire spectrum of the psychoanalytic psychotherapies through the contributions of self psychology.

A certain type of encounter between patient and therapist inevitably establishes a therapeutic relationship—the self–selfobject matrix—within which the patient's thwarted needs and thwarting fears can find expression. It is the patient's progressively less hampered expression of these needs, in the face of the ever-present fears of retraumatization, and the therapist's responsiveness to these needs and fears (mainly through "understanding" and "explaining" them) that are the core of psychoanalytic psychotherapy—irrespective of the nature of the patient's clinical condition. Instead of speaking of different "techniques" for different conditions, we speak of, and focus on, the nature of the therapist's responsiveness to the various constellations of emerging needs and fears in the treatment process.

In a nutshell, for us, it is the *genuine presence* of the therapist and his or her *empathic responsiveness* to the patient's subjective experiences that characterize psychoanalytic psychotherapy. Technique, that is, translating our understanding into proper responsiveness within the self–selfobject matrix of the treatment situation, is dictated by and subordinated to the evolving selfobject transferences. It is thus the nature of the relationship and the experiences within it that determine how we respond. And in that sense we do not simply apply a technique but enter into a relationship and participate in an experience that requires our genuine presence and responsiveness. Interpretation (in the broadest sense, the therapeutic conversation in the interpretive mode)[1] is a key aspect of this responsiveness. Not empathy versus interpretation, as is so often misunderstood, but empathy as a precondition for effective interpretation.

What we do and how we do it can best be articulated by describing the main components of the interpretive process. The interpretive process (the therapeutic conversation in the interpretive mode) is predicated on the nonjudgmental, noncondemning acceptance of what the patient brings to the treatment setting and consists of two familiar, interrelated steps: understanding and explaining.

1. *Understanding,* as the first step in this two-step process, contributes to structure building and has specific self-affirming, self-enhancing, and self-cohesion-providing functions. A self-structure that is thus strengthened is enabled to fill in some of its defects and as a result is also enabled to resolve some of its conflicts. Feeling understood—simple as this may sound—in reality has a profound effect on the state of the self. Feeling understood is the adult equivalent of being held, which on the level of self-experience results in firming up or consolidating the self. It is this consolidation of the self that permits—at first temporarily and then more sustainedly—the experiencing as well as the expression of affects, which on account of their intensity and/or particular content previously could not be tolerated. In relation to the defenses, the consolidation of the self, as this occurs in the self–selfobject matrix, permits the suspension of habitual defenses—again, at first tentatively and later on more sustainedly (P. H. Ornstein and A. Ornstein, 1985).

2. *Explaining,* as the second step in this two-step process, contributes a deeper understanding in that it places immediate experience in its longitudinal, genetic-developmental context. Explanation deepens the patient's own empathic-accepting grasp of himself or herself; Kohut (1984) says that it strengthens the trust in the reality of the bond of empathy that is being established between patient and therapist. The therapist's effort to explain what he or she understands can generate insight, but such insight is not something the therapist can *give* the patient; it is only the patient who can attain it.

The *conduct* of treatment refers to all the arrangements the therapist makes and all the behaviors (verbal and nonverbal) that he or she introduces to create the requisite clinical atmosphere, the therapeutic

---

[1]See the next chapter for a detailed definition and illustration of speaking in the "interpretive mode."

ambience within which the work can most fruitfully proceed. The *process* refers to what all the arrangements, the ambience as well as what is said and done by both participants, evoke in each of them—and how all this then determines their respective inner experiences. These inner experiences constitute the emerging therapeutic process and reflect the effect patient and therapist have on each other and how this effect becomes expressed in the meaning of their transactions.

One important point about the process needs to be stressed. The encounter between patient and therapist automatically and inevitably evokes in each of them certain feelings about and experiences of the other—an instant rapport, a feeling of great distance and mistrust, a feeling of acceptance and admiration, a wish for closeness and intimacy (or its opposite), and a whole host of other experiences that will unfold almost irrespectively of what they actually talk about with each other. This process could also be described as the latent meaning of the patient–therapist interaction.

A striking example of this was recently evident in a patient, who was treated by Paul Ornstein, and was missed by the therapist for quite some time. The patient brought in many dreams and diligently worked on searching for their deepest meaning. The therapist participated with him as best as he could to further the patient's own considerably creative, often stunning ability, to unearth the various meanings of his dream. And yet, on each of these occasions the session ended with the patient feeling that, as he put it, "the dream didn't work for me," and he left with a certain degree of apathy, depression, and hopelessness. We later recognized that the dream and its meaning did not matter to him—although he insisted that it be thoroughly understood each time on many levels and he always proceeded in his interpretive work without any prodding from the therapist. What the patient sought from the interaction about his dreams—and what was the central motive of all his communications and most significant to him—was to evoke admiration from the therapist for his unusual creative capacity. Nothing else would do, no other response would suffice. Without that recognition on some level (either in the therapist's tone of voice or gestures, or the manner in which he had asked questions), the patient did not feel understood. Without an appreciation of his brilliant performance, the patient could not benefit from otherwise "correct" (his word) interpretations of his many dreams. It was mandatory that the therapist recognize what the patient needed and wanted, and accept these as legitimate in the transference in order to make therapeutic progress.

The experiences within the process, as we have just sketched them, constitute the core of the therapeutic conversation. To put it differently, what is experienced within the process (preconsciously or unconsciously) has to be raised to the level of awareness and ultimately discussed by the patient and the therapist.

How does treatment have to be conducted—we may now ask—to ensure the emergence of those experiences within the process that are the requisite elements for the cure of the patient's unique psychopathology? There is a short and a long answer to this question. We should begin with the short answer: A well-defined therapeutic ambience is necessary for the mobilization of the pathognomonic transference (the transference that is characteristic of the psychopathology in question), which is activated through this process. The long answer involves a more detailed description of the therapeutic ambience and the mobilization of the transference—it is to these that we should now turn.

THERAPEUTIC AMBIENCE AND THE TRANSFERENCE

As long as drive theory dominated the psychoanalytic approach—whether in the context of ego psychology or object relations theory—treatment was conducted in a particularly austere emotional atmosphere. There was great concern about the inadvertent or sub rosa gratification the patient might derive from the analyst's or therapist's friendly and genuine presence. The idea was that if drive needs or drive wishes were gratified through ordinary, everyday acts of friendliness, they would become unavailable for scrutiny in the transference. As far back as the early 1930s, Michael Balint (1932, 1935) raised an objection to such an emotionally depriving atmosphere, saying that it created a false baseline of behavior on the part of the analytic therapist from which to determine the intrapsychic meaning of the patient's behavior. He felt that the artificially depriving atmosphere gave rise to reactions that were in response to the actual, arbitrarily introduced frustration and could not be used as valid clinical data on the basis of which to reconstruct earlier traumatic experiences in the patient's life. This, in spite of the fact that Balint retained drive theory as part of his overriding object relations theory.

Once drive theory no longer dominates the psychoanalytic therapeutic endeavor, the ambience in the analytic therapeutic situation will change drastically. When there is no longer any fear that ordinary, everyday human courtesies will undermine the success of treatment—in fact, they might contribute to it—a freer and more openly friendly atmosphere might prevail. The arbitrary distance that was to guard against overtly or covertly satisfying drive needs or wishes might give way to a more natural, genuine presence on the part of the therapist or analyst. Kohut

(1977) expressed this necessary and felicitous change with a highly evocative metaphor when he said that there has to be a minimum amount of oxygen in the consulting room for the patient to breathe. The baseline of a normal atmosphere is not the absence of oxygen—not the analyst's emotional withdrawal—in which case one can only observe the patient as he or she is desperately gasping for air. Under such circumstances the analytic therapist cannot view the patient's internally determined emotional struggle and discover the genuine transference.

The friendly, nonjudgmental, noncondemning acceptance of what the patient brings into the treatment situation will create the needed feeling of safety. The patient may then begin to let down his or her guard and risk expressing long-thwarted needs and wishes and his or her now maladaptive, lifelong, protective defenses against them. The strongest inner obstacle to progress in the remobilization of the transference is the patient's fear of being retraumatized by the therapist in response to his or her openly expressed needs and wishes or the patient's own inability to perceive and respond to the analyst's empathic understanding. The recognition and acceptance of this fear as justified in the light of earlier traumata goes a long way toward creating the proper climate for the progressively fuller emergence of the transference and its interpretive working through.

A colleague consulted one of us (Paul Ornstein) on a very difficult treatment process. He related the frequently recurring accusations of his woman patient that he was disinterested, detached, and often bored and that he probably regretted taking her on as a patient. The only reason he continued with her, she felt, was because he wanted to do the referring physician a favor. She also felt at times that her therapist hated and despised her. Finally, the therapist found it difficult to listen to all of this and asked for a consultation. He felt compelled to try to set the record straight and gently and tactfully show the patient that her accusations resulted from misperceptions, called "transference distortions" in our (perhaps defensive) analytic parlance. The consultant suggested that the patient may have had her own good reasons to feel the way *she* did, just as he had his good reasons to feel the way *he* did, but that pitting his subjective experience against hers is a complex, coercive procedure, with many potentially adverse side effects. The consultant recommended that, instead, he should accept the patient's accusations as valid in the transference, without challenging them as to their accuracy. He could then explore the experiences the patient had in sessions with him that had given rise to her feelings. He could merely say that if she felt he hated her, he could understand why she could not open up to him and would feel that treatment was just as painful to her now as growing up was when she felt that her mother or father hated her and felt unwanted.

In other words, the consultant counseled the therapist to be curious about the patient's earlier experiences that left her with the specific sensitivities that now emerged in the transference and to reflect on his own verbal and nonverbal behavior to detect in what way he might have inadvertently reactivated these early experiences. Freud discovered the kernel of truth in some severe paranoid delusions—it behooves us to recognize such kernels of truth in each instance in any therapeutic process. Nothing is more rewarding for putting a stalemated treatment back on track than the recognition of how we as therapists have inadvertently contributed to the stalemate.

In a psychoanalytic psychotherapy conducted along the lines just indicated, each individual treatment process potentially contains a number of significant curative factors, intertwined, in various combinations, and buttressing each other's effectiveness in bringing about the therapeutic results (P. H. Ornstein, 1988). Not all possible therapeutic factors are present, nor do they need to be present, in each treatment process. What is activated within each therapeutic dyad depends on certain key characteristics of each of the participants. On the part of the patient, it is the nature of the psychopathology and the capacity to mobilize it (beyond merely talking about it), in relation to the person of the therapist, that will determine at what level and with what therapeutic factors in operation the treatment will proceed. On the part of the therapist, it will be the capacity for sustained empathic listening and for resonating with what the patient brings to the treatment that will determine at what level and with what therapeutic factors in operation the treatment will proceed. The particular set of theories that guide the therapist in his or her capacity to listen and to resonate with the patient's experiences will significantly influence the nature of the treatment process, and the curative factors operative in it. We should now turn our attention to a brief survey of these curative factors.

THE MULTIPLE CURATIVE FACTORS IN EACH TREATMENT PROCESS

We used to rely on brief, highly evocative epigrammatic statements to describe the essential elements of cure. Early on (and for quite some time) in psychoanalysis "making the unconscious conscious" would suffice to characterize what was the most important feature of the cure. Making the unconscious conscious was said to have led to insight, which was considered to be the cardinal point of cure. Factors other than insight that contributed to the curative process were viewed as merely supportive, not leading to "real cure." When topographic theory gave way to structural theory (ego psychology) the preceding epigram changed to "where id was there shall ego be" to characterize the insight-based structural change. Such descriptions no longer seem to do justice to the complex and multilayered curative processes envisioned in the contemporary psychoanalytic psychotherapies. Neither is it sufficient to call attention to the transformation of a "rigid, punitive superego" into a "more flexible and benign" one, as Strachey (1934) conceived of the core of psychoanalytic cure. In the same vein, the supreme position of insight as a curative factor par excellence may now also be questioned, because a more basic "corrective emotional experience"[2] is seen as the broader, more encompassing portrayal, a sine qua non, for psychoanalytic-psychotherapeutic cure (P. H. Ornstein, 1988).

Insight alone, without the simultaneous affect-laden experiences of the patient within the transference, does not bring about cure in most instances. Even where insight alone seems to be responsible for change (such as is claimed in uncomplicated neuroses), closer examination reveals that effective insight is only possible in the context of a particular emotional experience within the transference.

Kohut's work underlined the primary significance of structure building (through "transmuting internalizations") and the recognition that insight may precede, follow, or go hand in hand with structure building, that is, "cure." He initially viewed this as the ultimate curative process, subsuming all others listed before as contributing factors, but not yet, in and of themselves, curative.[3]

Later on, after Kohut recognized the need for selfobjects throughout life, he introduced the idea of the curative value of (re)establishing empathic contact with one's own infantile and childhood self, as well as the (re)establishment of empathic contact with one's childhood selfobjects. Through these internally established changes—through the establishment of a continuity between past and present that was disrupted by traumatic experiences—perhaps for the first time the patient could finally forge a relationship to a network of contemporary (mature) selfobjects, as the supreme expression of cure (A. Ornstein, 1994).

[2] "Corrective emotional experience" has a bad reputation among some psychoanalytic psychotherapists because of Franz Alexander's recommendation that the therapist should take on the opposite role vis-à-vis the patient from what the parents' pathogenic behavior might have been. This prescription aside, however, psychotherapy should always provide a corrective emotional experience, without which we cannot conceive of a "cure."

[3] By "transmuting internalization" Kohut (1971) meant that potentially available innate, archaic, budding capacities mature in the course of development and gradually become transformed within an empathic self-selfobject matrix into permanent psychic structures. He thought transmuting internalization was triggered by "optimum frustration." Current views consider "optimum gratification," "optimum responsiveness," or "empathic responsiveness" as more appropriate concepts in this context.

Kohut, too, had an epigrammatic formulation of the nature of cure, which did not negate the contributions of other previously identified factors or processes, but did place them in a subordinate role in the total therapeutic process. In *How Does Analysis Cure?* Kohut (1984) wrote that "while structure formation via transmuting internalization is still a major part of the developmental process toward health, and in the analytic-therapeutic process toward cure, we now had to recognize that the gradual acquisition of the ability to maintain the self within the matrix of mature self–selfobject relationships, i. e. *the acquisition of empathic contact with selfobjects, is the essence of psychoanalytic cure*" [italics added].

CONCLUDING REMARKS

If therapists listen to patients from the vantage point of the patients' own subjective perspective and simply respond by recognizing and reflecting back to them what they hear, rather than focusing on what *they* think patients might be withholding from them, then each patient will teach his or her therapist about the proper therapeutic approach to the patient's own highly idiosyncratic problems.

To summarize:

Contemporary psychoanalysis encompasses a larger variety of possible curative processes than earlier views were able to do. The therapeutic relationship (variously conceptualized in its form and significance) is now widely recognized as the matrix for the achievement of insight. Such insight is no longer considered as the exclusive avenue to cure. Instead of holding on to the usual dichotomy between structural change through insight and structure building through a therapeutic relationship, we have indicated how the two processes necessarily dovetail or are actually one. They cannot be arbitrarily separated in our conceptualization of cure, since there is no insight without a therapeutic experience in the relationship, and no meaningful therapeutic experience can be devoid of insight. The necessity to work on "both tracks" and to make each enhance the other is the greatest challenge to the therapist and potentially of the greatest benefit to the patient [P. H. Ornstein, 1988].

REFERENCES

Balint, M. (1932), Character analysis and new beginning. Read at the 12th International Psycho-analytical Congress, Wiesbaden. Published in German in *Internat. J. Psychoanal.* (1939). Reprinted in English in *Primary Love and Psycho-analytic Technique.* New York: Liveright, 1953.

—— (1935), Critical notes on the theory of the pregenital organization of the libido. Read to the Vienna Psychoanalytical Society on May 15. Reprinted in *Primary Love and Psycho-analytic Technique*. New York: Liveright, 1953.

Kohut, H. (1971), *The Analysis of the Self*. New York: International Universities Press.

—— (1977), *The Restoration of the Self*. New York: International Universities Press.

—— (1978), Reflections on advances in self psychology. In: *Advances in Self Psychology* ed. A. Goldberg. New York: International Universities Press, pp. 473–552.

—— (1984), *How Does Analysis Cure?* ed. A. Goldberg & P. Stepausky. Chicago: University of Chicago Press.

Ornstein, A. (1994), Trauma, memory and psychic continuity. In: *A Decade of Progress: Progress in Self Psychology, Vol. 10*, ed. A. Goldberg. Hillsdale, NJ: The Analytic Press, pp. 131–145.

—— & Ornstein, P. H. (1975), On the interpretive process in psychoanalysis. *Internat. J. Psychoanal. Psychother.*, 4:219–271.

—— & Ornstein, P. H. (1977), Clinical interpretations in psychoanalysis. *International Encyclopedia of Neurology, Psychiatry and Psychology*, ed. B. Wolman. New York: Aesculapius, pp. 176–181.

Ornstein, P. H. (1988), Multiple curative factors and processes in the psychoanalytic psychotherapies. In: *How Does Treatment Help? On the Modes of Therapeutic Action of Psychoanalytic Psychotherapy*, ed. A. Rothstein. Monograph series of the American Psychoanalytic Association, *Monog. 4*. Madison, CT: International Universities Press, pp. 105–126.

—— (in press), Heinz Kohut's vision of the essence of humanness. In: *Psychoanalytic Versions of the Human Condition*, ed. P. Marcus & A. Rosenberg. New York: New York University Press.

—— & Ornstein, A. (1980), Formulating interpretations in clinical psychoanalysis. *Internat. J. Psycho-Anal.*, 61:203–211.

—— (1985), Clinical understanding and explaining: The empathic vantage point. In: *Progress in Self Psychology, Vol. 1*, ed. A. Goldberg. New York: Guilford, pp. 43–61.

Strachey, J. (1934), The nature of the therapeutic action in psycho-analysis. *Internat. J. Psycho-Anal.*, 15:127–159.

7

II. Speaking in the Interpretive Mode and Feeling Understood

Crucial Aspects of the Therapeutic Action in Psychotherapy

Anna Ornstein and Paul H. Ornstein

What psychoanalysts consider to be the critical aspects of the therapeutic action in psychoanalysis may be articulated in abstract, metapsychological terms or in terms of the patient's and analyst's experiences in the crucible of the therapeutic moment. When analysts resort to metapsychological explanations, it is hard to tell whether these explanations are the products of clever theorizing or were arrived at in the clinical situation. And even with our best efforts, when our conceptualizations remain close to the clinical data, we still do not know what it is that is curative, what the decisive factors may be in any given treatment situation. Modell said (1976)—and we agree—that in a successful treatment there are so many complex processes acting in concert that it may be impossible to know which particular element is responsible for therapeutic change. One important reason for our uncertainty is related to what Kris (1950) stated so well, namely, that the essential aspects of the analytic work are done by the patient's own unconscious thought processes and all that interpretations do is reawaken the flow of primary process connection, which may lead to change without insight. In other words, even if our understanding of what may be curative is based on clinical data, we cannot be certain how the changes in the patient's behavior may be related to our interventions.

Still, we would maintain that a theory of cure is essential for the conduct of psychotherapy that has as its aim the alleviation of patients' suffering and the achievement of their life's goals. Without an image of what could potentially make a contribution to the healing process, interventions would be offered in an arbitrary manner, unrelated to the therapist's theory of psychopathogenesis.[1] In our view, all aspects of the treatment, as experienced by the patient, ought to make a contribution to the healing process: the ambience the therapist and patient create, the level of meaningful engagement they achieve, and the interpretive process.

There are even greater difficulties encountered in ascertaining what the curative factors are in psychotherapy than in psychoanalysis. The answer to the question of what may be curative in psychotherapy has been sought by comparing and contrasting psychotherapy and psychoanalysis to learn how these two treatment modalities may be similar and in what way they may be different regarding their respective potential for change (Bibring, 1954; Gill, 1951; Frank, 1961; Dewald, 1964; Ekstein and Wallerstein, 1972; Malan, 1976; Kernberg, 1984; Luborsky, 1984; Strupp, 1984).

In contrast to psychoanalysis, psychotherapy has lacked uniformity in its method and technical recommendations; only in the manner in which psychotherapy was similar to psychoanalysis was it expected to bring about lasting structural changes.[2] Wallerstein (1969), one of the members of the Menninger Psychotherapy Research Team, raised the question of whether there was a scientific psychotherapy apart from psychanalysis. Answering the question of whether psychotherapy could or could not bring about structural change became important as more and more psychoanalysts were doing psychotherapy—a treatment modality that they could not reconcile with their depth psychological orientation. Under these circumstances—and as a result of the increasing demand for short-term treatment—psychoanalysts doing psychotherapy, by and large, retained the recommendation that was the legacy of ego psychology, according to which in once or twice weekly, face-to-face interviews, unconscious childhood wishes were not supposed to

---

[1]The theory of cure had always been correlated with the theory of pathogenesis. This was the case when healing required the reversal of the pathogenic effect of forgotten memories by insisting that the patient recall them with the help of hypnosis. Later—with the recognition that defenses (resistances) are also unconscious—the recommendations for resistance analysis had to be followed. More recently, in keeping with the theory of pathogenesis as it is formulated by object relations theory and self psychology, the emphasis has shifted to the importance of the therapist–patient relationship. In all instances, the aim of treatment has been to *reverse* the process that was assumed to have caused the illness.

[2]Psychological structures have different meanings in different theoretical contexts. However, they all refer to something in the psyche that is enduring and not subject to rapid changes and fluctuations.

become remobilized. At the same time, a "certain amount" of transference was considered to be necessary for "therapeutic leverage." This meant that transferences had to be "regulated" with specific forms of interventions. These interventions were to strengthen patients' defenses; patients were consequently encouraged, praised "and in general, given narcissistic support for those ego activities in which defense is combined with adaptive gratification, and discourage by subtle or direct techniques those activities which are maladaptive gratifications, whether or not they are combined with defense" (Gill, 1951, p. 66). Today, we would eschew such recommendations and consider them highly manipulative, as would Gill himself. In keeping with Freud's prediction, psychoanalysts felt compelled "to alloy the pure gold of analysis freely with the copper of direct suggestion" (1919, p. 168).

In our view, the difficulty these researchers had—in determining what may constitute the critical factors in bringing about psychological change in psychotherapy—was related to the fact that traditional psychoanalysis maintained that only those with psychoneurotic conditions, that is, patients who had reached the oedipal phase, developed interpretable transferences. Because such transferences were not expected to develop in patients who entered psychotherapy, treatment strategies— such as suppressive, supportive, relational, and insight-oriented treatment—were decided on the basis of the nature of the manifest illness and justified primarily on the basis of the patient's history. Those who used techniques guided by the nature of patients' psychopathology failed to appreciate the now generally accepted fact that what becomes available for therapeutic change does not depend only on the nature of the psychopathology (whether or not it is oedipal or preoedipal in nature) but also on what transpires between the two participants in the treatment process. The failure of psychotherapists to recognize transferences that were characteristic for patients with various forms of structural defects and deficits (patients who present with relatively severe forms of personality disorders) prevented the evolution of a treatment process[3]—a process that could be tracked, systematically

---

[3]"A distinct property of psychoanalysis is its character as a process with a notion, however loosely defined, or progressive development over time in a definite direction" (Kris, 1956, p. 445).

Merriam-Webster's *Third New International Dictionary* gives the following definition of process: ". . . the action of moving forward progressively from one point to another on the way to completion; the action of passing through continuing development from a beginning to a completed end; the action of continuously going along through each of a succession of acts, events or developmental stages; an actual, progressively continuing development marked by a series of gradual changes. . . ."

taught, and studied. Without a process that could be systematically investigated, no discoveries could be made regarding the curative factors in psychotherapy.

It is the thesis of this chapter that the introduction of self psychology, specifically, the recognition of selfobject transferences, profoundly affected the *practice* of psychotherapy. The recognition of specific transferences enabled therapists to respond to patients in the interpretive mode, which facilitated the evolution of a therapeutic process. We are now better able to recognize some of those factors that make a contribution to the healing process in psychotherapy.

SELFOBJECT TRANSFERENCES AND SELF-COHESION

The theory of psychoanalytic self psychology was formulated on the basis of the analysis of patients with narcissistic personality and behavior disorders. It was in the course of the analyses of these patients that Kohut (1971) recognized the selfobject transferences—transferences that were not based on intersystemic conflicts but were related to defects and deficits in the organization of the self. At first, the recognition of selfobject transferences only added to the spectrum of analyzable psychological conditions. It was with the passage of time that we began to appreciate how the discovery of these transferences could also revolutionize the conduct of psychotherapy. Recognizing the selfobject transferences (merger, mirror, and the various manifestations of the idealizing transferences) made it possible for psychotherapists to use interpretation as their primary tool of intervention and retain their depth-psychological orientation.

The mobilization of selfobject transferences, which arise as a result of of developmental arrests, does not depend on an "analytic regression." Rather, patients with various degrees of defects in their self-organization are engaged in an ongoing search for empathic responsiveness, acceptance, and understanding in order to complete development and achieve a sense of cohesion and wholeness. Patients "use" others in their environment to consolidate their fragmentation-prone selves or to enhance their capacity to regulate their self-esteem. Expectedly, in nontherapeutic relationships, using others for self-enhancement, even in subtle ways, burdens patients' relationships and leads to disappointments, with the result that the problems with which patients had entered their relationships may become worse rather than better. Psychotherapists, however, who immerse themselves in their patients subjective experiences and make an ongoing effort to decenter from their own selfobject needs, are able to recognize the specific ways in which patients make use of the psychotherapists' verbal and nonverbal communications. Empathic interpretive responses, which include acceptance, understanding, and explaining, facilitate the establishment of one of the selfobject transferences that, in turn, brings about an increase in self-cohesion. It is the patient's increased self-cohesion, secondary to the establishment of one of the selfobject transferences, that makes the working through of symptomatic behavior possible.

In relation to the interpretive approach to symptomatic behavior, our technical recommendations have to be distinguished from those offered by therapists who are guided by traditional psychoanalytic or object relations theory. The difference involves the way in which the function of symptoms in psychic life is viewed by the various psychoanalytic theories. In self psychology, defenses (denial, repression, projection, disavowal, and the ways in which these may be combined in the various forms of personality features and symptomatic behavior) are not viewed as obstacles that patients put in the therapists' way as resistances to the uncovering of aggressive and sexual impulses and their related unconscious fantasies. Rather, "resistances," in keeping with the original understanding of the developmental function of defenses, are considered to be protecting a vulnerable self from further traumatization (Kohut, 1984). Therefore, defenses, rather than being challenged, have to be interpreted in a manner that acknowledges their significance in securing a degree of functional capacity at least in some sectors of the psyche.

In the following, we shall detail the interpretive process in psychotherapy, in which the therapist strives to maintain an empathic contact with the patient's subjective experiences.

SPEAKING IN THE INTERPRETIVE MODE AND FEELING UNDERSTOOD: TRANSLATING THEORY INTO PRACTICE

"Speaking in the interpretive mode" means that the therapist does not wait until all parts of the puzzle have fallen into place but offers understanding and explanation from the beginning of treatment; the aim is to articulate the patient's experiences that the therapist could empathically encompass. We consider such a dialogue interpretive in nature because defenses are commented on not in isolation but always so as to include the motive for a particular defense or the symptomatic behavior. When such comments are articulated in a tentative and open-ended manner, they serve as invitations for the patient to correct the therapist's understanding or to elaborate on what has been said so far. At first, the therapist's responses can only encompass the patient's current experience (the here and now, the level of understanding), but with the passage of time, the momentary self-experiences can be given meaning in light of the patient's past (the level of explanation). Early in the process, when one's understanding is still very sketchy, an open-ended statement is best introduced by saying "This is the way I understand you so far; help me understand this or that better" or "This is what I hear you say; is this what you had in mind?" This manner of speaking indicates that therapists rarely "hit the nail on the head" and that what is required is a series of negotiations in which both parties make an effort to focus their attention on the affectively most highly charged issues with which the patient is dealing.

Speaking in the interpretive mode has considerable advantages over repeated questioning, no matter how tactfully the questions may be raised. Repeated questioning or inquiry is reminiscent of a diagnostic interview, based on the medical model, in which the data provided by the patient allow the doctor to arrive at the proper diagnosis on the basis of which the proper treatment can be instituted. However, the delineation between diagnosis and treatment in psychotherapy is an artificial one. As far as our patients are concerned, for them treatment begins with the very first encounter, whether this occurs in person or over the phone; psychotherapists are always engaged in a therapeutic–diagnostic dialogue.

The therapist's tentative understanding and its open-ended articulation facilitate the treatment, and with it the healing process, in several ways: (1) The phrasing of interpretive comments facilitates the patient's understanding of the particular way in which the therapist has organized the meaning of the patient's communications, which is always determined by theoretical orientation, personal biases, countertransferences, and other unconscious motives. (2) Hearing how his communications are understood offers the patient the opportunity to correct the way he is being heard and gives him a chance to further elaborate on what he has said so far. (3) Speaking in the interpretive mode, that is, articulating our tentative understanding and explanations, deepens the therapeutic process as ever-increasing dimensions of the patient's psychic life can be articulated by both participants. This is why it also proves to be most effective in illuminating the unconscious and barely conscious aspects of the patient's psychological life, which are the most enduring features of the personality. (4) Making an effort to understand the patient in depth demonstrates the therapist's genuine involvement. (5) In addition, in treatments of relatively brief duration, this mode of conversation helps locate the focus early in the process, which—when repeatedly checked against the patient's psychic reality—serves as a guide in making increasingly better focused interventions.[4] (6) The therapist's speaking in the interpretive mode promotes a feeling in the patient of being understood. Feeling understood facilitates the therapeutic engagement and the development of one of the selfobject transferences. In our view, feeling understood constitutes one of the most essential elements in the healing process. Conveying understanding and acceptance is what Winnicott meant when he said that "Holding the patient often takes the form of conveying in words at the appropriate moment something that shows that *the analyst knows and understands the deepest anxiety that is being experienced*" (Winnicott, 1965, p. 240; italics added).

The patient, whose treatment we shall use to demonstrate the points we have made so far, was in a brief, focal psychotherapy (with Anna Ornstein). The relatively detailed reporting will illustrate how the therapist's phrasing of interpretive comments facilitated finding the focus early in treatment and how her speaking in the interpretive mode permitted the working through of some of the most problematic features of the patient's personality. Follow-up interviews helped therapist and patient to appreciate the limits of such a brief therapeutic encounter.

CLINICAL EXAMPLE

Ms. Hoyt is a 41-year-old single woman, a student at a local art institute. Because of the patient's description of her apathy and of her difficulty in completing her thesis, and because of her family history of depression (her mother committed suicide when the patient was 11 years old), the referring psychiatrist put her on an antidepressant and asked the patient to keep in touch with him regarding the medication. He stressed, however, that what she really needed was psychotherapy.

In the first interview, Ms. Hoyt spoke rapidly, like someone who wanted to cover a lot of ground in a short time; she also appeared anxious and made poor eye contact. After telling me that she was very ambivalent about the recommendation to seek psychotherapy, she launched into a rather detailed description of her current problems and her understanding of their sources. She had gained these "insights" in the various group treatment programs she had participated in over the years: Overeaters Anonymous, EST (Erhard Systems Training), Transcendental Meditation, and Adult Children of Alcoholics. She joined the last group because her mother was addicted to pain killers and because she considered hers to have been a dysfunctional family. She felt that the

[4]The focus refers to that particular area of the patient's problems that best explains the current difficulties—both the symptoms and personality features—on the basis of which the current symptoms have arisen.

groups were helpful but that she had become too dependent on them and was unable to make a decision for herself. She knew how to explain her difficulties—she knew all the right words—but most of these explanations were formulas that were supposed to explain the difficulties of anyone who grew up in a dysfunctional family.

Ms. Hoyt was born and raised in a relatively wealthy suburb of an Eastern city. As an adult she had lived in a variety of places and held various temporary jobs. She came to town to get a degree in art and was living on a trust fund that was established by her father, who had died a year before. She has been very unhappy here as a result of what she experienced as a "pseudointellectual" climate at the art institute. As soon as she heard my accent on the phone, she decided that I must be part of the same pseudointellectual scene. She described to me her experiences with her teachers and advisers—all of which were characterized by a great deal of animosity; she had the reputation of having a "sharp tongue" and of being intolerant.

In her tone of voice and manner of speaking, I heard a haughty attitude that was a mixture of anger, envy, and an air of pseudo-superiority. I also heard her vulnerability—how easily she would feel hurt and would then impulsively retaliate or withdraw in rage. Some of the descriptions of her relationships, especially with the women at the art institute, had a paranoid tone; she was now hardly on speaking terms with anyone and was spending long hours—sometimes all day—in her room watching television. The patient rarely gets up before noon, and then settles down to watch television—only to feel disgusted with herself at the end of the day. This has gone on for about a year, in spite of her consciously held wish to finish her thesis and get out of the city. She appears to be greatly distressed about her inability to concentrate on her work and to put an end to her procrastination.

Ms. Hoyt's next associations involved her father's passivity, specifically his inability to keep his business going; he ended up as a recluse, immersed in the philosophy of an obscure religion. This is the image she now has of herself: she too will end up unrecognized, withdrawn, and unhappy. In her self-help groups, she was told repeatedly that she was condemned to repeat her father's life.

Ms. Hoyt is the middle of three children. She has very poor relationships with both of her siblings; she is not in touch with her older sister and rarely sees her younger brother. She considers herself to be the black sheep of the family, always struggling with jealousy in relation to her sister, who was her mother's favorite, and playing second fiddle to her more popular and successful siblings and schoolmates. This feeling has been with her all her life—she feels that everyone is always more appreciated then she is, she feels mistreated by her advisers and peers, and she believes that she will never be able to think of herself as "a star." Ms. Hoyt finds herself preoccupied with incidents in which she has been hurt and is always ready to strike out at anyone who, she feels, is pointing a finger at her.

When she paused, I said that she might want to know what I was thinking as I was listening to her. I said that in her story I heard her fear of being condemned to repeat her father's life. I also heard her struggling against feeling that she can only be second best in everything she does, a feeling she seemed to have carried from childhood into her adult life. It sounded to me, I said, like the struggle had become difficult and she had withdrawn into solitude where she felt safe but emotionally very isolated.

Ms. Hoyt appeared to consider what I said but did not respond directly. Instead, she told me that she was confused about her reasons for seeking a degree in art. She said that she did not think that she had natural gifts and it was her fear that she could not make it as an artist that prompted her to try to get a degree in art. However, she also doubted that she could get a teaching job and she did not particularly like teaching. She finds herself committed to something she does not see much point in doing. Several times she interrupted her narrative with a sigh, saying: "Oh, what's the point, it's a mess!"

Rather than responding to my comments regarding my understanding of her state of mind, the patient offered an explanation of her own as to what might be responsible for her apathy, her procrastination, and her difficulties with the faculty and her peers at the institute. She thought these were owed to her inability to invest herself in her thesis work because she really was not motivated to receive a teaching degree. I considered that while, on some level, my understanding of her current state of mind may have been close to what she felt, my comments were too encompassing and did not create in her a feeling of being understood.

Ms. Hoyt continued her narrative and spoke about her relationships with men. She had many short-lived relationships. She finds it easy to seduce men, especially men she does not look up to and can easily wrap around her finger. She said, "This is just an other example of how *shitty* I feel about myself. Men I could admire are beyond my reach."

As the hour was coming to an end, I referred back to her ambivalence about psychotherapy and said I could understand that she would have difficulty considering another attempt at treatment; she obviously had a great deal of group therapy experience and quite a bit of insight into the nature of her difficulties—it must be disappointing that in spite of this, she continues to repeat a pattern that blocks her from attending to her work and making satisfactory relationships. Again, she seemed to have dismissed my comments and, with irritation in her voice, asked about our financial arrangement, a matter we had thoroughly discussed over the phone prior to her first hour. I reminded her that I had told her I would not be able to accept her student insurance but had offered a reduced fee, which she had accepted over the phone. In a cold, detached voice she said that she would have to see what her insurance would cover before she made another appointment.

My feeling was that she came to look me over and I did not pass the test. I believe she experienced my bringing up her ambivalence, at the end of the hour, as questioning her commitment to treatment; anticipating rejection, she became angry and was ready to make her exit. This brief but emotionally significant exchange concerning the fee brought one of Ms. Hoyt's lifelong problems into the treatment—when she feared rejection, she responded quickly and with a great deal of anger.

Four days later, the patient telephoned and said that she called Dr. Neal, the psychiatrist who referred her to me, and he encouraged her to give me an other chance. She told him that I was not present with her for half of the hour and agreed to see her only for the money. Dr. Neal told her I did not need the money, because I was a well-known psychiatrist, but that I worked like a surgeon with a cold knife because I had to get to the bottom of her problems. He explained to her that this was her problem; her difficulty in trusting others had to do with the way she was treated as a child and it was for this that she needed treatment.

I was not happy with Dr. Neal's description of my approach to psychotherapy but I did not correct it because it was important that I not question the patient's perception of me and that my focus remain on her psychological reality. The only way I could understand her taking the advice of the referring physician and returning to see me was that she was troubled and could have—if ever so marginally—experienced my comments as indicating that I made an effort to understand her current state of mind.

I told Ms. Hoyt that I was glad she called me and that she told me about the phone call to Dr. Neal. I was also glad that Dr. Neal reassured her about my qualifications but I felt bad about her experiencing me as not having been emotionally present during the whole hour. After all, she told me a great many things about herself, all of which were very important—she must have felt terrible for not feeling listened to. The patient said she would like to understand what happened and we made an appointment for the next day.

I started the second hour by commenting on the disappointment she experienced the week before. To my surprise, Ms. Hoyt took the blame for her perception of me as cold and emotionally uninvolved. She was groggy, she said, because she did not have coffee before our session and could not listen to me very well. Also, as she said before, she tended to be critical of everyone. I took note of the fact that she had taken responsibility for experiencing me as emotionally absent and said that, at this time, it would be important for us to appreciate *her* perception of me—whatever the reasons for it might have been.

Ms. Hoyt returned to speaking about her childhood and described herself as having been "a good child," not argumentative like other members of her family. It was after she attended EST and various other self-help groups that she began to feel her rage at her family and felt empowered to express it. With a faint smile, she commented that she can well imagine why her advisers and peers think that she has a "sharp tongue" and is "intolerant." But just spewing out her rage has not been helpful to her—it has in fact made her relationships more tentative and much more difficult.

I had initially missed the meaning of this communication, namely, had she not attended EST and other self-help groups, she would not have gotten angry with me and dismissed me so quickly. My response to her came from my own agenda, which was my concern regarding her commitment to treatment. I said that I understood that seeking treatment this time was related to the fact that in spite of the many explanations she was given about her difficulties, neither her professional nor her personal life had improved. As a matter of fact, I can see how the expression of anger at her peers and advisers had only increased her emotional isolation. The patient responded by telling me that in EST meetings she experienced the group's encouraging her to express anger as supportive, but that this expression of anger worked only for short periods. Still, the fact that people always took her side made her feel very attached to the group and she still calls some of the members for "a quick fix" when she feels particularly low. She reflected on the difference between groups and individual treatment; she was always in large groups where everybody's problems were treated identically, this was the first time her problems were being looked at individually. Just before leaving, she said that she wanted to make an other appointment. Even though I realized that in this hour the patient's experience was very different from her experience the first time we met, I heard myself suggesting that she may want to take time out to think further about working with me, that she may regret it later if she made a decision under the impact of the successful hour. So we agreed that she would call me and tell me what she had decided. As she was leaving, I could see that she was disappointed with my suggestion; nevertheless, the patient left without my offering her another appointment.

Over the weekend, I found myself thinking about the way we parted. I thought of this woman's vulnerability to rejection and felt bad for not having offered her an other appointment. When I was thinking about my reason for leaving it up to her to call me, I had to confront the fact that my countertransference had gotten the better of me: I felt rejected by the patient after the first hour and needed to be reassured by her asking me *explicitly* to treat her. I was relieved to find that she had tried to reach me the day after we met and again the following week when I returned to my office.

In this third hour, Ms. Hoyt appeared very well put together: her hair was carefully combed, she was neatly dressed, and she had on some make-up. Sitting down, she sighed and asked: "Where should I begin?" After warning me that she might simply rattle off the things she learned about herself in the many groups that she had attended, she began by telling me about an experience that had happened about 4 years ago and about which she still had a lot of feelings. The experience was (and still is) very distressing to her: She fell in love with a young man who was prominent in art circles. The man paid no attention to her and, in desperation, she followed him around wherever he traveled in the country. She believes that she was "truly crazy" at that time. Many people in her current life knew about her behavior and she thinks that they are still holding it against her. She asked whether I had an idea as to what may have happened to her to make her behave that way. I said that I could not be sure, but that it reminded me of what she told me about the kind of relationship she had with one of her closest childhood friends. (This was a girl who won all the awards in school while the patient was a perpetual "runner-up." It was in relationship to this girl that Ms. Hoyt experienced herself most strongly as a "second fiddle." The success of this friend filled her with envy but as if she had been glued to her, she was deeply attached to this girl and the two remained best friends for many years.)

I said that from her description I inferred that the close, almost exclusive relationship with this very prominent and successful school friend provided her with reflected glory. If this was indeed the case, it could help us understand her clingy and possessive behavior with her friend as well as in relation to the young man. Ms. Hoyt appeared thoughtful and said that she felt a sense of relief that her behavior made sense to me; she had been worried that it meant that she was crazy then and could become crazy like that again at any time. Further confirming associations followed: She thought that many of her difficulties at the art institute were related to her not being part of the in crowd, but that as long as she is not viewed as "star material," she does not think she has a chance. "[It is] the same with men," she said. "When it comes to actually having an affair, I will find a man who is even less successful than I am." The patient then recalled the atmosphere in her home during her mother's severe depressions. After her mother's suicide, she turned to her older sister who, being a teenager herself, could not be a mother to her. This confirmed the patient's feeling that neither her sister nor her mother found her lovable, a feeling that has remained with her in her relationships with other people.

Ms. Hoyt may have been encouraged by our conversation and my level of understanding, and hastily mentioned another disturbing area of her current life that she would like to understand—watching television all day when, consciously, she wants to finish her thesis and get out of the city. I suggested that now that we understood her state of mind a little bit better, we might be able to understand what meaning the compulsive watching of television might have for her.

In the next hour, she focused on this issue, wondered why she would do something so destructive to herself as spending her days watching television when she was worried about time passing and running out of money before she would be able to finish her thesis. I said that I could have only a tentative understanding but that I would share this with her in the hope that together we could find the answer to her question. I said I thought that because she experienced the people around her as hostile and frustrating and herself as angry at them for making life so difficult for her, she withdrew in order to protect herself from these experiences. However, being alone in the apartment day after day she was lonely and the television had become company for her. This was a simple explanation that made sense to her and she hoped that just knowing this might help her break this very self-destructive habit.

At this point in the process, "making sense" of her behavior, such as following a man around and spending her days in seclusion when she consciously wanted to finish her thesis, helped her overcome the self-recriminations and profound shame over that behavior. The patient gave another example of just how angry and isolated she has been: She met two of her professors in the hallway the other day. They passed without greeting her and she didn't greet them, which led her to think, "They hate me and I hate them."

In the next session, Ms. Hoyt came in looking excited. She was in an upbeat mood: She had bought a computer and all the equipment she needed to get started on her thesis. Also, she was able to get together a group of women who were in a similar situation regarding their theses and it appeared that they would be able to form a support group. It sounded like Ms. Hoyt, missing her group experiences, had created one for herself—an active step in overcoming her sense of isolation and very different from the apathy she was experiencing when we first met. She said that she was feeling a great deal better and that her head felt clearer. She thought that this might be due to her having stopped taking antidepressants; she had run out of the medication and decided not to renew the prescription. It was not clear to me what part the medication had played in the patient's improvement, but she was very definite in her decision to discontinue it.

Much of this hour's conversation was related to the clingy obsession she developed for the famous and popular man she had told me about in previous sessions. As we took the meaning of this experience apart, she could better appreciate how this incident exposed many important aspects of her focal problem: her ambition to be known and admired and her feeling that she herself could never achieve that status and therefore had to be associated with someone who was admired by others.

My understanding of the meaning of this experience was influenced by my appreciation of the fact that this young woman was deprived of the developmentally crucial experience of having idealizable parents: Her mother was severely depressed and committed suicide and her father was considered passive and ineffectual. This made "the rejection" by her older sister potentially traumatic.[5] Ms. Hoyt said that she still feels the sting of humiliation from this young man's failure to pay any attention to her. "Is this a wound I carry around?" she asked. I said that the word "wound" seemed to capture the feelings she has been experiencing around this matter: her feeling that she always plays second fiddle, seeking reflected glory in the shadow of someone whom others recognize as accomplished and successful. I thought she may have chosen this word because there was so much pain involved in these experiences. Experiences like these are humiliating for Ms. Hoyt on at least two accounts: she is being rejected by those whose favors she is seeking and, in addition, others are witnessing the desperate way in which she clings to these "stars." From my statement, Ms. Hoyt could strongly identify her resentment of having to be a "second fiddle" to more successful people: "This is how more and more of them (her peers) became my enemies and I was left without friends, no one was supporting me. . . ." I said that it made sense to me that feeling this way, she would withdraw into the safety of her home. She thought that when people in the self-help groups told her that she was repeating her

---

[5]Traumatic interference with idealization in the course of an individual's development results in a compelling need to merge with powerful objects later in life—a characteristic feature of patients with narcissistic personality disorders (Kohut, 1971).

father's life by isolating herself, they saw only the tip of the iceberg; they could not see that her current difficulties were related to an old wound she carried around. She could now appreciate that her current problems were more complicated than could be explained by a simple identification with her passive and dysfunctional father. She spoke of her father with sadness. She could understand him better now; she had never before considered that it was his vulnerability that made him escape into an esoteric religion and that he too had to isolate himself from life because he could not deal with its challenges.

As the process deepened, I could appreciate better that in addition to having been deprived of idealizable parents, she suffered the consequences of feeling that her mother preferred her sister. What made the word "wound" so useful in our dialogue was that we could both appreciate the patient's efforts to heal her lifelong wound by attending various self-help groups. In her professional and personal relationships, however, the wound would be repeatedly reopened: Feeling clingy and needy and expecting rejection, she would test others' acceptance of her. Because Ms. Hoyt was sensitive to any indication of nonacceptance, she would express frustration and anger either by a haughty withdrawal or by a verbal attack on the nonaccepting other.

In the next hour, Ms. Hoyt continued to feel excited about the developments in her life and in rapid succession told me about all of the things that she was doing now. She looked and sounded energetic; she had been working on her thesis regularly and had gotten into a fairly steady relationship with a young man, with whom she had embarked on what she hoped would be a successful business undertaking.

I was both pleased and bewildered by these rapid changes. I did not think that they could be lasting and certainly did not think that they indicated structural change. However, the progress in the treatment process was real insofar as our dialogue appeared to facilitate the establishment of an idealizing merger transference. The ensuing increase in self-cohesion gave Ms. Hoyt an opportunity to be self-reflective without self-condemnation and to achieve an increasingly more accepting attitude toward her own previous behavior. This development represented a significant aspect of the curative process: the capacity to be empathic toward the "sick" or infantile aspect of one's personality greatly reduces the shame and guilt that perpetuates maladaptive behavior. Self-acceptance is also responsible for the increasing ability to relinquish defense organizations that protect a vulnerable self. In Ms. Hoyt's case, this meant a lessening of her haughty withdrawal into the safety of her home and a decrease in the imperative need to retaliate for actual or perceived hurts by verbally attacking others.

The patient may have been thinking along similar lines when she suddenly turned to me with the question: "How does psychotherapy work?" She said that she was surprised we did not go into her history more. This is what Dr. Neal said we would do. I said that the answer to the question as to how therapy works may best come from her: What had she experienced so far? Ms. Hoyt thought that what helped her most was that we could identify why she went "nuts" over that man—why she wanted him to pay attention to her and why she was preoccupied with that experience for years. She fell silent and then commented that the way that she sees psychotherapy working is that she had told me various stories and I picked out the ones that helped me understand what was bothering her *now.* I thought that this was a very good explanation and that, indeed, I have tried to understand those experiences that have continued to have meaning for her and, over the years, become a heavy emotional burden to her. I again referred to the emotional wound she experienced when she obsessively pursued the young man. She wondered whether, in the end, that experience was really useful to her: She had to face the fact that because she lacked serious talent in art, her decision to acquire a degree in teaching was a compromise that she resented and that was why she was very poorly motivated to work toward it. What she really wanted was to become a recognized artist herself.

As I was now confident that Ms. Hoyt was well engaged and that progress was being made, I was not prepared for the affect storm that occurred in the next hour and that could have destroyed this brief treatment process.

When Ms. Hoyt first entered the office, she did not appear angry or unhappy, so I was surprised when she told me that since she had seen me last, she had been in New York and the friend who originally insisted that she needed psychiatric help had talked her into coming back to see me. At this point, with a great deal of affect, she repeated some of the things she had told her friend: "I don't like this woman . . . coming here doesn't do a thing for me . . . all she does is make money off of me . . . I don't want to spend my father's money on conversations that lead nowhere. . . ."

It appeared that my assessment of the patient's progress did not correspond to hers. I also had to consider whether the conversation she had with her friend had something to do with the dynamics of their relationship and her disparaging me may have been related to that as much as to whatever may have transpired between the two of us.

There must have been restrained anger in my voice when I said that she must feel some obligation to this man to have come back here, feeling the way she did about her treatment with me. My comment infuriated her and she said that I obviously want her to run to the door and slam it, that my comment indicated that I hoped she would leave. "This would be exactly what has been happening to me all my life. When I dare to tell people how I feel about them, the next thing I know, they throw me out."

Though I had no idea what had infuriated her or made her feel that our conversations led nowhere, she had now apparently put herself into a position where she could have repeated an old pattern—she could have provoked me to reject her.

I said that the last thing I would want is for her to leave because I know that this is exactly the reason she came to see me, to see if there is any way she could escape this cycle of repetition in which she gets caught in angry feelings and provokes rejection.

This statement calmed her some and she reminded me that her big problem is rage and paranoia. I said, yes, I know that it is difficult not to feel enraged when she experiences a situation in which her interests are not being attended to and, instead, she feels exploited. This is how I understand her feeling about my charging her a sum beyond what the insurance company would pay. It is difficult to manage anger that is triggered by strong feelings of injustice. I also commented that, obviously, the issue around finances had not been adequately resolved between us.

Her belligerency gone, she somewhat sheepishly asked what she should do with her rage, which had already destroyed most of her relationships and family contacts. She was also briefly reflecting on what happened between herself and her friend in New York that prompted her to give him such a negative evaluation of her work with me. She thought that she may have been angry at him because he made her look bad by suggesting that she needed psychiatric help and she wanted to prove to him that he was wrong, that treatment did not do her any good. She added that this was a fairly typical experience for her—anger was one feeling that she had learned to rely on whenever she felt emotionally trapped.

I found myself pleased with this turn of events. I felt validated by her associations and was now convinced that we were dealing with issues in the transference that were responsible for some of the most intractable features of her personality. Rather than advising her on "anger management," I wanted to be sure that she realized that I understood and accepted her anger within the transference. This was the time that transference interpretations were not only possible but necessary.

I reminded Ms. Hoyt that when she first heard my accent on the phone, she thought that I must be a member of the same group of people that she felt had not treated her fairly and were not helpful to her. She had some reason to believe that, because I am a member of the university community. Her own anticipated feelings about me were contradicted by Dr. Neal, whose opinion she valued, which must have been confusing to her. Maybe Dr. Neal's comments about my being well known put me into the category of "stars" and that increased her ambivalence toward treatment: She would be associated with somebody whom others respected and she would have to feel inferior to her. Also, she would run the risk of becoming clingy and dependent, something she did not want to reexperience. The issue of money apparently was a convenient way to deal with this conflict—it confirmed her expectation that I was not interested in *her,* only in the money she would pay. Ms. Hoyt appeared to listen attentively. This encouraged me to continue and I added that her anger over the money may represent her resentment toward many other people who, she felt, had failed to appreciate her predicament and had taken advantage of her.

Ms. Hoyt's response to my lengthy interpretive comment indicated that the contact we had just established was more meaningful than any of our other contacts. She spoke of her disappointment in her sister, who, at the time of their mother's death, made her feel that she ought to be able to take care of herself. At the time of their mother's suicide, Ms. Hoyt's sister was 15 years old. However, for the 11-year-old girl, her sister was a "grown-up" and ought to have been able to take over the mothering. I commented that what appears to be posing a very difficult challenge to her is the fact that at the time of her mother's illness and death, she could not express (and possibly not even experience) anger and sadness, but that these feelings now seem to dominate many of her current relationships. I remembered that at one time she told me that her biggest problems were anger and paranoia: we are now understanding better where these feelings may have come from. "I am glad," I said, "that rather than running away, you stayed so that together we could understand your anger at me now."

This time, I passed the test: I was not the rejecting sister; I knew that she needed me. As long as she considered my fee as a form of exploitation, her anger in the transference was "legitimate." This was an experience in which the patient could better appreciate how her anger had become a powerful form of self-protection; this was the affect that protected her from experiencing helplessness and a sense of abandonment. As our time was up and I reached for my appointment book, Ms. Hoyt said "Yes, I want an other appointment, this was a very good hour."

The following hour was a calm one; I thought that we had reached a still deeper level of engagement. Ms. Hoyt spoke of her difficulty in getting the business that she had started with the man she was involved with off the ground. She complained that she still was not using her time well enough, that there was great pressure on her to make money (as she was rapidly depleting her trust fund), but that she did not want to neglect her art and hoped to be able to work on her thesis as well. Obviously, there were drastic changes in her day-to-day behavior; the daily television watching had stopped and she was doing a great many things during any one day. However, subjectively, she still experienced herself as not being productive. I wondered what that indicated. Ms. Hoyt explained that as her energy level increased and she began to spend long hours on her thesis work, she became panic stricken that this meant she was giving up hope of becoming an artist, which was still her dream and ambition. Fearing that her art would be irretrievably damaged if she stopped practicing it, she began to spend more and more time on her art. "This then is a different problem," I said, "it is difficult to find time to work on your thesis, practice, and make money, all at the same time." With satisfaction in my voice, I told her that I could see that she had a conflict, but that this was very different from her previous problem when she was unable to leave her room, or work on her thesis, or practice, or improve her financial situation. She agreed and was puzzled why good feelings, feelings of satisfaction with what she has been doing, were still eluding her. In spite of the many things she does, she is still left with the feeling that she has not done what "really needed" doing. Before leaving, Ms. Hoyt repeated what we had discussed as if she wanted to take something with her as we parted for a fairly lengthy summer break. We set up two appointments for September.

Ms. Hoyt had a very busy summer, but she did not make the kind of progress on her thesis that she thought she should have. Nor did she make any headway with her business venture. Instead, she spent more and more time on her art and felt relatively satisfied with that. She had been invited to participate in exhibitions that exposed her and her art to a greater audience than ever before. This, she agreed, represented a change in her perception of herself; she began to entertain the idea of pursuing art more vigorously even at the expense of attaining the degree she had originally come to town to earn. Now that she felt more comfortable at the academy, she did not experience the same urgency about this as she had when she first came to see me. Her financial situation had worsened and she asked if it would be acceptable to me if we did not meet for the second scheduled hour and postponed it for a later time. It would take her some time to take care of her bill as it was. This was acceptable to me and I told her that I hoped that we would not lose contact with each other.

I did not hear from Ms. Hoyt, and after about two months I called her. She was clearly pleased to hear from me. There were no major changes in her life other than that she had been traveling more, which was good for her artistic development but delayed the completion of her thesis. She was still in a relationship with the same man, who wanted to marry her, but she did not feel ready to marry anyone. She said that she felt as if she had lost 20 years of her life and was now beginning to make up for it; she did not trust her ability to love any man well enough to marry him. I told her that I was aware of her worsening financial situation but hoped that she would feel free to call if she thought a conversation with me would help to clarify matters for her. In answer, she asked if I had a fax number. She was leaving the country for an extended period and thought that she might fax me a note about how she was.

I did not hear from her while she was abroad and had one phone conversation after her return, which I considered to be a follow-up interview. After returning from her trip, Ms. Hoyt began work on her thesis again. She greatly reduced her initial plans for the work, which she recognized as having been much too ambitious. Consequently, she thought that she now had a better chance of finishing her thesis within a reasonable time. Her biggest problem was that she had very little money left; her ambitious plans for a business with the man in her life never materialized. In a matter-of-fact manner, she thanked me for keeping in touch with her and we said good-bye.

DISCUSSION OF THE CLINICAL VIGNETTE

This brief, focal therapy, which lasted 14 hours and included two phone calls and a follow-up interview over the phone, demonstrated that a selfobject transference may develop even in a relatively brief treatment process. The presence of the transference brought the essential aspects of the patient's psychopathology (narcissistic vulnerability and chronic and acute rage expressed either directly or indirectly, by making others feel guilty for her victimized position) into the treatment situation. The disruptions in the transference, which had occurred early in treatment, were crucial aspects of the process that could have either led to premature termination or facilitated progress in the treatment. It was at times of disruption that the therapist's clinical-theoretical orientation (the maintenance of the empathic listening perspective and speaking in the interpretive mode) appeared to be particularly important. It is difficult to make an effort to retain the empathic listening perspective when one becomes the target of the patient's rage. However, pointing out one's own psychological reality under these circumstances not only escalates the patient's rage but also denies the therapist the opportunity to interpret the nature of the anxiety and its attendant defenses, which had now become manifest in the transference. Once the acute episode subsides, disruptions offer optimal opportunities for meaningful interpretations and the therapeutic work that follows usually occurs on a deeper level of engagement than before. These are times when most of the working through of habitual defense organizations occurs; the structural changes that accompany this process manifest themselves in the lessening of the patient's symptomatic behavior.

We are not maintaining that in such a short time, deeply anchored personality features can be undone. However, a successful treatment experience can set in motion a process in which the patient's own healing tendency can more actively participate. We maintain that it was the therapist's acceptance and empathic interpretations of the patient's revengeful behavior in and out of treatment (and tracing this to its genetic roots), that reactivated the patient's ambition to pursue her career in art. Though the working through of the defensive structures had to be limited, it still permitted the emergence of the patient's curative fantasy to become an artist, a star in her own right (P. H. Ornstein and A. Ornstein, 1977; A. Ornstein, 1992). It was unexpected that the treatment, rather then helping her finish her thesis work, would result in Ms. Hoyt's increased confidence to pursue a career as an artist. The therapeutic action in this case appears to have resided in removing the obstacles that were preventing the patient from pursuing her original dream.

SUMMARY

In order to answer the question of what factors contribute to the therapeutic action in psychotherapy, we examined the potentially curative factors that are inherent in the therapeutic dialogue itself. We recommended that rather than offering interpretive comments only when all aspects of a complex case fall into place, therapists' speak in the interpretive mode, that is, make open-ended statements that convey acceptance and understanding and include the motivations for the symptomatic behavior. The aim of such a dialogue is to create in patients a feeling of being understood, an experience that promotes the development of one of the selfobject transferences. Such transferences, in turn, enhance self-cohesion. It is the relatively well-consolidated self that is then capable of self-reflection and the working through of habitual defense organizations—a process that offers understanding as well as explanations of the genetic sources of the patient's current difficulties.

It would be foolhardy, however, to expect that a treatment—even when conducted from an empathic perspective—would not have disruptions and the patient would not develop resistances. Once archaic transferences are mobilized, their attendant defenses can create rather disturbing disruptions. Such disruptions of the transference bond provide not only opportunities to recognize habitual behavior patterns but also times when the working through of these patterns can take place most meaningfully within the transference.

REFERENCES

Bibring, E. (1954), Psychoanalysis and the dynamic psychotherapies. *J. Amer. Psychoanal. Assn.*, 2:745–770.

Dewald, P. (1964), *Psychotherapy: A Dynamic Approach*. New York: Basic Books.

Ekstein, R. & Wallerstein, R. S. (1972), *The Teaching and Learning of Psychotherapy*. New York: International Universities Press.

Frank, J. D. (1961), *Persuasion and Healing: A Comparative Study of Psychotherapy*. Baltimore, MD: John Hopkins University Press.

Freud, S. (1919), Lines of advance in psycho-analytic therapy. *Standard Edition*, 17:159–168. London: Hogarth Press, 1955.

Gill, M. (1951), Ego psychology and psychotherapy. *Psychoanal. Quart.*, 20:62–71.

Horowitz, M. (1979), *States of Mind: Analysis of Change in Psychotherapy*. New York: Plenum.

Kernberg, O. F. (1984), *Severe Personality Disorders: Psychotherapeutic Settings*. New Haven, CT: Yale University Press.

Kohut, H. (1971), *The Analysis of the Self*. New York: International Universities Press.

——— (1984), *How Does Analysis Cure?* ed. A. Goldberg & P. Stepansky. Chicago: Chicago University Press.

Kris, E. (1950), On preconscious mental processes. *Psychoanal. Quart.*, 19:540–560.

——— (1956), On some vicissitudes of insight in psychoanalysis. *Internat. J. Psycho-Anal.*, 37:445–455.

Luborsky, L. (1984), *Principles of Psychoanalytic Psychotherapy: A Manual for Supportive-Expressive Treatment*. New York: Basic Books.

Malan, D. H. (1976), *Toward the Validation of Dynamic Psychotherapy: A Replication*. New York: Plenum.

Modell, A. H. (1976), The holding environment and the therapeutic action in psychoanalysis. *J. Amer. Psychoanal. Assn.*, 24:285–307.

Ornstein, A. (1992), The curative fantasy and psychic recovery. *J. Psychother. Practice & Res.*, 1:16–28.

Ornstein, P. H. & Ornstein, A. (1977), On the continuing evolution of psychoanalytic psychotherapy: Reflections and predictions. *The Annual of Psychoanalysis*, 5:329–370. New York: International Universities Press.

Strupp, H. & Binder, J. L. (1982), *Time limited psychotherapy: A treatment manual*. Unpublished manuscript.

——— & ——— (1984), *Psychotherapy in a New Key*. New York: Basic Books.

Wallerstein, R. S. (1956), Concepts on the psychotherapy research project of the Menninger Foundation. *Bull. Menninger Clin.*, 20:221–280.

—— (1969), Introduction to panel on psychoanalytic psychotherapy. *Internat. J. Psycho-Anal.*, 50:17–126.

—— (1975), *Psychotherapy and Psychoanalysis*. New York: International Universities Press.

Winnicott, D. W. (1965), Psychiatric disorders in terms of infantile maturational processes. In: *The Maturational Processes and the Facilitating Environment*. New York: International Universities Press, pp. 230–241.

8

Mode of Therapeutic Action

Joseph D. Lichtenberg

The hypothesis for my conception of the mode of therapeutic action of analysis is that a strong correspondence must exist between techniques empirically found to be effective in facilitating and providing positive change and processes that ensure or stimulate growth. I identify three growth processes: self-righting, shared expanding awareness, and the rearrangement (recategorization) of symbolic representations. Since growth occurs across many domains, I look for correlations between biological, neurophysiological, and psychological development.

SELF-RIGHTING

Clinically, self-righting refers to an intrinsic tendency during psychoanalysis to rebound from an altered (lower level) state of functioning to a more adaptive state. As analysts and therapists we depend on the capacity for self-righting to enable a patient (and ourselves) after an hour of intense affective involvement to resume a state of adaptive functioning needed to leave and return to other occupations (and to clear our own minds for the next hour). Within the clinical exchange after a disruption into an aversive state triggered by an experience of empathic failure, the restoration that takes place illustrates self-righting with a return to engagement and exploration.

As a factor in development, self-righting refers to an inherent tendency to rebound from a deficit with a developmental advance when a positive change in an inhibiting condition occurs. The term self-righting was coined by Waddington (1947), an embryologist who observed that a genetic program in surrounding cells will turn off a developing tendency toward abnormal growth, allowing a rebound toward normal cell structure. Numerous examples exist of a normal developmental step—in physiological regulation, attachment, exploration and assertion, control

of aversion, and sensual-sexual seeking—that had not been taken becoming possible under favorable circumstances.

A dramatic example is that of infants raised in the Guatemalan high-
lands. These babies, while always close to their mothers, are restricted
for over a year inside a windowless hut, often in a back sling with no toys
and little human interaction. At one year they are quiet, unsmiling,
minimally alert, and physically passive. They are far behind U.S. children in cognitive development. In the middle of the second year, however, when they become mobile and are allowed to leave the hut, their
development leaps forward dramatically. When the children were tested
at 10 to 11 years, their cognitive and perceptual abilities were at the same
level as American, urban, middle-class children.

Within the clinical experience, self-righting occurs in response to
many nonexploratory aspects of the treatment. The analyst's reliability,
willingness to accept responsibility, to listen with care and concern, and
to be tactful, individually and together, may constitute a positive change
in an inhibiting condition for patients who have experienced a deficit in
these relational qualities. The self-righting that ensues constitutes a
corrective emotional experience (Marohn and Wolf, 1990). In addition,
self-righting occurs in response to the specific endeavors of the analyst
in responding to those disruptions in the ongoing treatment process that
follow the patient's experience of an empathic failure. The analyst helps
in the recognition of the altered self state and, if possible, in identifying
the triggering source of the disruption, including the analyst's participation and contribution. "The reliable and apt recall of details from the
patient's previous discourse is part of what convinces him that we hear,
think, and care about him; he can now begin to experience himself as
worth paying attention to, understanding, and caring about" (Levin,
1991, p. 6). The continuity of the effort to recognize, understand, and
identify will often in itself lead to self-righting. Commonly the self-
righting to a restored state facilitates the expanded awareness of the
meaning of the disruption rather than the understanding leading to the
self-righting.

Weiss and Sampson (1986) explain the state change we call self-
righting through their postulate of a largely unconscious plan of patients
to change their pathogenic beliefs by testing them in their experience
with their analyst. "If the analyst's responses to the tests are experienced
by the patient as disconfirming the pathogenic beliefs, the patient is
likely to become less anxious, more relaxed, more confident in the
analyst, and bolder in tackling his problems" (p. 223). Weiss and Sampson note that generally analysts do not set out specifically to discon-
firm the pathogenic beliefs since often they only become aware of them

after the test has been passed by the analysts' empathically directed responses. As the danger anticipated in the pathogenic belief is disconfirmed, the patient's inherent inclination to reduce anxiety and move forward (self-right) is activated. *After* no longer feeling endangered, the patient "was able to experience the contents fully, think about them, and use them therapeutically" (p. 185). In our terms (Lichtenberg, Lachmann, and Fosshage, 1992), the analyst's successful employment of the empathic mode of perception led to self-righting. In turn, the state change of self-righting permitted greater access to inner experience and the ability to communicate and thus to expanded awareness of both analyst and patient. The expanded awareness is then confirmed by the interpretive sequence that *follows.*

What guides self-righting? Waddington (1947) suggests that for cells self-righting is guided by the genetic plan and the influence of the existing structure. In broader biological terms, if, for example, puberty is delayed because of illness or malnutrition, when the illness or malnutrition is reversed the genetic design will guide the self-righting recovery. But what guides the adult to a restoration of sleep, or friendliness and trust, or the willingness to explore, or a renewed interest in sexuality after a wounding rebuff? I suggest the form of the self-righting is oriented to approximate an optimal prior state. As each motivational system organizes and stabilizes, state changes occur. The state changes that self psychology refers to as selfobject experiences of maximum cohesion and vitalization (Lichtenberg, Lachmann, and Fosshage, 1992) become an intrinsically valued goal for re-creation. These states of physiological regulation, attachment intimacy, exploratory-assertive efficacy and competence, and sensual satisfaction when recreated become hallmarks of desired self-experience. During analysis, we can expect the forms of self-righting to be guided both by prior optimal states of each motivational system and the self (even if fleeting) and by optimal states guided by genetic potential that have been achieved because of the especially favorable conditions during the analysis itself. The disconfirmation of pathogenic beliefs represents one example of the especially favorable conditions that occur during analysis (and other psychotherapies).

I consider self-righting to be a powerful growth process that facilitates positive change across the spectrum of supportive, expressive, exploratory psychotherapies as well as psychoanalysis.

SHARED EXPANDING AWARENESS

Expanding awareness refers to the growth of knowledge about the self. Traditionally the focus of analysts was centered on insight into specific complexes, conflicts, or compromise formations regarded as causes of the illness. The traditional focus portrays one person, the analyst, who points out to another person information about that person's psyche. The view I hold is that two people are concurrently developing an expanding awareness of self with and apart from the other. And because of the need to discover the nature of a transference configuration (a new creation influenced by a prior experience), each is seeking to find the self as experienced by the other. The model for this conception of expanding awareness is based on the ordinary attachment experiences of caregivers and developing children. A parent tries to discover who his or her baby is and a baby tries to seek and confirm an identity through and with his or her parents. This mutuality of search impels the acquisition of information. The most significant information sought for is the unconscious and conscious sensing of the subjectivity of the other organized as emotion-laden perceptions and memories of events and procedures. In analysis, in contrast to ordinary life, a consistent effort is made to bring into conscious awareness the impact of procedural and event interchanges and to struggle against collusions in deception and denial. To quote Pulver (1992) about psychic change in analysis, *"an understanding relationship cannot be maintained without insight into the dynamics of the relationship itself"* (p. 204). While searching is joint, what is searched for is uneven. Analyst and patient seek to find the *patient* through the *long axis* of the patient's life (and maybe one or two generations back) as a narrative construction in the minds of both. Analyst and patient seek to find the *analyst* principally through the *restricted axis* of their shared experience as an intersubjective construction in the minds of both. Expanding awareness must work against and learn about the motives for using the vulnerability of the patient or the privileged position of the analyst to restrict recognition and revelation.

My understanding of the nature of expanding awareness derives from studies of cognitive and memory organization and of neural networks. Lived experiences are abstracted and categorized in the form of discrete events—eating, going to the store, playing with mommy, playing with my toys, going to sleep. Salient features by which categories are formed are extremely simple at first: the hunger-satiety cycle, mother's face and voice during play, the actions in a sequence. Asked to tell about making cookies, a child of three responds, "Well, you bake them and eat them" (Nelson, 1986, p. 27). The current understanding of memory is that a "memory" or a "trace" does not exist in a single brain locus. Rather maps or networks are formed based on one or another criterion for categorization. Perceptual stimuli alone are insufficient to activate categorization. An affective dimension is essential for creating and categorizing memories. These perceptual-affective-action maps have a continuous relationship with external stimuli, the differing nuances of which activate other maps. As the maps interact with one another, information is constantly recategorized (Rosenfield, 1988). When a stimulus is repeated, such as the recognition of a pattern of an experience of mild empathic failure, the strengths of the connections that produce pattern awareness are increased, making recognition easier to arrive at on subsequent exposures. Since each pattern varies somewhat in context and texture, no response will be exactly the same, thus *each recollection is a new creation* (Poland, 1992). What is stored is not a replication of the category or event but is the capacity to generalize associatively and then to narrow consequential behavior to achieve a motivational goal. Studies of brain mapping indicate that the capacity to categorize perceptually and generalize associatively is more complex in infancy than previously thought involving the brainstem and cerebellum (Levin, 1991). Even at this level generalization can involve commonality of feature, response, or history, any one of which can act independently of the other—"small biases in internal states can lead to large changes in responses" (Edelman, 1987, p. 258).

Still further complexity occurs with the addition of simultaneous alternative modes of processing as the frontal hemispheres become myelinated and "come on line." The influence of language and other symbol systems, mediated by a complex sense of self, multiple changing motivations, and the influence of culture, gives to exchanges during analysis a dynamic transformational quality. "At the level of concepts, categorization, is carried out neither by rigorous, nor by logical, nor by universal criteria. Indeed, there may be no single general means by which categories are formed at this level" (Edelman, 1987, p. 246).

I believe the dynamic transformational quality of the expanding awareness that takes place during analysis is the result of the facilitation of *two* individuals sharing affective experiences triggered by event descriptions and gestural and linguistic renderings of self-experience. The networks that mediate the relevant experience of each expand in conjunction with the affective arousal. At moments, analyst and analysand experience affect attunement and shared comprehension of meaning. However, moments of coincident perspective while confirming, informative, and intimate are responsible for only part of the momentum of analytic change. A dialectic tension exists as analyst and patient become convergent and divergent in their sense of knowing the subjectivity of each other. Boesky (1990) observes that "[i]f the analyst does not get emotionally involved sooner or later in a manner he had not intended the analysis will not proceed to a successful conclusion"

(p. 573). Benefit to the patient is not limited to receiving "correct final answers. The patient benefits from the process of the mutually attempted, partly successful, and partly failed efforts to understand. The way in which we, as analysts, misunderstand, and we always misunderstand a lot, is highly communicative to the patient, and this misunderstanding is by no means only or always regrettable" (pp. 577–578) (see also Poland, 1988). Preoccupied with concerns about the analyst's serious errors, "we have failed to appreciate that the conflict of the analyst can lead to . . . useful outcomes" (p. 578).

Most attention has been focused on the analysand's developing self-awareness, insight, and narrative continuity. Less attention has focused on the analyst's ability to form an associative generalized network about each individual patient. These two ever-changing, somewhat parallel schemas or networks are the source of the rich, deep (sometimes seemingly uncanny) perceptive sensitivities that grow in analyses (Major and Miller, 1984; Simon, 1984). Two explanations (Levin, 1991) have been offered for the impact of joint awareness of transference configurations. One is that the relevant network or map becomes enlarged through a linkage between higher cortical levels and the affect-rich limbic system and the cerebellar memory system. This enlarging of the map is achieved because the gated brainstem nuclei "no longer block out specific limbic and/or cerebellar or other inputs" (p. 51). "A second possibility is that the patient's style of coordinating his hemispheres . . . has been altered by his awareness of the analyst's style" (p. 52) of being open to playful integrations of right and left brain–processed information.

Levin implicated language as the carrier of dynamic affective-informational sharing as exchanges with metaphoric potential "tap multiple levels of experience" (p. 12) in analyst and analysand. Levin (1991) speculates that

> one's natural language, once assimilated, permanently and decisively alters brain organization. Language may not only facilitate the development of the genetic plan for psychological organization, but it may also allow for adaptive reorganization as a solution to problems requiring novelty and for the manipulation of modules of knowledge. . . . it is possible that our natural language also contains recurrent hierarchical elements that can be decoded as instructions to the brain's operating system, [allowing the brain to] "communicate with itself" [p. 117].

We have tended to believe that understanding during analysis follows a linear path—an interpretation leads to the patient's insight, which in turn leads to change. Brain studies give us a view of why the nature of communication involves gestural, verbal and affective modalities but moreover is governed by the richness of context between the two participants. Levin (1991) states:

At least three systems are critical for the kind of discriminate learning that we associate with human behavior at its most complex level: the system of the right hemisphere, with its preferential attachments to the limbic system; the left hemisphere, with its motor system dominance; and the vestibulocerebellar system. . . . Critical brainstem nuclei can either glue together or unglue these major subsystems [p. 80]. *When the arousal level is below a certain threshold of excitement, the patient's cortical activity appears to be limited to only one cortical (sensory) association area at a time.* . . . [I]f a threshold of interest is exceeded, the brain becomes activated *as a whole,* and . . . the various associative cortical (and presumably also the subcortical) parts of the brain come into communication with each other [p. 12].

Like self-righting, shared expanding awareness occurs across the full spectrum of psychotherapies. In supportive and expressive or cognitive therapies it is likely to be more restricted. Shared expanding awareness is central to the design of both exploratory investigative psychotherapy and psychoanalysis. A rearrangement of symbolic representations often occurs during exploratory psychotherapy. As I will describe, the *systematic* attentional focus on transference configurations distinguishes psychoanalysis as the therapy par excellence for facilitating this particular type of positive change.

REARRANGEMENT OF SYMBOLIC REPRESENTATIONS

The rearrangement of symbolic representations during successful psychoanalysis results, I believe, from particular experiences that increase arousal to a level that activates the brain as a whole. By rearrangement of symbolic representations I refer to a change in the manner in which the self and/or a significant person (or situation) is represented (categorized). Especially when the categorization is rigidly held, the changes at first may be imperceptible, requiring many repetitions and variations of the transference configuration to achieve flexibility of representation and plasticity of responsiveness.

The rearrangement of symbolic representations that occurs during treatment has as its precursor changes that take place at the transition point of every stage of development. The big boy who can use the potty and wear training pants, the big girl who can sleep in a bed, the youngster who can go off to school without mother and the mother who no longer watches over him so carefully, the adolescent who can decide when to go to bed and the parent who can leave her in the house alone at night all represent transitions in the manner in which self and significant others are experienced and represented. In this process the sense of self and the sense of others are reorganized and transformed into later versions while early versions remain.

Lichtenberg et al. (1992) state:

> During psychoanalysis, we identify two processes involving transference that lead to the reorganization of symbolic representations. The first is the analyst's assisting the analysand to recognize the manner of his or her response to the analyst's perceived benevolence or malevolence. The second is the patient's edge of awareness of unconscious appreciation of contrasting perceptions of the analyst. One perception of the analyst arises when an affectively laden transference fantasy, belief, or interaction dominates the analysis. The patient's other perception of the analyst derives from the analyst as empathic listener-observer-interpreter of the transference [Lachmann, 1990].
>
> One perception may involve the full affective sense of being specially preferred and loved by the analyst. The other perception recognizes that the analyst interprets the meaning of being special, ends the session at a prearranged time, and charges a fee. One perception may involve the full affective sense of the analyst as hated and hating, blamed and blaming, deprived and depriver. The other perception recognizes that the analyst listens to and interprets what he or she can identify as triggering acts involving hate, blame, or deprivation, thus making the experience open to shared consideration and reflection. The one representation involving self and analyst is largely organized in a primary process mode, the other largely in a secondary process mode, the discrepancy probably appreciated largely unconsciously in both modes for full effectiveness [p. 146].

For example, a patient who was planning to complete both her doctorate and her analysis in a year was extremely angry with her analyst for taking a longer than usual time away during the fall. During the hour after his return she stated that his being away for three weeks confirmed her in her belief he didn't care about her. In this way, he was felt to be similar to her mother in only wanting to be rid of her. In order to arouse his guilt and hold his interest on his return, she felt she had to tell him she had been miserable the whole time and had hardly completed any of her dissertation. Actually things hadn't gone that badly, but she was slowed down. Even going slowly wasn't so bad, as they had worked out many times—fast meant being reckless like her brother, mother's favorite. Slow, careful, and thorough meant being like the analyst, but she didn't feel that closeness now.

In the next session she noted that even though she hadn't finished the number of pages she intended to, she was pleased with what she had done since yesterday's session. (In the analyst's view the patient had self-righted from a deeper depressive affect and had restored a positive image of herself and of him that had been gained in their prior work and lost in her aversive response to her "abandonment.") She had received a disturbing phone call about her brother's sons, who were doing poorly in school and getting into trouble. She had advised psychological testing and treatment but her brother refused, claiming lack of funds. She was frustrated. She was also disappointed with the dean's effort to help her get a job. No one seemed to want to help—the dean with his recommendation or the analyst in providing the time she needed. The analyst acknowledged her sense of hurt but wondered about it in the light of a prior statement she had made that the dean's letter had been very positive. She agreed but concluded she couldn't believe it was authentic—only a pat on the head. Why should anyone want to help her? The analyst stated she seemed to discount the possibility that, besides fondness for her, it would be in the dean's and his (the analyst's) self-interest to have her succeed. She answered that she knew that intellectually but couldn't believe it, although she didn't know why. She had had two dreams. In one, someone said "they are not our kind of people." In the other, because of money the analyst had had to move out of his office and was seeing her in a parking lot behind a garage. It was strange and upsetting. She was puzzled because she knew she had paid her bill.

In the next session she began wondering about the snobbery in her dream of not our kind of people. She recognized in it her mother's attitude toward her father's family. The analyst added: And her brother's attitude about therapists—hers and someone for his children. She replied: No, it wasn't his snobbish attitude about people who are weak and dependent that stopped her brother but his lack of money. He wasn't really snobbish. Actually, he lived in a run-down, working-class neighborhood and was friendly with the people there. (This was the first time in this long analysis that she had mentioned this information about the often discussed, much-admired brother). Highly interested, the analyst invited further details. She stated that the people in the brother's area had been badly affected by the recession. Because he and his wife hadn't moved when they could have, the property values had dropped and they were stuck where the schools and all services were underfunded and inadequate. The analyst said: As in her dream where he saw her in a parking lot behind a garage. He had lost his money and couldn't provide properly for her to be able to progress. No, she stated, my brother didn't lose his money—in fact, he is one of the few people there who has kept his job. The reason they don't have any money for treatment is because they've spent their money for pleasures as soon as it came in. The analyst then "corrected" the view of himself portrayed in her dream: He hadn't lost his money; rather he had been spending it for his pleasure. Angrily, she retorted, "You take my money and spend it to go away!" The analyst added, No wonder she couldn't believe he would regard it as in his interest as well as hers to see her progress; he's busy spending her money for his pleasure. The patient on leaving looked a combination of angry and sheepish.

In this example, analyst and analysand are engaged in exploring an unconsciously determined pathogenic belief (Weiss and Sampson, 1986) that the analyst, like her brother with his children, and her parents with her, was an impoverished, inadequate, unmotivated provider of care. The awareness of each is expanded as they understand the way the negative image of the analyst has reappeared—first as the familiar abandoner, then as the failed sponsor of her future, and finally in a new version as a selfish spender. I believe that the expanding awareness of the motivations, meaning, and causal linkages of the shared experience moves the treatment forward. But the key to the specific power for positive change lies in the simultaneous experiencing of two contrasting subjective realms. In one, the analysand fully experiences the analyst as implicated in her distress. In another he is the person she is talking to, being open with, and having her view acknowledged and affirmed by. In the words of Atwood and Stolorow (1984), "Every transference interpretation that successfully illuminates for the patient his unconscious past simultaneously crystallizes an illusive present—the novelty of the therapist as an understanding presence" (p. 60). I believe the pathogenic representation embedded in the transference configuration may be softened (derigidified) by the consistent alternative sense of the analyst as empathic coexplorer.

Looked at from the standpoint of the brain, I believe the intensity to activate the whole brain does not derive from affect alone. An affect state might trigger only right hemisphere–limbic system processing. I believe whole brain activation results from the vitality of the joint exploration and assertion of analysand and analyst working in tandem. Reviewing suggestions of Galin (1974) and Basch (1983), Levin (1991) notes that mental events in either hemisphere can become disconnected functionally from the other. Affect states might block out left hemisphere logical categorization and when an affective self-experience is aversive, right hemisphere responses might be disconnected. But with the whole brain activated, communication can take place between hemispheres and with the vestibulocerebellar system as well, bringing in past experience (mother as abandoner, brother as [over] idealized successful favorite). The special quality of an energetic transference interpretive experience creates a tension between the more logical categorization of the analyst by the left hemisphere and the representation by the right hemisphere linked to the vestibulocerebellar input that draws on related past experience. The discrepant categorizations require reconciliation (hierarchical rearrangement) as part of the continuous problem-solving effort of the brain. Levin (1991) believes the functioning of the prefrontal cortex creates "meaningful relationships between complex input and output variables, even when these relationships are not obvious or do not appear logical" (p. 90). The prefrontal cortex makes use of motivationally relevant experiences of self and others to compare possible future states with current goals in order to test out the sufficiency of proposed solutions—what Kent (1981, p. 18) calls a "forward search" strategy. In matching possible future states with goals, the optimal symbolic representation may change from that of self with an abandoning or selfish other to that of self with an available or empathic other. That is, in the recategorization of experience that follows the intense transference attribution of abandoner or self-server, a hierarchical rearrangement may make the next episode of recategorization that of someone who is available or empathic. Of course, as we know about transferences, a renewed context of a perceived empathic failure may trigger a reactivation of the aversive symbolic representation, but hopefully less "cast in stone."

To summarize, unlike the early psychoanalytic assumption of recovering fixed memories from repression, current brain research along with recent analytic studies indicate that all perceptions are to some degree creations, all memories are part of an ongoing process of recategorization and imagination. Psychoanalysis leads not simply to knowing more but to reworking, recategorizing, and rearranging. When this process is successful, symbolic representations and all other information are generalized and recast in new, freer, and more imaginative ways.

REFERENCES

Atwood, G. & Stolorow, R. (1984), *Structures of Subjectivity.* Hillsdale, NJ: The Analytic Press.
Basch, M. F. (1983), The perception of reality and the disavowal of meaning. *The Annual of Psychoanalysis,* 11:125–154. New York: International Universities Press.
Boesky, D. (1990), The psychoanalytic process and its components. *Psychoanal. Quart.,* 59:550–584.
Dorpat, T. & Miller, M. (1990), *Clinical Interaction and the Analysis of Meaning.* Hillsdale, NJ: The Analytic Press.

Edelman, G. (1987), *Neural Darwinism: The Theory of Neural Group Selection.* New York: Harper & Row.

Galin, D. (1974), Implications for psychiatry of left and right cerebral specialization. *Arch. Gen. Psychiat.,* 31:572–583.

Kagan, J., Kearsley, R. & Zelazu, P. (1978), *Infancy: Its Place in Human Development.* Cambridge, MA: Harvard University Press.

Kent, E. (1981), *The Brains of Men and Machines.* Peterborough, NH: BYTE.

Lachmann, F. (1990), On some challenges to clinical theory in the treatment of character pathology. In: *The Realities of Transference: Progress in Self Psychology, Vol. 6 ,* ed. A. Goldberg. Hillsdale, NJ: The Analytic Press, pp. 59–67.

Levin, F. (1991), *Mapping the Mind.* Hillsdale, NJ: The Analytic Press.

Lichtenberg, J., Lachmann, F. & Fosshage, J. (1992), *Self and Motivational Systems: Toward a Theory of Technique.* Hillsdale, NJ: The Analytic Press.

Major, R. & Miller, P. (1984), Empathy, antipathy, and telepathy in the analytic process. In: *Empathy II,* ed. J. Lichtenberg, M. Bornstein & D. Silver. Hillsdale, NJ: The Analytic Press, pp. 227–248.

Marohn, R. & Wolf, E. (1990), Corrective emotional experience revisited. *Psychoanal. Inq.,* 10:285–458.

Nelson, K. (1986), *Event Knowledge.* Hillsdale, NJ: Lawrence Erlbaum Associates.

Poland, W. (1988), Insight and the analytic dyad. *Psychoanal. Quart.,* 57:341–369.

—— (1992), Transference: An original creation. *Psychoanal. Quart.,* 61:185–205.

Pulver, S. (1992), Psychic change: Insight or relationship. *Internat. J. Psycho-Anal.,* 73:199–208.

Rosenfield, I. (1988), *The Invention of Memory: A New View of the Brain.* New York: Harper & Row.

Simon, B. (1984), Confluence of visual image between patient and analyst: Communication of failed communication. In: *Empathy II,* ed. J. Lichtenberg, M. Bornstein & D. Silver. Hillsdale, NJ: The Analytic Press, pp. 261–278.

Waddington, C. (1947), *Organizers and Genes.* Cambridge: Cambridge University Press.

Weiss, J. & Sampson, H. (1986), *The Psychoanalytic Process.* New York: Guilford.

9

Optimal Responsiveness

Its Role in Psychic Growth and Change

Judith Guss Teicholz

In Tony Kushner's (1992) play, *Angels in America,* a character asks, "How do people change?" The answer comes back: "[I]t's not very nice. God splits the skin with a jagged thumbnail from throat to belly . . . plunges a huge filthy hand in . . . grabs hold of your bloody tubes and . . . pulls . . . til all your innards are yanked out and the pain! We can't even talk about that . . ."(p. 79). This grotesque imagery seems to capture what analytic treatment is like for some individuals who have suffered severe deprivation or trauma in childhood. These patients, whose early trauma is part of their adult psyches, know that their treatment will be painful: They feel legitimate terror that our thumbnails will be jagged or our hands dirty. Our theory can help us, as analytic therapists, to file our jagged nails, and to pull gently rather than yank at our patients' psychic innards. By pulling gently we can provide conditions under which early environmental failure, and other forms of trauma that have been translated into "negative introject" and "intrapsychic deficit," can be modified or compensated. When this arduous task has been accomplished, the patient can continue in his or her development and self-understanding, achieving through the analytic treatment enough internal balance and resilience to endure and respond to the inevitable frustrations of life.

OPTIMAL RESPONSIVENESS: ORIGIN OF THE CONCEPT

The concept of *optimal responsiveness* evolved within self psychology as the result of an effort to reconcile an apparent contradiction in Kohut's writings (1971, 1977, 1984): on the one hand, his emphasis on *empathy* as the primary mode of analytic observation; on the other hand, his insistence on *optimal frustration* as a necessary precondition for the transmuting internalizations that contribute to the formation of self-structure. To the extent that empathy and frustration of any kind are seen as mutually exclusive, these coexisting elements in Kohut's work present a theoretical and technical conundrum. In the observations that follow, however, the empathic/introspective stance is seen as only a first step in the journey toward optimal responsiveness. Empathy is a *guide* to analytic action. It can lead the analytic therapist in a number of possible directions with potential for a broad range of alternative interventions. These interventions include but are not limited to clarifications and psychodynamic, psychogenetic, and interpersonal interpretations and reconstructions. Although informed by empathy, optimal responsiveness does not necessarily coincide with doing what the patient asks: With some patients, it involves setting firm limits on the patient's behavior, or on the therapeutic relationship, which to an outside observer might seem unusually harsh; it may also involve *the transient provision of missing psychic function* for the patient, which she cannot ask for, because she does not yet know what she lacks.

Optimal responsiveness can only theoretically be separated out from the rest of what goes on in an analytic treatment. It is a quality of the analytic relationship and of the analyst's interventions. The psychological provision that is sometimes included in optimal responsiveness is only one aspect of the richly textured, complex, and multifaceted treatment process, but it is in some cases a prerequisite to, or a backdrop for, the many other elements that contribute to psychic change. In the imagery of Stephen Mitchell (1994), it is one of the "platforms" on which the patient might need to stand, in order not to be left trying to pull herself up by her own bootstraps.

Critics of this viewpoint sometimes mistake it for "niceness," fuzzy-mindedness, or indulgence on the part of the analyst. They are concerned that the analyst's responsiveness enables the patient to avoid confrontation with the harsher realities of life and of treatment; or that the "responsive" therapist will create an atmosphere incompatible with expression of the patient's most anguished and rageful feelings, especially when such feelings are experienced in relationship to the analyst herself. But paradoxically, it is exactly *because* of the intense psychic pain and rage of some of my patients that I have arrived at the ideas that I'm about to set forth here. Although many analysts (such as Bacal 1988; Ornstein, 1988; Terman, 1988; Wolf, 1992) have found the concept of optimal responsiveness to be a useful one, none has suggested that the optimal quality of empathy, or of functional provision, can save our patients from the everyday conflicts, hurts, and frustrations of life, nor from the random and tragic losses to which we are all vulnerable. Not only is there no analytic stance that can make psychic change painless, but more particularly, regardless of the analyst's stance, the anguish of analytic treatment seems inevitably to match the anguish of the original developmental conditions. This is because those conditions have become part of the internalized structure and "climate" that the patient carries with her, until the treatment has done its work.

OPTIMAL RESPONSIVENESS AND INTERNALIZATION

In human development, optimal responsiveness constitutes the safety zone between the dangerous environmental extremes of deprivation and indulgence. But where these zones shade together, it is not always clear what will facilitate, and what will curtail, development. Questions of frustration and gratification are significant for psychic development and change, because many patients seek treatment, having had in childhood not enough of the "good," or growth-*promoting* experiences that they needed, while at the same time having gotten too much of the "bad," or growth-*disruptive*. As parents or analysts, we seek the optimal balance between frustration and gratification, because this balance contributes positively to the internalization processes leading to structuralization of the personality in original development, and to the creation or reorganization of psychic structure entailed in analytic cure. Frustration and gratification are highly individual and subjective experiences, which are profoundly affected by the intersubjective context in which they occur; therefore, both the analyst's stance and the patient's prior experience will contribute to what is felt as optimal for each particular patient at any given point in a treatment. This means that we must ask ourselves anew with every patient: At what point do the unavoidable frustrations of life slide over into deprivation and trauma? Or, under what conditions with this patient might the satisfaction of needs become harmful?

Although these questions have been thoughtfully addressed in the past (see Freud, 1912, 1915, 1919, 1927, 1930; Balint, 1953, 1968; Winnicott, 1958a, Kohut, 1977, 1982, 1984; Stolorow, Brandchaft, and Atwood, 1987, 1992; Bacal, 1988; A. Ornstein, 1988; Wolf, 1992), I come back to them because some of our most challenging clinical judgments as analytic therapists are based on our assumptions about how much of what kind of frustration is optimal for psychic development or change. For instance: When does our neutrality or abstinence provide a potential space within which the patient can find or create her own solutions; and when does it produce a harmful repetition of the patient's childhood deprivation? How do we know when our silence will show respect for the patient's internal process, and when it will mean only traumatic abandonment? When do we maintain a purely analytic stance in response to our patient's transference requests, and when do we stretch ourselves in response to what our patients ask of us? How do we know when our limit setting will protect the patient from internal chaos or harmful enactment, and when it will serve only to diminish his sense of dignity or autonomy? How do we listen and communicate from within the patient's own cognitive-affective framework, and yet recognize the moment when a particular patient needs to be confronted with a different, more external reality? How do we know when to use an intervention that, with one patient, might constitute a growth-inhibiting indulgence, while with another, might make the positive difference between cohesion and fragmentation, or between life and death? My clinical material will bring us back to these questions later.

We know that internalization is a process central to psychic development and change. But what kinds of experiences foster internalization? And what *is* it that gets internalized? In original development, the child has only one source for what can be internalized, that source being the interactions between the infant and her primary caretakers. In contrast to original development, the patient in analytic treatment has two sources for internalization: one that derives from the early experience as it is transferentially relived, interpreted, and reconstructed in the analytic process; and the other, which derives from the interaction with the analyst as a new object in the here and now. In analytic treatment these two sources of internalization interact with and enhance each other.

In normal development, the child's psychological potential selectively unfolds on the basis of the interaction of genetic endowment, biological preparedness, and environmental responsiveness to the child's unique qualities and to her basic needs. This responsiveness includes, among other things, essential physiological care and basic psychological functions reliably performed by the caretakers, in countless repeated interactions with the child: These are what gets internalized, or taken over by the child, as development proceeds. Although infant research (Lachmann and Beebe, 1992) points to mutual regulation between infant and caretaker, we must still recognize the greater impact of the adult caretaker's more highly developed patterns of functioning on the emergent organization and functioning of the infant.

This limitation on the mutuality of regulation applies not only to parent and child but to the treatment dyad as well. Patients enter analysis or psychotherapy with differing capacities to negotiate relationships—

differing capacities for establishing comfortable closeness or distance, for maintaining firm but flexible boundaries, for collaborating on a task or working toward common goals, for playing and for humor, and for grieving losses. These and other capacities are the goals of analytic treatment. To begin moving toward these goals, each patient has certain basic psychological needs that must be met. At the outset of treatment, the analytic therapist is the only partner to the dyad in a position to meet these needs. This reality constitutes one of the asymmetries of the therapeutic dyad, which changes only as a result of the treatment itself.

Where early environmental provision of psychological requirements has failed, analytic treatment offers the adult patient a second chance at internalization. Through the ordinary interpretive-reconstructive process of a good-enough analysis, some patients can refind positive aspects of the earlier environment, and of the self, that were originally lost or distorted and now can be beneficially clarified and integrated. But for patients whose early histories involved gross deprivation or trauma, psychoanalytic psychotherapy often provides the first chance for internalization of a good-enough environmental provision (Winnicott, 1960a). This provision includes the cognitive-affective reworking of the destructive experiences of childhood, leading to modification of the early toxic introjects. The reworking and modification of "bad internal objects" is possible both because of the interpretive process itself and because the therapist, within the protection of the analytic frame, is, at least to some extent, experienced as a new object, different from the original ones (Loewald, 1960; Greenberg, 1986).

But the more depriving and damaging was the patient's early environment, the more the treatment may at first feel like a psychic "Catch-22" for both patient and analyst—a situation in which the patient is unable to use interpretation of the transference without first taking in aspects of the analyst's psychological functioning, but at the same time is unable to take in anything positive from the environment until some of the damaging effects of the early destructive experience have been interpreted, reconstructed, and transformed. In these cases we must shuttle among several different kinds of intervention: interpretation, genuine engagement, and psychological provision, often combining them in a single intervention.

OPTIMAL RESPONSIVENESS AND PSYCHOLOGICAL PROVISION

What do we mean by psychological provision? Part of what is internalized, both in original development and in the further development entailed in successful analytic treatment, is the environmental provision of specific psychological functions. These might include various aspects of *ego* and *superego* functioning, such as impulse control (this is what Otto Kernberg, 1994, and others, recommend that we provide for the borderline patient who is dangerously out of control), containment or elaboration of affect, reality testing, problem solving, decision making, judgment, and modification of guilt. We also provide various *self* functions such as "holding" or omnipotent merger; mirroring or affirmation; availability for twinship experience or affect-sharing; and idealizability. When needed, we provide any or all of these complex psychic functions as an aspect of our analytic attitude and optimal responsiveness, which in turn get internalized by the patient in treatment. The analyst's analyzing function, and her stance and attitude toward the patient, will be internalized as well. Thus, it is both the *content* of the analyst's interpretations and reconstructions, and the analyst's psychological *functioning* in interaction with the patient, that together provide the stuff that internalizations are made of.

This focus, beyond interpretation, on what the analyst must *provide* would seem to fly in the face of Freud's whole concept of necessary privation for psychosexual maturity, or to fuel the work of analysis. But when Freud saw frustration as a constructive force toward development, he was referring to frustration of instinctual impulses: the libidinal and aggressive wishes relating to bodily-based drive discharge. In contrast, I'm referring to provision in the sense of meeting basic developmental needs. I suggest that it's the meeting of such needs which makes possible the development of psychic structure, in childhood or in treatment. (Included among universal developmental needs is the need to have normally occurring libidinal and aggressive strivings optimally responded to by the human environment.)

Freud (1927) defined *frustration* as the nonsatisfaction of instinct. Therefore, the language of frustration and gratification is the language of instincts and does not belong in discussion of developmental needs. Self psychology offers the alternative concept, of optimal responsiveness, to represent the frustration–gratification continuum where developmental need is concerned. In treatment, optimal responsiveness involves the analyst's affective attitude, and her psychological functioning, in relation to the patient. Where instinctual strivings are concerned, optimal responsiveness does not coincide with direct gratification, because we know that the sexual or aggressive strivings of the child or patient must be accepted and understood but not directly gratified. In contrast to instincts, where basic developmental needs are concerned, optimal responsiveness and direct gratification do coincide. Among the developmental needs that are directly fulfilled by optimal responsiveness are the needs for containment of affect, for acceptance, and for understanding, as well as many other self and ego needs which I'll later elucidate.

Whether in response to developmental need or in response to instinctual strivings, the optimal responses of containment, acceptance, and understanding are rarely experienced as indulgent or overstimulating. Rather, repeated interpersonal experiences of such provision tend to facilitate in the patient the capacity first to deepen and expand upon, then to modify and to integrate, the previously split off or previously overwhelming aspects of the self. Well-timed, empathically conveyed interpretation of disavowed or repressed experience can provide a profound sense of being understood. But some patients need a period in which they are not understood to the depth that effective interpretation can penetrate. With some patients, at certain points in a treatment, *just the consistent affirmation of whatever the patient brings,* and the analyst's genuine engagement with it, can lead to spontaneous emergence of previously disavowed experience, with little interpretive work necessary. This still leaves plenty of analytic work to be done, especially the painful, lengthy, and difficult process of working through the feelings that emerge. Working through involves the capacity to examine previously disavowed experience with increasing awareness as it emerges within and outside of the transference, placing it empathically in its personal historical context, toward acceptance and integration. This process eventually changes the impact on the individual's life of what is being examined. And of course, as treatment proliferates, expands, and deepens self-awareness, there are ever new aspects of previously disavowed experience to be worked through.

Over time, the analyst's containment, acceptance, and understanding of the patient's instinctual and affective experience, and of need, are internalized by the patient and, together with the reworking of the parental relationships, become the stuff—or the structure—that the patient's own ego, superego, and more robust self are made of. The robust self includes the modulated sexual and aggressive self, and the fullest range of differentiated needs and affects.

INSTINCTS, AFFECTS, AND DEVELOPMENTAL NEEDS

Optimal responsiveness avoids the destructive overstimulation involved in premature or cross-generational fulfillment of libidinal and aggressive wishes. It is a significant alternative to either frustration or gratification, because while it postpones instinctual fulfillment, it directly fulfills a constellation of more basic, psychological needs. Over time, optimal responsiveness provides the patient with an increasing repertoire of internalized psychological capacities for processing and managing her own instinctual and affective life, and for recognizing and acting upon her own need. This has a salutary effect on the capacity to negotiate relationships, and to set and work toward personal goals, sometimes even when the patient does not directly address these extratransference issues in treatment.

Although containment, acceptance, and understanding have always been integral to the analytic attitude, few analysts have been comfortable conceptualizing the analytic process as one in which basic developmental needs are directly met. Winnicott and Kohut were pioneers in their emphasis on *environmental provision* in response to developmental need: Winnicott in his concept of maternal ego support, to protect and facilitate the unfolding of the infant's ego; and Kohut in his concept of selfobject functioning, needed for the establishment, maintenance, and enhancement of the self. While Winnicott saw the mother's holding as essential to the infant's ego development in the first year of life, Kohut saw parental mirroring, twinship, and idealizability as functions essential to self-development in the second and third years of life. These needs evolve into more mature forms, but persist throughout life, continuing to require some basic minimum of environmental input that may vary situationally and from individual to individual. When not met in childhood, developmental needs are split off from the developing personality, leading to functional and structural deficit, and calling forth debilitating defenses as the individual, thus handicapped, tries to proceed through life. Successful treatment involves the dissolution of the defenses, together with the emergence and full flowering of the previously unmet needs and related affects, leading to their modification and integration.

Winnicott explored the relationship between ego needs and instinctual experience, saying that instinctual experience can overwhelm the immature ego except in the context of maternal holding. Before the child gains the ego strength to use instinctual experience as a resource, such experience can only weaken the ego (1960b). This is one of many reasons that externally introduced sexual experience is destructive to the developing child. A clinical application of this understanding might lead a therapist to postpone interpreting associative material that seems to signify latent sexual or aggressive wishes, especially in the transference, if these come up at a time when the patient's ego functioning or self-cohesion is judged too fragile to tolerate this recognition. Winnicott also distinguished between instinctual regressions and regressions to dependency (1958b, p. 187), exhorting the analyst to meet the regressed patient's dependency needs (p. 192). *This can be done through emotional availability, but must include clearly established boundaries.*

Winnicott (1960b) also told us that before the infant can signal his needs to the mother, maternal care must be based purely on empathy. After the child can communicate his needs, the caretaker must wait for the signal and respond only to it, thus avoiding impingement. This has relevance for treatment, because although our adult patients can use language *cognitively,* many cannot yet use *affect as signal* (Russell, 1994). These patients are at first dependent on the analyst's capacity to recognize and differentiate affect, and to help them use it as a signal of need.

OPTIMAL FRUSTRATION AND OPTIMAL RESPONSIVENESS

We have just reviewed some of the many areas of psychic functioning for which Winnicott and Kohut emphasized the *environmental requirements* needed to facilitate the child's or the patient's achievement of structural development. In the context of this focus on environmental provision, Kohut's (1977) concept of optimal frustration has sometimes been a source of confusion. It has even been understood by some analysts to be compatible with Freud's emphasis on renunciation as a maturational value. But perhaps Kohut intended the emphasis to be on the qualifier, *optimal,* and not on the concept of frustration as a value in itself. Kohut saw frustration, in development or treatment, not as something actively to strive for, but rather as something inherent to the human condition. In Kohut's view, the parent's or the analyst's task was to keep the inevitable frustrations of life within optimal limits, for the sake of the developing individual. Kohut's choice of the word optimal tells us that he recognized a continuum, at either end of which were dangers for the developing child, or for the patient. The frustrations Kohut saw as optimal were those which were stage-appropriate, were affectively manageable, and which occurred within a context of an ongoing empathic bond (1977, 1984). Under these conditions, unavoidable frustration can play a constructive role in early development or in analytic progress. When these conditions are not met, frustration can become a disruptive, rather than a growth-promoting, force in the individual's development or treatment.

Kohut's phrase, optimal frustration, seemed to lend itself to misuse by those who would emphasize frustration as a developmental value, in and of itself, outside the context of an ongoing empathic bond. Several self psychologists therefore suggested that this phrase be replaced with the concept of optimal responsiveness. Among these were Stolorow,

Brandchaft, and Atwood (1987, 1992); Bacal (1988); A. Ornstein (1988); Emde (1990); and Wolf (1992). These innovators saw optimal responsiveness as a crucial environmental provision in childhood or analytic treatment, one which contributes to the normal or reparative development of psychic structure. Psychic structure accrues not on the basis of frustration, but on the basis of having developmental needs reliably enough responded to over time. When frustration does occur it is significant in a positive way, not because of the privation itself, but for the opportunity it presents for making repairs in the disrupted empathic bond between infant and mother or patient and analyst; and, in the view of this author, *for the practice afforded the developing individual in managing her own distress in small doses, having an available object within reach.* In this view, frustration becomes not a positive developmental principle in its own right, but an inevitable concomitant of the human condition, to which specific environmental response is required in order to help the developing child, or the patient, master otherwise overwhelming affective experience.

At first this mastery depends entirely on the emotional availability and responsiveness of the parent or analytic therapist. Gradually, the complex psychological functions involved in such tasks as containing, differentiating, and integrating affective experience become part of the increasingly autonomous functioning of the child or patient. Until the child or patient has achieved adequate functioning in these areas, the absence of emotional and functional availability of the object, or selfobject, will necessitate in the developing individual a reliance on primitive means of managing painful psychic experience. These means tend to include splitting, denial, projection or projective identification, and self-destructive action. Thus, when developmental needs are not met, we speak not of frustration, but of "environmental failure" (Winnicott, 1960b, p. 52).

Winnicott's concept of environmental failure, and Kohut's of empathic failure, remind us that there is a standard to which the caretaker, or analyst, must adhere in meeting the child's or the patient's developmental needs. To the extent that such needs are not met in childhood, they will emerge in the analytic transference of the patient in treatment. To the extent that they are not met in treatment, the analytic reworking of the damaging relationships of childhood will be indefinitely postponed. The modification of "negative introjects" and the redressing of "structural deficit" always proceed hand-in-hand in treatment, because they are two interrelated aspects of the same development gone awry. Internalized object relations and self structure are each an integral part of the human psyche and are closely interwoven: the health or the psychopathology of the self and of the internalized objects cannot be separated.

OPTIMAL RESPONSIVENESS AND AFFECTIVE DEVELOPMENT

Infant research has confirmed Winnicott's and Kohut's concepts of basic need, to which the human environment must respond, especially singling out the early development and integration of affect. This centrality of affect is seen in the infant work of Sander (1980), Stechler and Kaplan (1980); Emde (1990), Stern (1985), Demos and Kaplan (1986), Demos (1988), Eisler (1989), and others. Through this research, which has been supported by clinical observation, instincts have gradually been replaced by affects as the biologically given, primary unit of experience in psychoanalytic theory. Early psychic development is understood to involve countless interactions in which the caretaker provides containment, organization, and affirmation of the infant's otherwise overwhelming and chaotic affective experience. In healthy development, this leads to increasing self-regulation by the child, in which differentiated affect has meaning, value, and communicative function and becomes an intrapsychic guide to action.

With recognition of affect as central to development, Strachey's 1934 interpretation at the moment of *instinctual* urgency becomes our 1994 interpretation at the moment of *affective* urgency. As an example of this: A patient became disorganized and suicidal but did not connect these feelings with my impending vacation. He dreamed his truck hit a patch of black ice. He lost control, skidded off the road, and got out to ask a stranger for help. The patient had no associations to the dream and asked me what I thought it might mean. I said to him: ''Perhaps because of my vacation, I have become the black ice—dark, slippery, and dangerous, when you thought you had solid ground beneath you. You feel out of control and derailed. I'm also the stranger to whom you must turn for help, because you no longer recognize me as the person you knew and trusted.'' Though still distraught by my impending absence, the patient became more organized and less suicidal; he said this was because I had understood and accepted his feelings, and by speaking them, I had helped him do the same.

We see now that much of what changes in analytic treatment is the patient's relationship to his affective life. Another example: Shortly before setting a termination date, a patient dreamed that he was walking with a friend in the forest at dusk. He noticed a fire burning alongside the path but then saw that the fire was contained and that it would light his way. As he walked with his friend by the light of the fire, they were engaged in lively dialogue. The dream seemed to signal that this patient, who had been painfully inhibited, constrained, and convinced that his passions were dangerous, now felt they could be contained and useful, as well as enlivening in a way that enhanced his relatedness. The previously disavowed passions included his loves, his hates, his ambitions and rivalries, and his ideals, all of which now were enriching his life and strengthening and deepening his sense of self.

This dream points to the centrality of affect development and integration for the structuring of personality in treatment, as well as original development. But we know that the analytic path to such integration is neither linear nor unidimensional; that for many patients, becoming aware of affects, even through transference interpretation, will not be adequate for cure. Overwhelmingly intense affect may need first to be contained; and previously disavowed affect may need to be not just identified through interpretation, but also elaborated on, affirmed, and placed empathically in its historical context by analytic reconstruction. The analyst's inability to provide these and other functions when necessary represents not a growth-promoting frustration of the patient's wishes, but an environmental failure in response to developmental need.

A BROADER VIEW OF HUMAN MOTIVATION

Although all this might sound dangerously simple, the parent's or the therapist's optimal responsiveness calls upon a constellation of psychological functions which are as complex and multifaceted as human development itself. The parent first, or the analytic therapist later, must respond optimally to as many different aspects of the child's or patient's functioning as there are developmental needs, affects, and motivations interwoven or clashing in the fabric of the human psyche. Lichtenberg (1989) has identified at least five broad motivational systems that encompass all the needs and instincts previously singled out in Freudian, object relations, and self psychological thought. Lichtenberg's motivational systems include the need for physiological fulfilment, the need for attachment and affiliation, the need for exploration and self-assertion, the need for aversive reaction through antagonism or withdrawal, and the need for sensual and sexual satisfaction. We now have a broader and richer sense of the range of human needs, affects, and motivations than ever before. But such knowledge can serve only as templates to help us organize our analytic listening or amplify our empathic functioning. Ultimately, the individual patient is the first and final source of usable knowledge in the analytic interchange.

As analytic therapists we respond to each need constellation as it emerges with an eye to acceptance, understanding, and integration, but never with the thought of renunciation. Each patient finds his own way to grief. Ultimately, our optimal responsiveness allows our patients spontaneously to renounce what they no longer need, to find or create appropriate channels for fulfillment of needs that remain, and to better contain and tolerate what the environment cannot provide.

OPTIMAL RESPONSIVENESS AND THE TRAINING WHEELS OF LIFE

I offer an analogy, that of the child learning to ride a bicycle. The child whose bicycle is equipped with training wheels is building muscle power even though she has support in place. When the training wheels first come off, the parent *runs* to hold the child's bicycle upright and only gradually lets go. In the parental letting go, the child discovers her own balance and pedal power. If the parent continues to hold on, the child never gets to discover that she can achieve her own balance or use her pedal power alone. This would seem to be an argument for optimal frustration, symbolized by the taking away of the training wheels or of the parental support.

However, if that child had not started, years earlier, first being pushed in a four-wheel carriage, then in motion by herself on a three-wheeler with parental coaching, then on a bicycle with training wheels, then without the training wheels but with someone to hold her until she's ready to be let go—if all these stages of support and their gradual, phase-appropriate diminishment had not been patiently attended to by the environment, then the letting go would become only an abandonment, nothing more than an invitation to trauma.

It is therefore a mistake to say that internalization leading to psychic structure comes about as a result of the optimal frustration inherent in nontraumatic empathic failures, unless we mean by that, that each nontraumatic failure functions like the appropriately timed parental removal of the training wheels, or the letting go of the parental hold on the child's first solo bicycle ride. When done at the right moment, the removal of support can serve to crystallize the gains made in the previous years of parentally supported and guided practice.

What makes a frustration optimal is its timing and manageability in terms of the child's or the patient's functional capacity, and its absolute infrequency against a general background of environmental responsiveness. Small frustrations within an ongoing context of reliable responsiveness to need can become the occasion for developmental leaps forward, and for recognition of functional capacities not previously known. However, it is not these manageable frustrations that actually create the structure. The structure is created out of the repeated transactions in which the individual's needs for responsiveness are met

(Terman, 1988). The failure of responsiveness should be no more than a flash of lightning that reveals whether the previous sustained periods of reliable responsiveness have led to the laying down of structure or not. Clinically, the analyst's summer vacation might constitute the environmental failure, or lightning flash; and the previous year of sustained psychoanalytic adequacy might have enabled the patient to make structural gains which would now be visible in her new capacities for coping with the analyst's absence.

The writings of Winnicott (1958a,b; 1960a) and Kohut (1984), as well as my own work with patients, lead me to emphasize *explicit functional provision* in early development and in treatment, rather than to focus on empathic responsiveness by itself. In Kohut's (1982) words: "[E]mpathy . . . is never by itself . . . therapeutic. . . . [E]ven if a mother's empathy is . . . accurate . . . it is not her *empathy* that satisfies her selfobject needs. *Her actions, her responses to the child* will do this . . . *guided by* . . . accurate empathy" (p. 397; italics added).

BRIEF CASE ILLUSTRATION

A brief vignette might illustrate provision of function in my work with Dr. S, an M.D.-Ph.D. whose recurring nightmares were her daily reminders of childhood emotional and physical abuse by her alcoholic mother and sexual abuse by her mother's (extramarital) lover. Her more emotionally responsive father, a performing artist, had often been absent as long as nine months at a time. This patient had felt all her life that she could rely on no one but herself. She complained of having to take all the responsibility in every personal and professional setting. Eventually she came to feel that the same was true of the analytic setting as well and berated me, particularly, for being unwilling to give her advice.

In her second year of treatment, Dr. S became involved in her first relationship with a man that was not dominated by mutual sexual betrayals. She felt grateful that she had finally established a connection with someone who felt solid and who was supportive of her professional interests and development. For months, however, she had thwarted her fiancé's wishes to set a wedding date because she dreaded the thought of a ceremony at which her divorced and warring parents would make a scene, but at the same time she was unable to bear the idea of a wedding without both of her parents present. Her fiancé began to feel that she really did not want to marry him. I asked her if this were so, and she answered passionately that she wanted to be married to him more than anything in the world. I then asked her if she saw any contradiction between what she had just said and how she'd been behaving by postponing her wedding plans. Much to my surprise, she experienced my question as the helpful and long-awaited "advice" she'd been asking for, and she was immediately able to make wedding plans that excluded her parents, setting up separate, small celebrations with her mother and father for after the marriage. After these events, she told me that my "advice" about her marriage had been a turning point in her treatment, the kind of thing she'd been asking for all along. She hoped that I would continue to do more of this. For a period of several months thereafter, she explicitly sought "advice" about many large and small details of her life.

In searching for the optimal response to these requests, I recognized the absence in her development of an available and idealized parental figure to whom she could turn for guidance. I recognized also that one of the central ways in which she had adapted to this absence, and to the abuse that had filled the void, had been with what had become a characterological hypervigilance and counterdependency. I therefore tended to see, as a developmental step forward, the newly emergent capacity of this high-powered and very competent woman to trust enough to seek any kind of help from me within the treatment. Had I chosen to *interpret* her demands for advice, my interpretation would most likely have been experienced by Dr. S as a repetition of her parents' tendency to comment negatively on every aspect of her personal self-expression. I therefore responded to her requests for "advice" by walking her through her decision-making process, in each case asking her what she knew that was relevant about the specific situation, about her self, and about *her feelings,* that might guide her toward a good choice or decision. After she had experienced my "help" in making several decisions in this way, I was able to help her place the experience of asking for and receiving this help in the context of her personal history. Her requests for this kind of guidance, or "borrowed" psychic function, receded and disappeared spontaneously after a few months, at the same time that Dr. S first inquired about the possibility of converting her twice-a-week therapy to an analysis.

Many analytic therapists understandably share a concern that this degree of responsiveness might be growth inhibiting, or might thwart the analytic process. Some analysts even fear that direct responsiveness to a patient's needs will lead to an interminable regression (Shabad, 1993). Shabad has suggested that the frustrated needs of childhood are reborn as "impossible-to-fulfill" wishes, which must be renounced as such. Although his theoretical construct is interesting, original, and seems to match the intrapsychic dynamics of some individuals seeking treatment, his formulation seems to ignore the distinction that others have made between felt need that derives from essential caretaking functions which were not provided in infancy or childhood, and wishes (whether felt as needs or not) that derive from incestuous or destructive impulses which cannot safely be directly gratified. The importance of the analyst's or therapist's capacity to make the necessary fine discernments between what is genuinely needed and what is only desired cannot be overestimated. Nevertheless, the differences between Shabad's technical recommendations and my own, in response to our patients' needfulness, calls for additional dialogue about this aspect of our analytic work. Such dialogue must especially address the qualities of responsiveness that enable patients to do the analytic work, in contrast to those that would tend to lead to unproductive or irreversible regressions.

Tentatively, I believe that the quality of responsiveness that will facilitate growth and will not lead to "malignant regression" (Balint, 1968) has something to do with the therapist's or the analyst's own sense of internal safety and *boundariedness,* and her capacity to convey this to the patient or analysand, even in the context of direct response to developmental need. Thus, in carrying out a theoretical commitment to optimal responsiveness in clinical work, the analytic therapist must be possessed of clarity as to the rationale for her interventions and have the capacity for firm intrapsychic and interpersonal boundaries herself. Furthermore, she must be at all times attentive to the effect of her interventions and be prepared to retract or redirect her communications based on the patient's response. Keeping these concerns in mind, it has still been my experience, in the case I have presented as well as in others, that certain *developmental* needs that continue unmet in treatment can become the biggest obstacles to analytic progress, whereas those that are transiently and symbolically responded to tend to resolve themselves, making room for further evolution of the therapeutic process. These interactions can become part of what is analyzed and worked through, at later points in the treatment.

Lichtenberg (1989) has suggested that need satisfaction is fundamental to the establishment and maintenance of self-cohesion. I think that this is an essential background guide to clinical functioning with every patient. Though it is only one of multiple curative factors, without it the cognitive gains of insight and self-understanding tend to become hollow psychoanalytic achievements. Once the interpretive-reconstructive process, in the context of need satisfaction, has led to the patient's increased self-cohesion, the analytic relationship becomes important in a new and different way, no longer a relationship in which one person so much needs the other for psychic survival. In my experience, the stance that I have presented tends to enhance the patient's capacity to engage in loving and hating more freely, in negotiating more satisfying relationships, in working or playing creatively, in pursuing ambitions, and in striving toward attainable ideals.

In order to provide a counterpoint to the clinical vignette in which I have highlighted the degree of therapist responsiveness to need, I will now present a case fragment that focuses on my inability and unwillingness to act in accordance with a patient's expressed wishes. This patient, whom I will call Mr. Q, came to once-a-week treatment following the death from cancer of his fifty-nine-year-old father. Mr. Q, aged 29, married, and father of a 2-year-old, owned and ran a successful small business catering to an educated and wealthy but countercultural clientele. In his initial session, Mr. Q reported that since his father's death, he could not remember the content of his dreams but recurrently awakened crying. He said that he had loved his father, who had felt like his only parent; and that he now felt left alone to take care of his mother, who had been a chronic source of pain for him.

Mr. Q had grown up a middle child in a highly educated, well-to-do family in a West Coast suburban setting. His father had been an overworked physician, whose return from work each day Mr. Q had awaited longingly throughout his childhood. Mr. Q felt that his father was kind and well-intentioned toward him, but that every time Mr. Q approached his father excitedly with any accomplishment, his father would snuff out Mr. Q's excitement with a warning about how important it was that Mr. Q not think too much of himself. His father seemed always to remind Mr. Q of whatever down-side might be lurking nearby whenever anything happy or promising happened.

In spite of these painful encounters, however, Mr, Q's father had been by far the preferred parent. Mr. Q described his mother as an "automaton," or as "cold steel." She did everything right. And she raised Mr. Q by the rules. Since Mr. Q had been an unruly child, being raised by the rules felt relentlessly crushing to him. His primary memory of his preteen years was of days spent alone in his room, serving out his mother's "sentences" for ever-new rules that Mr. Q had unwittingly broken. His one older and two younger sisters seemed much more easily to toe their mother's line. Mr. Q felt that everyone in the family, including his father, loved his perfect mother; and as a socialite and freelance writer, she was greatly admired outside the family as well. Thus, his inability to win her acceptance left him feeling hopelessly undeserving and unlovable. This feeling was exacerbated by his three sisters' seeming closeness to each other and to their mother; and by his hearing, every weekend afternoon, what he understood to be his parents' lovemaking, through their closed bedroom door.

Mr. Q started his once-a-week treatment by telling me that he needed from his therapy not the facilitation of insight, but rather the development of an authentic and meaningful relationship. This, he said, would be fostered if his therapist would adopt with him a less distancing professional demeanor and be less exacting about starting and stopping times. In addition, he said, he would need his therapist to give him a hug at the beginning and end of each session and to dress in blue jeans, instead of in skirts, so that she could sit on the floor with her patient. At no time did I ever say either yes or no to these requests. However, neither did I ever act on any of Mr. Q's requests. I told him that I wanted to understand his requests, and that I *accepted* his feelings and his sense of his own needs, whether or not I could actually meet them. We explored the meaning and roots of the longings behind these wishes. In spite of this frustration of Mr. Q's wishes, he never acted on his thoughts of seeking a different therapist, who would work in accordance with what he felt were his needs.

In exploring Mr. Q's wishes, we discovered that his requests felt important to him not so much as a desired source of gratification, but as a way of establishing me in his mind as a woman distinctly different from his mother. What he perceived as my conservative and "perfect" professional attire reminded him too much of the way his mother dressed. My sitting "properly" in my chair and starting and ending sessions precisely on time called to mind for him too much of his mother's rigid adherence to the rules. I therefore "interpreted" to him that in order for him to begin with me the process of seeking help and self-understanding, he felt the need for some tangible signs that I had the vitality, spontaneity, and capacity for responsiveness that he felt sorely lacking in his mother. I also told Mr. Q that I thought my inability to meet any of his initial requests had to do with limitations in my own personality, as well as with my professional training and identity; but that it was also based on what I thoughtfully and genuinely judged would enable me to be most helpful to him in the only ways that I knew how.

In my private processing of Mr. Q's requests, and my own analysis of how best to respond, I judged that for me to comply with his requests would entail changing my way of working (i.e., how I dressed, or how I managed my professional time), which I could not do without impacting on other patients. I thought that to hug him or sit on the floor with him might be overstimulating for him—might arouse in him anxieties, hopes, or expectations about escalating intimacy—and would most probably interfere with creating and maintaining a setting in which we could both focus on helping Mr. Q understand and resolve his life problems. His requests seemed, at least in part, to derive from unconscious instinctual wishes in relationship to his mother, or could easily have been confused with instinctual wishes, had I tried to comply with them. By the end of the first year of once-a-week, face-to-face therapy, Mr. Q's longings and transference demands had begun to shift.

Early in the second year of treatment, he told me that I no longer felt to him like the "cold steel" of his mother's character: that I now at least felt like *warm* steel. He began to trust more, and a period of idealization ensued. In particular he idealized my responsiveness and availability to him, articulating fantasies in which he would be lying on his deathbed and I would be by his side. Considering that I was ten years older than the patient and was treating him in once-a-week therapy, this fantasy seemed to entail the projection onto me of an omnipotence that evoked countertransference impulses on my part to disavow my capacity to be that available to him, or for that long. Within this countertransference-driven response were hidden (but not hidden well enough) my unresolved concerns about being needed more than I had bargained for, and my unresolved fears about disappointing my patient. My response felt to Mr. Q like a direct repetition of his father's regular attempts to ward off disappointments for Mr. Q by bursting his son's bubbles whenever he brought exciting experiences to be shared. Mr. Q had experienced these interactions in childhood as an expression of his father's lack of confidence both in himself and in Mr. Q. These experiences of his father's lack of confidence had also heightened Mr. Q's sense that his mother was the all-powerful one, and that his father could not save him or make up for the deprivation and humiliation that Mr. Q suffered in relation to her.

Meanwhile, my mild, unanalytic protests against Mr. Q's fantasies of my eternal availability had created both a repetition and a rupture in the treatment relationship. This turned out, however, to be a rupture that we were able to process fruitfully. It seemed that my *willingness to engage,* my taking Mr. Q's feelings and requests seriously, and my keeping them in the forefront of our communication contributed to making tolerable for him the frustrations entailed in his requests' not being directly met by me. He also said that it was very important to him that I took some personal responsibility for not being able to respond as he might have wished, rather than referring only to the rules. This aspect of our interactions, he said, helped him differentiate between the frustrations he felt in relation to me and those he felt at his mother's hands, in which she, the other family members, and the surrounding community held her up as a model of ideal mothering, while he himself felt abjectly unmothered.

At the beginning of treatment, Mr. Q seemed to be playing out much of the earlier relationship with his mother in relationship to his wife, who, although capable of considerable warmth, was more organized and oriented toward societal expectations than was Mr. Q. His wife was involved in the business with Mr. Q, in which he was the creative force and she was the person in charge of organization and handling of details. In both the business and at home, Mr. Q's wife was often disappointed and angry that he did not do his share of the "detail" work; and Mr. Q often reacted with his wife as if he were back in his mother's rule-bound clutches. The differentiating he did in the transference, between his mother and the therapist, eventually seemed to carry over to enable him to undertake a similar differentiation process between his wife and his mother.

Had I not responded to any of Mr. Q's initial requests but also not been able, through my stance and my level of interaction with him, to establish myself in his psyche as someone in significant ways different from the way he had experienced his mother (as warm steel rather than cold steel), I think Mr. Q would either have left the treatment in the first weeks or months, or would have spun his wheels with me in a "passive-aggressive" or masochistic repetition of the emotionally enslaved psychic position vis-à-vis his mother of childhood. As the therapy proceeded, Mr Q was able to change his old ways of relating to his mother, now widowed, and dependent on her son for many of the things that her husband had taken care of in their family before he died. Mr Q began monthly to fly to the city where his mother was living, so that he could help her with financial matters and take care of household maintenance. Although Mr Q's mother seemed not to have either warmth or nurturance in her repertoire, she began to treat Mr Q with a respect she had never shown to him in the past, and he felt less and less oppressed by his former attitude of supplication toward her. He also finally began to get closer to his sisters, all of whom eventually confided in him about their own need for psychotherapy.

Mr. Q's new assumption of responsibility in his mother's life affected his self-concept and seemed to lead to a shift between him and his wife, in terms of how they shared their family and business responsibilities. With Mr. Q carrying more of the burdens, and allowing his wife to participate in more of the fun and creative aspects of their work and their parenting, his wife felt less critical of him and the tensions between them eased. At the time of termination, Mr. Q and his wife were expecting their second child and were making plans to move to a different area of the country, where they expected a greater demand for the goods and services provided by their business, and where they had reason to hope that they would find more satisfying relationships with people who shared their special interests. Mr Q's therapy had lasted three years, and considering its relative brevity and the infrequency of our meetings, he seemed to have made some reasonable life gains. Because of the nature of his wishes and demands of me early in the treatment, I had judged that my understanding, acceptance, and interpretation of what he asked of me would be more useful and facilitative of the therapeutic process than any direct response to what he presented as his needs. However, it seemed important that I had, in essence, responded to his initial request for a genuine engagement, even though I did not enact the more material aspects of what he had felt that he needed at the outset. I see this treatment as an illustration of a circumscribed therapeutic success in the face of a necessary frustration of several of the patient's expressed wishes, which I understood as being intertwined with incestuous desires, but which were felt by him as needs, initially presented as preconditions for the treatment.

These two contrasting case fragments suggest an optimal stance on the part of the analytic therapist, one entailing thoughtfulness, self-discipline, and boundariedness, as well as openness, flexibility, and a nonjudgmental attitude toward what the patient presents as needs. These qualities of mind and attitudes can enhance the ever present challenge of arriving at a quality and degree of responsiveness that will fall within the optimal range for each patient at any given point in treatment. This is of course an analytic ideal, and something which we therefore accept will be always just beyond our reach.

REFERENCES

Bacal, H. (1988), Reflections on "optimum frustration." In: *Learning from Kohut: Progress in Self Psychology, Vol. 4,* ed. A. Goldberg. Hillsdale, NJ: The Analytic Press, pp. 127–132.

Balint, M. (1953), *Primary Love and Psycho-Analytic Technique.* New York: De Capo Press.

—— (1968), *The Basic Fault.* New York: Brunner/Mazel.

Demos, V. & Kaplan, S. (1987), Motivation and affect reconsidered: Affect biographies of two infants. *Psychoanal. & Contemp. Thought,* 10:147–221.

Eisler, E. (1989), An exploration of the ramifications of the organizing effect of affect in infancy. Unpublished doctoral dissertation, Massachusetts School of Professional Psychology.

Emde, R. (1990), Mobilizing fundamental modes of development: Empathic availability and therapeutic action. *J. Amer. Psychoanal. Assn.,* 38:881–914.

Freud, S. (1912), On the universal tendency to debasement in the sphere of love. *Standard Edition,* 11:177–190. London: Hogarth Press, 1957.

———(1915), Observations on transference love. *Standard Edition,* 12:157–171. London: Hogarth Press, 1958.

———(1919), Lines of advance in psycho-analytic therapy. *Standard Edition,* 17:157–168. London: Hogarth Press, 1955.

———(1927), The future of an illusion. *Standard Edition,* 21:3–56. London: Hogarth Press, 1961.

———(1930), Civilization and its discontents. *Standard Edition,* 21:59–145. London: Hogarth Press, 1961.

Greenberg, J. (1986), Theoretical models and the analyst's neutrality. *Contemp. Psychoanal., 22*:87–106.

Kernberg, O. F. (1994), Internalized object relations: Transference analysis and structural change. Presented at the conference on *The Therapeutic Action of Psychodynamic Psychotherapy: Current Concepts of Cure,* Boston, April 8.

Kohut, H. (1971), *The Analysis of the Self.* New York: International Universities Press.

———(1977), *The Restoration of the Self.* New York: International Universities Press.

———(1982), Introspection, empathy, and the semi-circle of mental health. *Internat. J. Psycho-Anal.,* 63:395–407.

———(1984), *How Does Analysis Cure?* ed. A. Goldberg & P. Stepansky. Chicago: University of Chicago Press.

Kushner, T. (1992), *Angels in America: Perestroika.* New York: Theatre Communications Group.

Lachmann, F. & Beebe, B. (1992), Reformulations of early development and transference: Implications for psychic structure formation. In: *Interface of Psycho-Analysis and Psychology,* ed. J. Barron, M. Eagle & D. Wolitzky. Washington, DC: American Psychological Assn., pp. 133–153.

Lichtenberg, J. (1989), *Psychoanalysis and Motivation.* Hillsdale, NJ: The Analytic Press.

Loewald, H. (1960), On the therapeutic action of psychoanalysis. *Internat. J. Psycho-Anal.,* 41:16–33.

Mitchell, S. (1994, April 9), When interpretation fails: A new look at the therapeutic action. Presented at the conference on *The Therapeutic Action of Psychodynamic Psychotherapy: Current Concepts of Cure,* Boston.

Ornstein, A. (1988), Optimal responsiveness and the theory of cure. In: *Learning from Kohut: Progress in Self Psychology, Vol. 4,* ed. A. Goldberg. pp. 155–159.

Ornstein, P. H. & Ornstein, A. (1980), Formulating interpretations in clinical psychoanalysis. *Internat. J. Psycho-Anal.,* 61:213–224.

Russell, P. (1994), Process with involvement. Presented at the conference on *The Therapeutic Action of Psycho-Dynamic Psychotherapy: Current Concepts of Cure,* Boston, April 9.

Shabad, P. (1993), Resentment, indignation, entitlement: The transformation of unconscious wish into need. *Psychoanal. Dial., 3*:481–494.

Stechler, G. & Kaplan, S. (1980), The development of the self: A psychoanalytic perspective. *The Psychoanalytic Study of the Child, 35*:85–106. New Haven, CT: Yale University Press.

Stolorow, R., Brandchaft, B. & Atwood, G. (1987), *Psychoanalytic Treatment: An Intersubjective Approach.* Hillsdale, NJ: The Analytic Press.

———(1992), *Contexts of Being: The Intersubjective Foundations of Psychological Life.* Hillsdale, NJ: The Analytic Press.

Terman, D. (1988), Optimum frustration: Structuralization and the therapeutic process. In: *Learning from Kohut: Progress In Self Psychology, Vol. 4,* ed. A. Goldberg. Hillsdale, NJ: The Analytic Press, pp. 113–126.

Winnicott, D. W. (1958a), The capacity to be alone. In *The Maturational Processes and the Facilitating Environment.* New York: International Universities Press, pp. 29–36.

——(1958b), Withdrawal and regression. In: *Holding and Interpretation.* New York: Grove Press, pp. 187–192.

——(1958c), *Through Paediatrics to Psycho-Analysis.* New York: Basic Books.

——(1960a), Ego distortion in terms of true and false self. In: *The Maturational Processes and the Facilitating Environment.* New York: International Universities Press, pp. 140–152.

——(1960b), The theory of the parent–infant relationship. In: *The Maturational Processes and the Facilitating Environment.* New York: International Universities Press, pp. 37–55.

Wolf, E. (1992), Abstinence, neutrality gratification: New trends, new climates, new implications. *The Annual of Psychoanalysis,* 20:115–129. Hillsdale, NJ: The Analytic Press.

III

An Integrative Approach to the Concept of Cure

10

When Interpretations Fail

A New Look at the Therapeutic Action
of Psychoanalysis

Stephen A. Mitchell

O ne of the most distinctive and fascinating features of psychoanalysis as a field is the centrality and perpetual presence of its
founder. There is no other intellectual, empirical, or clinical
discipline in which the ideas of one person have held sway for so long.
Think of Newton in physics, Darwin in biology. They made extraordinary contributions; yet, physics and biology have absorbed their impact
and moved on. Their disciplines have grown past them.

The relationship between Freud and psychoanalysis has been different. Freud's ideas, his vision, and the entire package of theory,
technique, and understanding that constitute Freud's psychoanalysis
has had remarkable staying power—inspiring generations of analysts
and serving as a perpetual take-off point and frame of reference for
virtually every dimension of the subsequent history of psychoanalytic
ideas. One has only to look at the photographs of Freud and his contemporaries to be aware of how much time has passed and how much has
changed from Freud's day to ours. Yet, his concepts are very much alive.
Why has the relationship between Freud and the discipline he founded
been so different?

Surely, one reason for Freud's durability is precisely that, unlike
Newton or Darwin, he founded his discipline. Physics existed prior
to Newton; biology existed prior to Darwin. There was no psychoanalysis before Freud. There had been protopsychoanalytic forays into
unconscious phenomena, expanded notions of sexuality, symbolic processes, and so on. But until Freud put it all together, nothing remotely
like psychoanalysis existed—as a system of ideas, a methodology for

psychological exploration, a technique for treating mental disorders. And because psychoanalysis, in its early decades, was so distinctively and thoroughly "Freudian," it is difficult to imagine a psychoanalysis that is wholely post-Freudian.

But there is more to it than that. Systems of thought, even the richest and most powerful, ordinarily have a life span. Think of the intellectual fashions that have illuminated and then faded from recent Western culture: Marxism, existentialism, structuralism, deconstructionism, and so on. What is different about psychoanalysis is that, in addition to being a system of thought, it is a treatment, a powerful treatment. Of course, there had been other treatments for so-called "nervous disorders," but psychoanalysis was something different—a sustained, in-depth, intensive exploration of the structure of the patient's mind, the complex tapestry of the psyche.

By inventing psychoanalysis, Freud created not just a treatment, but *a kind of experience* that had never existed before. Symptomatic treatments, like hypnosis, were highly focal and time-limited. A more radical cure required that the understructure of patients' symptomatic outcroppings be traced and delineated, which led Freud into the depths of patients' unconscious motivations and residues of childhood.

I do not think it diminishes Freud's achievement to suggest that he stumbled into something the power of which he had scarcely imagined. In his necessarily naive early associative tracing of patients' symptoms to their original contexts, Freud soon encountered the phenomena of transference and resistance, in all their passionate intensity. The tracing of neurotic symptoms led, step by step, into the deepest recesses of personal experience, into the remote past, the most horrifying impulses and fantasies, the most dreaded fears, the most poignant and delicate hopes and longings. Like a river explorer sucked into a whirlpool, Freud repeatedly found himself in the grip of forces beyond his comprehension, and classical psychoanalytic theory, as a system of thought, served to carry him through. The theory of infantile sexuality, drive theory, and technical recommendations regarding interpretation all became crucial parts of the conceptual craft that Freud developed to navigate the treacherous waters of the psychoanalytic experience.

The existence of so many analysts today, many years after Freud's original efforts, is evidence that clinical psychoanalysis works, both for analysands and for analysts. Patients get better; under the best of circumstances, they get better in ways more remarkable than Freud could possibly have envisioned. They get better in ways they themselves could scarcely have envisioned. At its best, psychoanalysis can assuage painful residues of childhood, release thwarted creative potentials, heal fragmentation, and bridge islands of isolation and despair. And not only is psychoanalysis a powerful, transformative experience for the patient; it also provides an extraordinary experience for the analyst. It is only in recent years, with the increasing openness in writing about counter-transference, that it has been possible to acknowledge how absorbing, personally touching, and potentially transformative the practice of psychoanalysis can often be for the analyst.

Thus, perhaps the most distinctive feature of psychoanalysis as a field is that Freud created not just a set of ideas or a treatment but also a unique, extremely powerful, personally transformative experience, for both parties. Because all analysts have also been analysands, we have lived that experience from both sides, and it has been compelling enough for us to want more and to want to offer more to other people.

To return to my original question, I would argue that one of the most important reasons for the durability of Freud's ideas over the history of psychoanalysis is that his system has made it possible for us to think that we really understand what happens in the analytic process and why people change in the often profound ways that they do. It is the central argument of this chapter that whereas Freud's explanation worked persuasively in his day, it can no longer work for us, and that we have had great difficulty in fully coming to terms with this.

Freud's explanation, stripped down to its bare essentials, goes something like this: Psychopathology results from repression, a blocking from awareness of disturbing impulses, memories, thoughts, and feelings. Repression is undone through insight, which bridges conscious ideas and unconscious impulses, memories, thoughts, and feelings. The analyst's correct and well-timed interpretations generate insight by creating the necessary bridges. Transferences and resistances, correctly understood, express the central unconscious conflicts with great intensity, so the competent analyst can always find just the right material to interpret.

This is a wonderful model—interpretation leads to insight and insight changes psychic structures—it must have been extraordinarily persuasive for analysts of Freud's day. The whole feel of it was consistent with the stunning developments and new technologies in the rest of science. Microscopy was enabling scientists to look into the subvisual world and view the underlying structure of both organic and inorganic matter. (It had been only shortly before Freud entered neurology that the neuron had been isolated in the study of brain function.) Telescopes were enabling scientists look into outer space and see planets, moons, and stars never viewed before. So, Freud too had invented a methodology for entering a previously invisible realm—the psychological structure of the human mind. Free association and the other features of the analytic setting had revealed the underlying patterning and fragmentation of psychic life, and interpretation seemed to be a wonderfully precise tool for excising and reworking faulty patterns and rejoining fragments.

Many things have changed since Freud's day, and these changes have made this model no longer very workable. I cannot explore these changes fully here. (They are discussed at considerable length in my 1993 book *Hope and Dread in Psychoanalysis.*) But I would like to note a few salient and, I believe, quite profound shifts.

1. Scientists of Freud's time could well believe they stood outside of what they were studying, observing its nature. Scientists of our time believe that to study something is to interact with it, that one's methodology partly creates the object of study. So, any analytic theory today—drive theory, object relations theories, self psychology—needs to be regarded as offering not a blueprint of the mind but a framework partially imposed by the analyst to organize data that could be ordered in many other ways.

2. The hopes of scientists of Freud's time that they would soon be able to grasp the smallest particles of matter or chart the broadest patterns of the universe seem, from our perspective, understandably naive. Considering the ever-expanding complexities of particle physics, astronomy, and cosmology, and considering that the human brain is the most complex natural phenomenon ever encountered, the confidence of Freud and his contemporaries that psychoanalytic theory would provide a comprehensive, ultimate blueprint of the mind seems wildly overly optimistic, if not fundamentally misguided.

3. The giving of an interpretation by an analyst to a patient in Freud's day was a very different event from an analyst giving a patient the same interpretation in our day, because the whole social context of our experience of authority is so different. In Freud's day, everyone invested the analyst with considerable authority; it made sense to do so. Thus Freud regarded what he termed the "unobjectionable positive transference" based on childhood belief in authority as a basic ingredient in the power of the analyst's interpretations. The patient grants the analyst a certain expertise, a certain power, even a kind of magic—but that's OK, because it helps the patient really consider the interpretation, creating the bridges that release repressions from their internal exile.

In our day, anyone who initially invests the analyst with that kind of authority has a serious problem. In our post–Watergate, post–Iran-Contra world, with all we know about the abuse of authority by political leaders, doctors, lawyers, priests, and so on, it makes no sense to grant the analyst the kind of authority that Freud was granted by his patients.

Or, rather, it makes a different kind of sense. The same behavior means something different in our time than it did then. Anyone approaching me with that kind of deference at the beginning of a treatment starts me thinking about the possible reasons for a brittle idealization, or, a kind of obsequious handling, or perhaps both. That sort of transference today *is* "objectionable," not in a moral sense, but in that it requires one to object, or to raise questions, because an interpretation accepted in such a mode is an act of submission. And it is less likely to lead to insight than the perpetuation of sadomasochistic object relations.

4. Since Freud's day there has developed a hefty literature on the outcomes of analytic and other treatments. This literature is complex, confusing, and hotly contested. But I think any fair overview of it would have to take into account two predictably recurrent findings that pose difficulties for the traditional model of therapeutic action—interpretation leading to insight: (1) patients even of highly successful analyses don't tend to remember or put much weight on the interpretations therapists give them; and (2) the particular theory or ideology of the therapist, and his or her repertoire of interpretations, has little impact on the outcome of treatment, whereas his or her personality or emotional presence has great impact. Now I know these kinds of findings can be explained; I have heard all the explanations. But I would suggest that what we analysts do when we do this is to explain away, rather than really explain, because it is bothersome, very bothersome, to think that analysis may not work on the basis of interpretation leading to intrapsychic insight.

Because of these developments since Freud's time, it is no longer compelling to think of the analyst as standing outside the patient's material, organizing it in some neutral, objective way. It is understandable that Freud and his patients saw it that way; it is no longer possible for us. As Donnel Stern has put it, "To these (some) contemporary analysts the interpretive model is uncomfortable. It feels stilted and unnatural. It is like walking out in the street wearing the clothing of a different era." Patients who today accept and internalize analytic interpretations the way Freud's patients did are not helping themselves get better; they are enacting their pathology. No matter how fond we analysts are of our theories and interpretations, and I (for one) am exceedingly fond of mine, we must deal with the fact that something else is going on.

There is a strong tradition in psychoanalytic thinking and writing that makes it very difficult to deal directly with this problem—a tradition that enshrines Freud's model of therapeutic action as a kind of holy relic, a relic that needs to be preserved untouched, rather than reworked and revitalized. Even some of the most progressive thinkers of our time add their contributions to the traditional model of therapeutic action as a credo. Thus, Fred Pine (1993) begins a recent article by proclaiming, "Arlow and Brenner (1990) see analyzing as the essence of the psychoanalytic process, and I certainly concur" (p. 186). Despite Pine's recent assimilation of the contributions of object relations theories and self psychology, he makes it a point to distinguish his approach from the work of more radical thinkers like Kohut by his loyalty to the credo. Pine states, "Although Kohut (1984) has quite a different view of the change process, in principle, I believe, one need not shift the view of the process even if one were to shift or expand the view of the significant mental contents that analysis addresses" (p. 187).

Otto Kernberg, who has broadened the content about which interpretations should be made to include early object relations, also preserves the traditional model of the therapeutic action, interpretation leading to insight, as if it were still serviceable in its pristine form. Thus, Kernberg (1992) recently referred to interpretation as "the basic instrument of psychoanalytic technique . . . the concept and testing of changes in conflictual equilibrium is central to psychoanalytic technique as well as to its theory of outcome" (p. 121).

As an illustration of why I believe the classical model of therapeutic action, interpretation leading to insight, can no longer serve us well in its original form, consider a moment in the very beginning of the treatment of a very disturbed young man. George had been in several nonanalytic treatments before, mostly centered around his problems with drug addiction. He was the son of an emotionally absent, workaholic, celebrity father who had an almost unimaginable amount of money. George's sense of self was remarkably merged, first with his father, and secondarily with his wife, whom he had married as an antidote to the power his father had over him, but to whom he had a similar, merged relationship, a blend of adoration and submission. He would recite aphorisms from both his father and wife (who were, incidentally, both devotees of psychoanalysis), as if they had been handed down on Mt. Sinai. The father had been the patient of a famous analytic researcher for many years, to whose research efforts he had donated great amounts of money. I do not know if the father's analysis did him any good, but there was no evidence of it in terms of his relationship with his son.

After several weeks of his not being sure what to talk about and my not being sure what to say to him, George began filling me in on characteristic details of his problematic negotiations with his wife. He liked to spend one or two evenings a week out with his male friends, at sporting events or playing poker, but that meant leaving her alone with their two children, because she was a devout believer in the ideological principle that small children should never be left without a parent. He felt he was never in any position to decide what would be fair, because he had demonstrated his unreliability in earlier years through his drug excesses. Further, he did not want to be the kind of absentee father and husband that his own father was. So, he had to leave it up to his wife to decide when he had the right to spend an evening out. When he did go out, however, he tended to stay out longer than she was comfortable with, drink too much, and arrive home in a state that seemed, in fact, to confirm his judgment that he was unable to make these kinds of decisions for himself.

I felt I might be able to say something useful here, and commented on his giving her a great deal of power over him in a way that, I imagined, might make him angry and resentful; I could understand how he might defiantly abuse his privileges on his evening pass. He acknowledged that this was precisely how he often felt. I tried to get him interested in the vicious circle aspect of this interaction, the way in which his submission made him angry, his anger made him self-destructively defiant, and his self-destructiveness convinced him further of his need for submission. I did not say this all at once and felt he was with me point by point. However, at the end of the session, he asked me to summarize everything I had said. He felt he had a tendency to misuse therapy, being lazy and forgetful, and this seemed important. He wanted to get it clear. I repeated what I had said. Then he wanted to repeat it back to me so that he could repeat it again to his wife when he returned home.

I had a progressively sinking feeling, as I imagined my interpretive description hanging, embroidered on their wall, with little flowers around it. I tried to say something to him about his doing with me precisely what we had been talking about his doing with his wife— treating my ideas as if they were some kind of precious, supernatural guide to living rather than something he and I were working on together. He became confused and clearly felt I was both criticizing and abandoning him. I backpedaled and, I think, was able to regain the prior sense that we had understood something important, although clearly on his adorational terms. I reflected on his need to believe I had all the answers and decided not to challenge that belief at this point, but expressed a curiosity about his need for that belief and the lengths to which he seemed prepared to go to maintain it. It seemed to me that my choice was between repeating one or the other feature of his relationship with his father: sticking to my interpretation of the transference and thereby abandoning him like the "bad" father, or somewhat passively allowing him to use me as the overly idealized magical father; the latter, I thought, might eventually offer more opportunities for growth.

What is happening in this interaction? I think I see something in the material the patient provides that is worth commenting interpretively on. This is what I have been taught to do. The same material surely could be described interpretively in lots of different ways—in terms of a wish and a defense, a developmental longing, and so on. I don't really think it would have mattered because what happened was that George did not really hear the interpretation as an interpretation; he heard it as something else, something familiar, something recognizable within the basic categories of his own frame of reference. I might have thought I was offering an interpretation; George thought I was handing down the 11th commandment.

Is George's transference "unobjectionable"? In Freud's day, it might have been defensible to think of it that way, but I do not think we can really get away with that. It seems fairly clear that George is relating to my interpretation much more like one of his father's aphorisms than my idea of what an interpretation is supposed to be about.

The contemporary Kleinians (e.g., Betty Joseph) have a solution to this problem, which concerns what they call the patient's "relationship to the interpretation." They make another interpretation, this time of the patient's relationship to the interpretation. This is in effect what I did by calling George's attention to the way in which he was doing with me what I described him doing with his father and wife. The Kleinians argue that the content of all other possible interpretations is irrelevant because of the way the patient relates to interpretations. Interpreting this mode of processing interpretations is the only way to get through. I find this a useful way of thinking, and it sometimes works. But most often it does not really solve the problem. You will remember that when I made such a second-level interpretation to George, he got confused and disoriented. I think it was clear that he was unable to really reflect on the way in which he attributed oracular status to my statements and instead felt I was delivering yet another, a 12th, commandment by raising questions, in an obscure and critical fashion, about his failure to defer properly to the previous commandment. Trying to interpret the patient's relationship to each interpretation can create an infinite regress from which the analyst can never disentangle himself or herself.

Because Freud could assume that the analyst, when making interpretations, stood outside the web of these kinds of sticky, repetitive transference–countertransference configurations, he never had to deal with this problem as such. Whatever other transference there was to the analyst's interpretations, the dimension of the "unobjectionable positive transference" was, as noted previously, considered an aid. The closest Freud came to dealing with the kinds of problems analysts are faced with today was when he discovered the importance of time, long periods of time, in effecting analytic change. Freud's early analyses lasted only several months. It seemed reasonable to assume that the analyst merely needed to arrive at the correct interpretive understanding and convince the patient of its correctness for curative insight to occur. Freud and subsequent analysts discovered that useful interpretations were not a one-shot deal. It takes time; lots of time. One makes the same or closely related interpretations over and over again. How can this be understood within the traditional model of therapeutic action? If the conflictual material is released from repression by the interpretation, why does it have to happen over and over?

Freud developed the notion of "working through" to try to account for the temporal dimension of the analytic process—the fact that the work takes time. I have always found this the most elusive, the murkiest of all Freud's major technical concepts. Laplanche and Pontalis, in *The Language of Psychoanalysis* (1973), note that "working through" takes place "especially during certain phases where progress seems to have come to a halt and where a resistance persists despite its having been interpreted" (p. 488). What does the analyst do to facilitate "working through"? Laplanche and Pontalis say that "working through is expedited by interpretations from the analyst which consist chiefly in showing how the meanings in question may be recognized in different contexts" (p. 488). This seems to amount to saying that during stagnant times when interpretations seem to fail, something useful sometimes happens when the analyst continues to make them. Can this be persuasively explained in the classical model?

Picture "working through" in terms of the spatial metaphors Freud relied on. Even after the original conflict is uncovered through interpretation, its derivatives need to be traced and eradicated, like the troublesome shoots of a complex weed system in a garden. Once the central roots are pulled up, one needs to follow the many shoots to prevent a reemergence of the plant. But this way of thinking about "working through" over time does not really explain how patients like George change. George could not really use more interpretations; George seems to need some different way of grasping and internalizing interpretations. My interpretation seemed to compound the problem, not cure it. In pulling up each root, the analyst is scattering seeds of the same weed; the very activity designed to deal with the problem perpetuates the problem. From our contemporary point of view, the analyst seems less like the surgeon Freud asked us to imagine and more like the sorcerer's apprentice.

Is this just a problem that comes up in the beginning of analyses? Or in especially difficult cases? I don't think so. We become most aware of the limitations of the therapeutic impact of interpretations when they fail dramatically, as with George, but the very same processes may be operating even when things seem to be going well.

A vivid demonstration of the limits of interpretations in everyday analytic work and therefore of the explanatory insufficiency of the traditional model of therapeutic action is to be found in an excellent and extremely important paper entitled "Penis Envy: From Childhood Wish to Developmental Metaphor" (Grossman and Stewart, 1976). This paper points to the way in which the common (perhaps it would be fair to say the traditional) interpretation of penis envy presumes, following Freud, that penis envy is a concrete, biologically based fact rather than a metaphor to be interpreted like any other piece of manifest content. The authors thoughtfully demonstrate that for two women who sought a second analysis, the "penis envy" interpretation from the first analysis had an antitherapeutic effect of gratifying various masochistic and narcissistic dynamics. In discussing one patient, Grossman and Stewart (1976) note that "[s]ince admiration always led to rivalry and envy, and sexual interest to aggression, the only permanent tie to the object was of a sadomasochistic nature. She chose the masochistic role and the defense of a mild paranoid attitude. Indeed, the 'helpless acceptance' of the penis envy interpretation in the first analysis seemed masochistically gratifying" (pp. 197–198).

Here is a very interesting situation. Grossman and Stewart are suggesting that while the content of the analyst's interpretation may or may not have been correct or relevant in one sense or another, what was most important was the way in which the patient experienced and internalized the interpretation (the patient's relationship to the interpretation). While the analyst thought he was offering an interpretation, the patient experienced it as a kind of sadistic attack or beating to which she was submitting, thereby enacting her central dynamics. While it looked like something new was happening, an interpretation that should create insight and effect psychic change, actually the patient was reenacting her same old masochistic surrender to men.

Second analyses are always wonderfully privileged vantage points from which to observe what went wrong in the previous analysis. But, in this case, the realization Grossman and Stewart arrived at, that the first analyst's interpretations had no real analytic impact because they had been processed through the patient's masochistic dynamics, did not help the second analyst very much.

Even to interpret her masochism posed the threat that the interpretation would be experienced as a "put down" and gratify her masochistic impulse; all interpretations, if not narcissistically gratifying, gratified masochistic wishes. They were felt as attacks in which her worthlessness, her defectiveness, and her aggression were unmasked. The analysis threatened to become interminable, one in which the relationship to the analyst was maintained, but only at the price of an analytic stalemate [p. 198].

This is a wonderful example of what I am arguing is the problem at the heart of every analysis. The analyst arrives at a way of understanding the patterns through which the patient organizes his or her subjective world and perpetuates the patient's central dynamic conflicts. The analyst delivers this understanding in the form of an interpretation. But the patient can only hear the interpretation as something else—it gets slotted into the very categories the analyst is trying to get the patient to think about and understand. The analyst makes an interpretation about the way in which the patient eroticizes interactions, and the patient experiences the interpretation itself as a seduction. The analyst makes an interpretation about the way in which the patient transforms every interaction into a battle, and the patient experiences the interpretation itself as a power operation. Or, in this case, the analyst makes an interpretation about the patient's masochism, and the patient experiences the interpretation as a put-down to be agreed to and feel humiliated by.

It is very common for the analyst not to realize that this is happening, but, as in the cases discussed by Grossman and Stewart, it often becomes quite apparent to the next analyst. Why is this? The patient and the analyst, as long as the analysis is ongoing, both have a great investment in thinking that the analyst's interpretations are something different, something new, part of the solution and not part of the problem. It is very easy for the patient to unconsciously organize his or her experience in analysis in a familiar, characteristic fashion while hoping and believing that something quite new and transformative is happening. It is often very difficult for the patient to let the analyst know that he or she is beginning to feel that the analyst, even when offering interpretations, is only the latest in a long line of those from whom they have suffered seduction, betrayal, abandonment, torture, pathetic disappointments, and so on. It is also very difficult for the analyst to pick up and hear the patient's hints in these directions, because the analyst wants so much to feel that the analysis is going well and that interpretations are truly analytic events rather than reenactments of chronic disasters. In fact, when the patient makes this sort of experience finally, unmistakably clear, there is usually a sense of great crisis in the analysis, and its value is called into question. So, most often the patient's experience of the interpretation does not get fully revealed and investigated until the patient is already working with the next analyst and the new analytic pair can operate under the illusion that this problem does not really pertain to them.

Because Grossman and Stewart (1976) laid out the issues so clearly, I was very interested to see what they would say next. Had they found a way out of this central dilemma? The next paragraph starts with: "Over many years the patient was able to recognize her need to be a mistreated little girl, rather than to face her disappointments as a grown woman" (p. 198).

The first time I read this I was convinced that my mind must have wandered and that I had missed a paragraph. No. Perhaps the typesetter dropped the paragraph? What had happened here? The authors lay out the problem so lucidly. They show that interpretations, in themselves, can't possibly solve the problem, because the patient organizes the interpretations into another manifestation of the problem. Yet they say that "over many years" something changed. But how? The implication is that the interpretations themselves eventually did the trick, that the traditional model of therapeutic action somehow prevailed. Yet, Grossman and Stewart have shown that in itself, interpretations cannot possibly have effected analytic change. There is a major problem here at the heart of the traditional model of therapeutic action. Something else must have happened.

The dictionary says that when we describe someone as pulling themselves up by their own bootstraps we mean that one has helped "oneself without the aid of others; use(d) one's own resources" (*Webster's New Universal Unabridged Dictionary,* 1989, p. 171). But this definition leaves out the paradox implied by that phrase. You cannot pull yourself up by your own bootstraps; try it. You are standing in them. To pull yourself up by your bootstraps, you would have to find somewhere else to rest your weight. You cannot be in them and pull yourself up by them at the same time. This seems to be precisely the problem that we have been tracing with the traditional model of the therapeutic action. Interpretations are credited with pulling the patient out of his or her psychopathology; yet, interpretations are deeply mired in the very pathology analysts use them to cure. There must be something else on which the analyst can rest his or her weight while tugging on his or her interpretive bootstraps. There is a missing platform somewhere.

When astronomers were studying the orbit of the planet Uranus, they noticed small deviations from the elliptical course they would have predicted. Even though the telescopes available at that time did not make it possible to see other planets, they realized that there must be something else out there pulling Uranus out of its predictable orbit. This reasoning made it possible for them to locate and eventually to see Neptune.

We are at an analogous point in the history of psychoanalytic ideas. There is something else, some other force, that must help the analyst to pull patients out of their customary psychodynamic orbits—simply making interpretations cannot possibly be doing the job. But whatever else it is out there, in the analytic situation, has been generally invisible to our available conceptual repertoire, and the preservation of Freud's now anachronistic model of therapeutic action, of interpretation leading to insight as the basic mechanism of change, lulls us into not really looking.

There have been several important strategies for shoring up Freud's model, and the concept of the "working alliance" developed within American ego psychology has been the most popular of these, particularly in this country. When interpretations fail, it is because there is no working alliance. Thus, Freud was right about how analysis works, but we have come to understand the preconditions necessary for an effective analytic process. With more disturbed patients, rather than making interpretations, the analyst builds a working alliance. With patients who are working well, a closer look reveals an underlying working alliance. Thus, the working alliance becomes the missing platform that makes interpretive leverage possible, a place for the analyst to rest his or her weight when making interpretations.

The concept of the working alliance begs all the most interesting questions of the problem we have been considering. Interpretations won't work unless the analyst is experienced as outside the dynamic web of the patient's transferences. You need to have a working alliance. But how in the world does the analyst establish a working alliance? A close reading of Greenson (1967), for example, reveals that the analyst actually establishes the working alliance largely by interpreting the transference. But how can the patient hear interpretations of the transference if there is no pre-existing working alliance? This concept has merely shifted the problem with the traditional model of interpretation to an earlier precondition for interpretation.

Parallel use has been made recently of many concepts borrowed from object relations theories and self psychology by writers like Pine, Kernberg, and Modell. Interpretation leading to insight is still the key process, but in order for interpretations to work, patients must experience the analytic setting as a "holding environment" or the analyst as truly "empathic." When interpretations fail, holding or empathy is needed; when interpretations work, holding or empathy is presumed.

But for "holding" or "empathy" to be genuinely analytic, the patient must experience it as something quite different from anything found in his or her customary object relations. How is the analyst able to establish something different? To presume holding and empathy is, once again, to beg the most central questions. For the patient who has grown up in a world of dangerous and deceitful others, the analyst's offer of empathy is likely to be experienced as dangerous and deceitful, and what the analyst might feel is an empathic understanding of this problem doesn't solve the problem because it is still embedded in it. Rather, it is in the long and hard struggle to establish an empathic connection that a particular patient can recognize as such and really use that the most fundamental analytic work is done, not in the effective interpretations themselves that presuppose its achievement.

Several lines of analytic thinking have directly engaged the bootstrap problem. Fairbairn (1952) anticipated our current struggles with this problem almost 50 years ago when he argued that the relinquishment of the tie to the bad object is the central transformative dimension in psychoanalysis. He suggested that in order for the patient to give up the "adhesive" tie to the bad object (to use Freud's wonderful descriptive adjective), he had to believe, through the relationship with the analyst, in the possibility of a good object relationship. However, Fairbairn left obscure and ambiguous the questions of exactly what a good object relationship is and how the analyst struggles through transferences to achieve it.

Important progress has been made on this problem by the interpersonalists, particularly those most influenced by Fromm. (Sullivan, although radically innovative in many areas, was quite conservative regarding therapeutic action and the analytic relationship; he considered analytic traction to rest on insight, delivered not through interpretations but through questions, from a therapist located outside the push and pull of transference and countertransference.) Fromm saw the analyst's role as more personal, and contemporary interpersonalists, such as Levenson, Wolstein, and Ehrenberg, locate the therapeutic action in the struggle of the analyst to find an authentic way of engaging the patient.

Self psychology also has made important contributions to the bootstrap problem. Whereas Fairbairn understood the adhesiveness underlying psychopathology in terms of ties to bad objects warding off unimaginable object loss and isolation, Kohut understood adhesiveness in terms of the need for selfobjects to ward off the experience of annihilation and disintegration of the self. In my view, Fairbairn's depiction of the untenable loss of all objects and Kohut's depiction of annihilation anxiety are two different ways of describing the same phenomenon.

Whereas Fairbairn was sketchy, Kohut was messianic; he often depicted empathy as if it were generic and easily achieved, a basic posture on the analyst's part that works for all patients. Kohut also seemed to suggest that self-object needs are primed, that is, in the patient all the time and waiting and eager to emerge. This view (like Winnicott's notion of a prefigured "true self") is problematic, because it once again presupposes rather than explains how the analyst finds, differently with each patient, how to be that patient's analyst. The classical model circumvented the bootstrap problem by assuming that interpretations provided a direct channel between the analyst and the patient that bypasses the patient's dynamics. Contemporary Kleinians assume that only interpretations of the patient's relation to interpretations provide a direct channel. What might be called the classical self psychology of Kohut assumes that the analyst's empathic stance provides a direct channel to the patient, bypassing the patient's conflicts and reaching developmental longings poised for growth if only provided the requisite environment.

I am arguing that it is not useful to assume such a direct channel, but rather to understand the interactions between the patient and analyst in terms of the patient's dynamics, that is, as manifestations of old patterns. Meaningful analytic change, in this view, comes not from bypassing old object relations, but from expanding them from the inside out (Bromberg). Recent developments in self psychology more directly address the bootstrap problem in their exploration of the repetitive dimensions of the transference (Lachmann and Beebe), the "dread to repeat" (Ornstein), the inevitability and utility of "empathic failures," and the fundamentally intersubjective nature of the analytic situation (Stolorow).

The point of convergence of these various lines of innovative thinking about therapeutic action, the missing planet of the analytic process, is to be found in the emotional transformation of the relationship with the analyst (Racker, Levenson, Gill, Hoffman, Greenberg). Interpretations fail because the patient experiences them as old and familiar modes of interaction. The reason interpretations work, when they are effective, is because the patient experiences them as something new and different, not encountered before. The effective interpretation is the expression of, and sometimes the vehicle for, something deeper and more significant. The central locus of analytic change is in the analyst's struggle to find a new way to participate, both within his own experience and then with the patient. There is an enormous difference between false empathy, facile and postured, and authentic empathy, struggled toward through miscues, misunderstanding, and deeply personal work on the part of both analyst and patient.

Thus, although I find enormous value in the developmental concepts of writers like Winnicott and Kohut, I think there is a danger in the developmental perspective of assuming new growth where subtle forms of repetition may be occurring. Of course, neither of these two different interpretative approaches can be considered simply right or wrong— they are ways of organizing ambiguous data that can be ordered in many ways. The more relevant question concerns not correctness but the consequences of holding one view or the other. Looking for repetitions, if it is done with sensitivity and tact, has two major advantages.

First, it helps the patient appreciate how deftly old patterns can be resurrected. Since none of us ever completely outgrows such patterns, and relative mental health entails an increased capacity to refind and emerge from them, I think this effort serves the patient well. It conveys to the analysand the sense that authentic living is achieved only through struggle.

Second, an alertness to repetitions shapes the analytic relationship in a way that I think is highly beneficial. It conveys a willingness on the part of the analyst to continually question his or her own participation, an openness to criticism and self-reflection, and a dedication to patients' getting the most possible out of their analysis and, consequently, their life.

Consider a point in the second analysis of a woman named Carla, whose first analysis had come to an anguished stalemate. I want to use this material because it involves a later point in work with a patient whose issues were somewhat similar to George's. I will elaborate my own struggles in the countertransference, because that is where I think a lot of the work was done.

Carla was the daughter of a brilliant, crackpot, would-be inventor who had lived in paranoid isolation, working on what he considered to be groundbreaking innovations. Carla and her siblings were forced to choose between their parents in the years preceding as well as following their divorce, and Carla felt deeply loyal to her father. She felt she was like her father in many ways, and cultivated a deep isolation from her own peers, which served as a sign of her superiority and her internal merger with her father. She was torn between her sense that her father's self-absorbed estimation of his own importance was wildly inflated, and her deep need to believe in her father and her link with him. Very little ever actually happened between Carla and her father, but through her identification and loyalty to him, Carla felt a precious, but very shaky, fantasied sense that she was following in her father's footsteps and that her father was taking care of her.

Central to Carla's resentments against her first analyst was her feeling that she had been kind of snookered into treatment from the very beginning. She had been sent to consult with this man by a friend and really did not know what sort of treatment would be preferable. Following an extended consultation, the analyst informed her that she would be suitable for analysis and offered to see her five days a week for a token fee. (Carla later suspected, of course, that the analyst was a candidate at an institute, and that she had become a training case, although this was never explicitly acknowledged.) In a certain sense, the die was cast from that initial moment, because a central feature of the transference was organized around the idea that the analyst had lured her into their analytic arrangement for his own needs.

The analyst seemed blindly devoted to psychoanalysis as a quasi religion. Carla experienced her own devoted daily attendance as an effort to worship at the analyst/father's altar, even though she had profound doubts about both the analyst and psychoanalysis. In return, she longed to be helped, perhaps rescued, at least talked to. Over the years, she developed an increasingly deeper sense of betrayal, abandonment, and outrage.

Carla initially came to see me for help in understanding what had happened in this treatment that had left her feeling so embittered. After several consultations, I had gotten enough of a sense of the features of the transference I have just recounted that I recommended that she begin a kind of trial analytic treatment with a new analyst, the purpose of which would be partly to explore what happened the first time around. We agreed it would be best for her to work with someone more experienced. This meant higher fees, and, since her income was limited, only one or two sessions per week. I told her that in my experience, working at that frequency was difficult, but often quite constructive. After thinking about it a while, Carla asked if it would be possible to work with me, and we set up an arrangement in which I saw her once a week at a somewhat reduced fee.

Many things happened over the course of the first six months of treatment that I cannot recount here because I will follow only the threads leading to the moment I want to describe. Generally, I felt the work was going quite well. Carla seemed deeply mired in her masochistic, narcissistic identification with her father, but we were working well together and I felt cautiously optimistic. Then she told me she had found out that she actually had an insurance policy that would pay a considerable amount toward her treatment, with a twenty thousand dollar lifetime limit.

Given the retrenchment in third-party payments these days, I regarded this news as roughly equivalent to a report that she had won the lottery. I envisioned expanding her treatment to three or four times a week. I found working with her very absorbing but also frustrating at once a week. This seemed like great news. I restrained my enthusiasm, and she herself wondered whether this meant she might come more often. What did I think? Being well trained, I dodged the question and asked what she thought.

Because so much reciprocal dodging ensued, I don't remember exactly who said what, but the basic outline of what was said went something like this: Being a lot more frugal than I am, she felt that this newly available money needed to be spent carefully. After all, the twenty thousand dollars would only last for several years; then it would be gone. So, she really needed to be sure that this work with me was *the* treatment for her; perhaps she would be able to afford only one such treatment in her lifetime, and she needed to know that this was it. And she had all kinds of doubts. Her life certainly hadn't improved noticeably over the six months. What did I think?

I felt increasingly uncomfortable. At first I thought that I was doing a good job as an analyst by dodging her question and solemnly taking the position that the decision was hers. We needed to explore what she thought. This position did not wear well, though. As we explored her sense that she needed to hear from me, my somewhat righteous analytic conviction that I was not called on to venture an opinion began to feel too easy, a bit irresponsible.

We explored her experience of my position that my opinion was not important. Why wasn't it, she wanted to know? After all, I was an expert to whom she was coming for professional help. I must have an opinion; it must be more informed than hers, or at least of some potential value in helping her make up her mind. My withholding my thoughts from her seemed to her to be deliberately hoarding and sadistic, like her first analyst's laconic style. To ask her to believe that it was really in her best interest seemed like asking her to defer to a principle that seemed to her exceedingly abstract and dubious and probably self-serving on my part. The more we explored her experience of my abstention, the more infeasible it seemed to be.

Well, I thought further, what do I really think? I could imagine going either of two ways.

One line of association about the question of whether this was the best treatment for her led to the thought: "Beats the hell out of me." Most of the people I've worked with have gotten a great deal out of the work and feel it was worth it, but not all. Would it work for her? I really didn't know. She would have to decide one way or the other and take her chances: "You pay your money and you take your choice." But that didn't feel right. It felt too facile. Did I really feel so casual about this decision? No. Maybe I should tell her to go ahead, and use the money for our analytic work. That was certainly what I would do. She was in serious danger of living an enormously compromised life. If our work took, it could make a great difference in the quality of her life, much more of a difference than having the money in reserve. She should go ahead, and I should tell her so.

But that didn't feel very comfortable either. For one thing, I tend to spend money somewhat impulsively. The next twenty thousand dollars I stumble across will surely pay for the tennis court I've been fantasizing about. Perhaps Carla's cautiousness was valid, particularly for her. Was I so sure our work would help her? How much was that belief an extension of my narcissism? Easy for me to say. Perhaps my very passion for the work was itself dangerous to her.

Further, I could imagine my clear stand on the desirability of analysis for her leading us into precisely the same sort of transference–countertransference impasse that destroyed her first analysis. Would I need to keep convincing her that the work was going well? Would I need increasingly to see it that way myself? The more confident I was that this would be good for her, the more she might need to defeat me by destroying the analysis. It began to feel like the alternatives were either to bail out on her, or to take the role of a snake-oil salesman, to sell a product with a greater certainty than I in fact had.

I began to feel suffocated, a feeling I have come to regard as an invariable sign that something important is happening. This situation is set up so that there is no way for me to be my idea of an analyst. If I abstain, she experiences it as an abandonment. If I encourage her, she experiences it as a seduction and, there *is* something in the way our interaction develops that draws me into wanting to make claims and implied promises I have no business making. We seemed to be at an impasse.

I have been struck by the frequency with which the term "impasse" has been used in the recent literature, generally with some prescribed route out. As I suggested above, the Kleinians (Joseph, Rosenfeld) regard interpretation of the patient's relationship to the interpretation as the solution. Some interpersonalists (Cooper and Witenberg) recommend detailed inquiry into the patient's history. Other interpersonalists (Ehrenberg) regard the self-disclosure of countertransferential feelings as the key. Self psychologists favor the reestablishment of an empathic stance. When things get difficult, everyone tends to rely on what they do best.

I have not discovered any general solution to situations like these; in fact, I don't believe there are any general solutions, for reasons I will explain in a moment. But one reaction to an impasse that I have sometimes found helpful is an outburst. I do not mean a countertransferential temper tantrum or retaliatory attack. I mean a reaction that conveys a sense that I feel somehow trapped and constrained, that I feel the analysand and I are both trapped and constrained, and that I want to burst out of the confines of options that all seem unacceptable to me.

So, in this situation, I told Carla about my sense of being stymied: I agreed with her that it did not seem fair to not say what I thought, but I could only think of two ways to respond, and neither seemed quite right. To say that I really didn't know if our work would be right for her left out my good feelings about what we had been doing and my sense of its possibilities. Yet, for me to say that she ought to simply go ahead seemed to imply a certainty and a promise that I couldn't make, a promise that I felt quite sure she would feel the need to defeat and feel betrayed by. As we spoke of these various options, I told her what I thought I would be asking myself if I were her: Did she feel the things we were talking about were at the center of what mattered to her in her life? Did she feel we were grappling with them in a way that seemed meaningful? What seemed to her to be a reasonable trial period for our efforts to bear fruit? And so on. The treatment went on, and what seemed important was that we had found a way to work together that allowed me to function in good faith as my idea of an analyst and allowed her to begin to conceive of a way of getting something important from me that did not require a self-betraying devotion.

The way constructive analyses overcome the bootstrap problem is that the analysand and analyst struggle together to find a different kind of emotional connection. There is no general solution or technique, because each resolution, by its very nature, must be custom designed. If the patient feels the analyst is applying a technique or displaying a generic attitude or stance, it cannot possibly work.

Sometimes making interpretations works analytically, not simply because of the content of the interpretation but because the patient experiences the interpreting analyst as alive, as caring, as providing fresh ways of thinking about things, as grappling deeply with what is bothering him or her. Sometimes refraining from interpreting works analytically, because the patient experiences the quiet analyst as alive, as caring, as providing fresh ways to be together that don't demand what may have come to feel like the inescapable corruptions of language. Sometimes patience is required, sustained involvement over time, as evidence of a different kind of relationship than past abandonments. Sometimes impatience is required, an exasperation that conveys a sense that the analyst can envision something better than the patient's perseverative patterns and cares enough not to take the easy way out and passively go along. What I am suggesting is that the central feature of the therapeutic action of psychoanalysis is the emergence of something new from something old. It can't be there in the beginning, because you have to find yourself in the old to create the proper context for the emergence of something new. It can't be in the application of a standard technique or posture, because then it wouldn't really *be* something new and would never strike the analysand that way.

Let us imagine what happened "over the years" with the patient discussed by Grossman and Stewart (1976). It can't be simply that the interpretations themselves gradually sunk in. There must have been something in the analyst's involvement over time, trying over and over, refusing to give up, declining again and again the easy role as sadistic humiliator that the patient granted him, which established him as offering a different sort of relationship than the patient had encountered previously.

Coming to terms finally with the inadequacy of the classical model of therapeutic action frees analysts to ask the most relevant questions, questions that Grossman and Stewart did not think to explore. The analyst had begun to feel that the analysis threatened to become interminable. That's interesting to me. Did he share that fear explicitly with the patient? Did the analyst know that the problems with the first analysis had reappeared in the second? What did the patient sense of the analyst's fears and frustrations? What was her sense of why he kept on trying to make something new happen when she kept organizing everything that happened in old terms?

There is no general solution or technique. At the heart of the work is the lived experience of constraint, discovering oneself in the confines of the patient's dynamics, which always reverberate with complementary features of the analyst's dynamics (Racker). Then analyst and analysand work together to find a way out. It can't be easy, for long, because then one has skipped over the most important part. Generally speaking, the analyst has to go first, to break out into a different emotional state, to want more, and then to find a way to get the patient interested. It is only when that new emotional presence appears that interpretations become truly new, truly analytic events rather than disguised repetitions.

Imagine one of Freud's patients returning many decades later, seeking further analysis. Would the procedure the patient was familiar with work now? Could the patient simply free associate, awaiting interpretations as a source of enlightenment? I think not. Today's analyst would want to know a great deal more. What did the patient do with the old interpretations? What was the fate of the analyst as internal object? What were they hoping to gain by returning? Why return to this analyst at this time? What were they leaving behind? The patient's relationship to the analysis would not be taken for granted in the way it was then. Analytic knowledge would be regarded not as impersonal truth but as an understanding always embedded in a relational context. Meaning would not be assumed but would have to be invented anew.

In many ways, Freud's patients lived in a simpler world than ours, a world in which authentic personal meaning did not have to be so individually shaped, so hard won. We ask more of our patients now, and, necessarily, have to ask more of ourselves.

REFERENCES

Fairbairn, W. R. D. (1952), *An Object Relations Theory of the Personality.* New York: Basic Books.
Greenson, R. (1967), *The Technique and Practice of Psychoanalysis.* New York: International Universities Press.
Grossman, W. & Stewart, W. (1976), Penis envy: From childhood wish to developmental metaphor. *J. Amer. Psychoanal. Assn.* (Supplement), 24:193–212.
Kernberg, O. F. (1992), *Aggression in Personality Disorders and Perversions.* New Haven, CT: Yale University Press.
Laplanche, J. & Pontalis, J.-B. (1973), *The Language of Psychoanalysis.* London: Karnac.
Mitchell, S. (1993), *Hope and Dread in Psychoanalysis.* New York: Basic Books.
Pine, F. (1993), A contribution to the analysis of the psychoanalytic process. *Psychoanal. Quart., A2*:185–205.

11

The Therapeutic Action of Play in the Curative Process

James M. Herzog

The poem of the mind in the act of finding
What will suffice. It has not always had
To find: the scene was set; it repeated what
Was in the script.
                          Then the theatre was changed
To something else. Its past was a souvenir.
It has to be living, to learn the speech of the place.
It has to face the men of the time and to meet
The women of the time. It has to think about war
And it has to find what will suffice. It has
To construct a new stage. It has to be on that stage
And, like an insatiable actor, slowly and
With meditation, speak words that in the ear,
In the delicatest ear of the mind, repeat,
Exactly, that which it wants to hear, at the sound
Of which, an invisible audience listens,
Not to the play, but to itself, expressed
In an emotion as of two people, as of two
Emotions becoming one. The actor is
A metaphysician in the dark, twanging
An instrument, twanging a wiry string that gives
Sounds passing through sudden rightnesses, wholly
Containing the mind, below which it cannot descend,
Beyond which it has no will to rise.
                                              It must
Be the finding of a satisfaction, and may
Be of a man skating, a woman dancing, a woman,
Combing. The poem of the act of the mind.
                          —Wallace Stevens (1982)
                          ''Of Modern Poetry''

I t is difficult to date the onset of development; it is impossible to specify the beginning of meaning. This chapter will address issues of representation, refiguration, mimesis, and aporia as these are encountered developmentally, and therapeutically, within the analytic *Spielraum*. That part of the analytic experience which involves reiteration has been extensively described; my focus shall be that part of the analytic experience which allows for new play, and the role of this component in intrapsychic change. The analyst's reality as well as those reality factors that shaped the analysand's preferred play mode and interactive repertoire will be seen to exert crucial influences.

I wish to posit an openness in the representational world, on the intrapsychic stage, to new experiences and subsequent refigurations which admits of therapeutic feasibility. In so doing, I propose that intrapsychic change occurs when such openness can be realized, potentiated, or even created in the therapeutic encounter. Such openness to mimetic mobility and new representation allows for ameliorative refigurations of the object relations inscape and thus for new modes of intrapsychic and interactive play. Such openness is a function of libidinal cathexis, object relationship, and the nature of the self–selfobject configuration. All of these simultaneous processes are contained in the nature of the love relationship between caregiver and child, the ways in which aggressive eruptions and disruptions are managed intrapsychically and interpersonally, concurrent relationships (for both caregiver and child), and evolving and repeating patterns of meaning. The above obtains in both development and treatment. The relationship between that which has occurred in development and individuals' subsequent capacity to utilize treatment differentiates a number of "schools" in psychoanalysis. This issue is most acute when analysis is conceptualized as primarily or exclusively dealing with replay; it is "complexified" by the "widening scope" perspective, self psychology, the question of "critical periods" versus sensitive periods in development, and conflicting definitions of what constitutes analysis or the analytic stance. Always, the relationship of replay to new play and to interplay occupies a central position conceptually and in regard to one's theoretical orientation and personal conviction.

By specifying conditions that tend toward mimetic occlusion (a lack of openness to refiguration), I wish to highlight their opposites, those conditions that can be utilized in the service of refiguring the object relations inscape. These conditions, both for stasis and dynamism, are a regular feature of development as well as of the therapeutic encounter. They figure prominently in transferential experience of both varieties; that which repeats earlier experience and pain and that which represents hunger for and openness to a developmentally necessary nutriment. I shall try to focus on healing as it occurs in the analytic encounter as a function of the resumption of hitherto derailed development, noting that even the most optimal endowment requires a reciprocating and attuned surround. This developmental principle, in turn, admitting as it does of varieties of attunement and reciprocity, lays the groundwork for therapeutic opportunity and, conversely, for unwanted mimetic occlusion.

I wish to advance the hypothesis that therapeutic dysjunctions (and developmental discontinuities) constitute both repetitions (e.g., transference as it is classically understood) and the opportunity for new experience (the second form of transference and the opportunity for mimetic refiguration) and as such are *the* critical moments in many an interventional dialogue. In what I have just posited, I wish to stress that I am speaking of both players in the analytic *Spielraum,* analyst as well as analysand, and of all three players in the developmental trialogue, child, mother, and father.

The self develops as a self-seeking entity. Process and being are in a sense the same. This interactive contingency means that the caregivers must have available selves with which the emerging self of the child interacts in vitalizing and development-maintaining ways. In both development and analysis such a meeting, an I–Thou encounter, can occur; something can happen. In both settings, tragically or seemingly inevitably, the obverse can and does occur. Developmentally this often results in deformation or at least in restitutive alteration of the self; in treatment such a nonmeeting often leads to clarification of previous derailment but may also feature a loss of hope and or the repetition of the very sort of mimetic occlusion that is conceptualized to reside at the core of the "pathology." Interpretation, itself, then may constitute an enactment, a painful repetition; understanding may seem ironic rather than growth enabling.

What is this phenomenon that I am calling "something is happening"? What does it look like developmentally and therapeutically? What are the essential conditions for its occurrence and what, if any, are the safeguards against its abuse? When does it not occur and then, in its absence, what transpires? I shall try to address these issues by presenting analytic experience as it has evolved in my work. Of necessity, these encounters will be of two (as in the Stevens poem), the analysand and the analyst, the you and the me. To enhance explicative clarity, I shall present such a happening from the analysis of a child. The opportunities for what Ricoeur, after Wittgenstein, has labeled *erlkaren und verstehen* declare themselves; the occurrence of what Simone Weil labeled *l'enracinement* is presented.

Etta is now 11 years old. She has been in analysis with me for three years. Her divorcing parents sought a referral from their pediatrician, who pronounced them "the most difficult caregivers I have ever encountered." Etta's parents are both nonproductive artists; Etta, in a sense, is their only creation. Earlier, they "shared" an analyst. Following this disaster, they became ever more furious with each other. They are now estranged, although occupying adjoining primary and vacation residences "for the sake of Etta." Neither works and each is enmeshed with the daughter. The mother and Etta share a bed; the father and Etta exchange flirtatious explorations that are grossly overstimulating. The father has accepted a referral to an analytic colleague. He often wonders if Etta should not see her also and is troubled by recurrent concerns about a sexual relationship between his daughter and me. The mother refuses to see anyone, although she is quite interested in the father's analyst and me. She states that she cannot afford treatment, which does not seem to be primarily a financial statement.

I meet with both parents approximately every three months to assess their concerns and to try and respond to their queries. Most of these meetings end up focusing on their battle and I have referred the couple to yet another analyst, who is available to discuss "co-parenting" issues with them. In addition, there are relatively frequent telephone conversations with the father when his agitation about either his daughter or her analyst reaches a point where it requires immediate reality testing. His analyst fully supports this contact with me. Etta and I meet four times a week.

I wish to describe my response to both Etta and her parents. You will hear a combination of my transferences, impressions, and irritations, as well as the limits on my availability. Etta is beleaguered and imperious. She is physically quite attractive—tall, blonde, and blue-eyed. Her play favors the mode that I have called "interactive enactment." I have previously posited that this mode, representing a regressive "shift to the left" in the ego function of play is often encountered posttraumatically (Herzog, 1992). She demands that the analyst do certain things. These vary according to the scenario of the day or week, but this feature is quite persistent. She is constantly preoccupied with self-regulation, which she delegates to me. The quality of this delegation is usually unpleasant; I feel put upon rather than as if I am a partner in a developmental dialogue designed to build her self-regulating inner structure. Stated somewhat differently, the feel of this interaction is of a transferential repetition rather than of a developmentally nutritive request. Yet, I cannot easily determine whether the repetition is of passive or active experience; what is being repeated is unclear, why it is being repeated in actual interaction with me is, likewise, not understood by me (*erklaren und verstehen*).

Concomitantly, her libido and aggression are much in evidence. Displaced play, when it occurs, features iterative clashes that are highly eroticized and often culminate in severe spankings. Considerable affect, mostly of excitement, accompanies this kind of play. Although usually assigned a role at such times, I feel rather peripheral, even though the scenario features seemingly intense action. Despite my inherent interest in both domestic loving and hurting, in intercourse and in spanking, I occasionally drift off during these interludes. This is quite noteworthy for me. After considerable self-investigation, I have tentatively concluded that it is because I am not really a part of this play. It is occurring in my presence, but, in a sense, without me. I could, perhaps, force my way into it; but, this does not feel to me as though it would make analytic sense.

I feel that I need to be alert and attentive at all times. Not only will Etta notice my inattentiveness, for which I am rebuked, but she is quite likely to take a swipe at me if I am not "on guard." I am very alert during our "interactive enactments," less so when the play is displaced. I regard this phenomenon with great interest as the displaced material is inherently and in terms of my own psychology much more interesting than the interactive enactment. I consider that I may be "checking out" defensively, but this does not feel right. It seems more likely to me that the interactive enactment is the scene of the action. At the moment, this mode and the material in displacement are divergent rather than convergent. My attunement and nonattunement are informative and related to the nature of the self–self dialogue that is being conducted.

The parents elicit strong feelings in me as well. The mother's anger is never far from the surface and her dissatisfaction with the course of the analysis is quite clear. She does not want Etta to leave her bed and resents my counsel that this constitutes a goal. I rarely feel that she and I are on the same wavelength but appreciate her contention that she must protect Etta from her father's overwhelming intrusiveness. The father is a flamboyant and unusual man. He seems to use almost no repression and expresses interested astonishment in observations such as "Even though Etta says she would like to examine your penis, it might be prudent to think about the meaning of her request before acceding to it." My response to the father is often that I cannot quite believe his naivete, or at least that I do not fully understand his thought processes. He is always rather polite to me, even when voicing his concerns about my morality. In nontechnical language, I find the father to be bumbling and inappropriate, usually responsive to suggestion, and not frightening. Etta's mother seems more frightening; she is misguided in her methods but understandable in her cognitive design. I feel that I have compassion for Etta in her daily interactive struggle, for the complexities, cacaphony, and impingement of her *Umwelt,* and that she and I have established, albeit it with difficulty, an analytic *Spielraum* in which the contours of her inner world can be divined and, perhaps, addressed. I am both closer to and at a greater remove from her than I am with many a patient. I like her, wish to be available, feel put off, do not fully understand the relationship of the play modes she utilizes, and feel that there is more to come. This seems crucially important. I feel neither demoralized nor as though the pace of our work has become asymptotic. Furthermore, Etta seems still to be productively at work.

I should now like to describe a therapeutic dysjunction, its unfolding and resolution, and the impact of these events on both analyst and analysand. I believe it is a "something is happening" encounter, and I hope it will suggest what is involved in aporia, mimetic openness, and subsequent intrapsychic refiguration.

Etta has been playing out a somewhat complicated scenario in which she and I are detectives. We are investigating the murder of a woman in a "random act of violence." The murder has been particularly gory, involving a beheading. Etta is insistent that this was accidental. The murderer only intended to kill the woman, not remove her head. I am assigned the role of co-investigator, but clearly expected to be a bumbling assistant. I suspect that I am being cast as the father and that the beheaded woman is the mother. In the play, we continually are looking for clues. Etta suggests that if there were children of the deceased, they might have something to offer. I am dispatched to consult the "register of children of murdered mothers." (There is an interesting exchange as I profess ignorance of the register and Etta harangues me for my stupidity. I immediately note to myself that I feel very much involved, alert, interested, and totally there.) This imaginary computer document does indeed prove valuable. There is a special section of it devoted to be-headed mothers and this allows us to construct most of the details of the victim's life and even of the events surrounding her death. We definitely seem to be on to something. Often at such moments in the past and now again, the syntactical play is interrupted by Etta's suggestion that we play a game of cards called "Spit." I have repeatedly observed this "interrup-tion of the action" aloud, wondering why it occurs. Etta scoffs and reprimands me for "playing analyst." This transition from displacement to interactive enactment is, of course, very familiar. Usually I experience it as *now the action is really beginning.* I wish that the action were in displacement. Today, however, the action is in displacement. We are both really there, or at least, I, the analyst, am really there. I note that I am really there in both play modes and that I wish that the displaced play had not been interrupted.

We play Spit. As often happens in the game, Etta is dissatisfied with the outcome and grabs the cards out of my hand and pushes me aside with considerable force as I try to win by being the first to put my remaining cards down on one of the piles. On this occasion, I not only protest but also remind Etta that we have agreed she will not do this. I explain to her that I injured my shoulder in another activity and that her assault has been quite painful. Etta expresses surprise and then apologizes. She promises me that it will not happen again. When I do not seem totally mollified, she raises the ante. She will give me her vacation home in Tuscany if I will resume the game. Moreover, she will give me the Ferrari, too, if she doesn't keep her promise and even inadvertently strikes me again. The hour ends on this note. Etta appears convinced that we will resume tomorrow. In fact, we leave the cards out, in the disarray that resulted from our interaction. I feel engaged, looking forward to the next hour and feeling as though we are in the middle of something important.

The next day, the play begins with a return to the murder. We learn more about the register of children of murdered mothers. There is a special section in the register, very small, of mothers murdered by fathers. By far the largest volume of the register is occupied by mothers murdered by their own mothers. This section is entitled *Killing in the Family: Children and Mothers*. I note the ambiguous title and wonder aloud how this is connected to the fact that most mothers are killed by their mothers. Etta screams at me to be quiet. "We are on a case," she says. My questions get in the way rather than forwarding our investigation. "Don't you know, stupid, that sometimes mothers and children look the same?" she screams. "Don't you have a brain in your head? Have I beheaded you?" As the play progresses, we try to learn whether the child of the beheaded mother had a father. "What is a father?" Etta has this imaginary child say. "I've never heard of that, of a father."

I think that the play is moving in a very interesting direction. I dimly comprehend that both play modes now reflect the same question: "What is a father, where is he?" At that precise moment, Etta turns to the cards and announces that we are going to play Spit. I wonder aloud about the child's question: "What is a father?" "Never mind that, come here and play," Etta responds. I comply and moments later there is a repeat of the "assault" of the previous day. I remind Etta of our agreement. She is annoyed but remembers. Several more promises are made. I say that I can see that she wants to continue to play Spit very much, but that I am unwilling to play. I shall not play Spit again. "Forever?" Etta asks in great agitation. "Not for awhile," I respond. Etta begins to cry. She is very shaken. The hour ends with Etta in evident distress but very engaged in the analytic process. I feel similarly engaged, no longer put off or put out. The intensity of my feeling that I am being asked to be a part of critical action, action that I need and want to be part of, is very striking.

The next day, we resume the play. We spend the entire hour reconstructing events in the life of the murdered mother's child. It turns out that she is a girl who had been forced to hear her mother's dreams every night in bed and could not stand anymore what was in her mother's head. She did not really wish to kill her mother but rather just to "dedream and demouth" her, behead her. Furthermore, Etta has rethought the paternal absence in the evolving story. The child reveals that she knew what a father was all along. She states that a father is a person who says yes by saying no, who says "come in" by saying "stay out." Etta does not suggest that we play Spit. She gazes toward the cards a few times and then resumes the play. For the next several weeks, we continue with this scenario. Deeper and deeper levels emerge. I notice that my role has changed. I am not disparaged as frequently. When I ask a question about motivation or meaning, it seems to be heard and is sometimes even responded to. Etta notes that it is easier to come to her analytic hour than it used to be. Her father tells me that his fears about what is going on between his daughter and me have ebbed. Furthermore, he shares that Etta has asked that he read her bedtime story downstairs before she changes into her bedclothes, rather than when she is already in bed as had been their practice. He is "mystified" by this request but interested in my counsel. I support his "interpretation" that Etta, like Virginia Woolf, may need a room of her own. Etta's mother reports that my waiting room is chilly and that the lighting seems to have deteriorated. It is no longer comfortable for her to read in so she will drop Etta off and do her grocery shopping during the analytic hours. Etta does not object to this change. I note that I now think I understand what has transpired and that the changes in each parent or for each parent seem good to me. Has something happened?

I would like to suggest that something has indeed happened. For both analyst and analysand, a shift has occurred. Feeling and doing have conjoined on both the level of displaced play and that of interactive enactment. The father has been found in the saying of no; the repetition compulsion has been confronted, aporia introduced, and the possibility for refiguration advanced.

Etta's analysis featured from its inception the complexities of multiple personae and multiple transferential dramas. This is often the case in child analysis and perhaps, also, in the analysis of adults. In both situations, adult and child work, the analyst needs to consider the ways in which content, interaction, and the analytic relationship reveal parallel, convergent, or divergent processes. We analysts often comment on the reality for the child of his or her relationship in the present with parents or others and of the analyst's capacity or propensity to be a real object and to have a transferential relationship with the significant others in the patient's life. We are, perhaps, less aware of similar processes with our adult analysands, particularly if we or they exclude their "nonneurotic" issues and self constituents from the analytic playroom.

It is a reality for our child analysands that life, average expectable and otherwise, prohibits them from excluding the "nonneurotic." It is a privilege for the child analyst to have such experience and a profound influence on his or her openness to such work with older, that is, adult, analysands.

I propose that the "something that has happened" involves the accessibility of Etta's inner world to the influence of the analytic encounter and to the analyst. Conversely, the analyst's availability is neither static nor to be taken as a given. For "something to happen," there must be an overlap between availabilities, the analysand's representational world must be enterable to be alterable; the analyst must be able to participate in this process. It is in the service of explicating this later condition that I have tried to share what was going on within me while I was with Etta. It goes without saying that biographical and conflictual issues within the analyst, hopefully subjected to analytic illumination, are at constant play as a factor in determining his or her availability. Here, however, I try to highlight those emanating from the analysand.

There had been many previous times when I had felt the need to prohibit Etta from doing something while in the direct interaction with her. Most of these occurred when I felt uncomfortable with what she was doing to me and concerned about her incapacity to modulate her own impulses. This time, it seemed different. I needed to protect my shoulder, but I sensed as well a self–self encounter that was fueled by both the displaced scenario, a reflection of Etta's unconscious fantasy life and mounting drive pressure, which could not be contained, and some developmental need for help. Etta could not stop the combined oral, anal, and genital compulsion for us to "spit and tussle" without the presence of a paternal introject that said "yes" to her separateness and competence (including the competence to elaborate the scenario in displacement) by saying "no" to her disregard for the well-being of the other. Beheading and heading (that is, structure building intrapsychically) were condensed in the question of a register—what will register and how? The Winnicottian notion of the "use of the object" is here revealed simultaneously in the two play modes. Disguised by reversal and condensation in displacement, it is enacted and verbalized more directly in the interaction. Understood, at last, by the analyst who could now fully attend. This last imperative condition, I would argue, is an outgrowth of the first two rather than an independent event reflecting the vagaries of the analyst's intrapsychic existence.

It felt to me as though a new attachment was occurring between us. Etta regarded me differently, with a new "essentiality"; with a kind of awe, I felt this shift. I was being asked to be a "no" sayer—in Chasseguet-Smirgel's terms, to stand for reality as a paternal principle in order to effect a further differentiation of self and other in the object relations world, on the representational stage (in this case between Etta and her mother). I felt both a pull toward returning to the displaced play, which seemed increasingly important, *and* a rising sense of both indignation and conviction about limiting the assault on me and about Etta's incapacity to do this on her own. I want to emphasize that this sense of "rightness" about the intervention, including my saying specifically that we would not play Spit again for quite awhile, felt loving to me. I also felt somewhat stern, a self state that I had not previously experienced with Etta. It is almost as if I were thinking to myself, which I was not: This is not good for Etta and therefore I shall prohibit it, no matter what. I say that I was not thinking this and that is true, but I was feeling it—strongly. This feeling was a component of an even stronger feeling that we were really at work. This was a core issue for Etta and the play modes had converged because she and I were now in a position to "get it, work with it, and do something about it." In this context, my stern feeling was particularly noteworthy. I do not usually feel stern, with or without Etta. Now, it felt not only right but also part of a larger picture. I would label my feeling as "loving and developmentally nutritive sternness." It is important to note that I would not call this a "corrective emotional experience," after Alexander. This feeling was not contrived. It was my experience, our experience in the play.

Such a strong feeling on the part of the analyst is often, perhaps always, an occasion for self-analysis, consultation, or, at the least, a deep breath. We analysts are accustomed to thinking about this sort of enactment with concern if not derision. It is also, however, one way in which "something happens," perhaps a critical way. The convergence of material in displacement and in interactive enactment signals a readiness for mimetic mobility, for a self-seeking-another-self encounter to occur.

The analysand's representational world is now open. If there is room on the representational stage (or template), then new internalization can occur. The interaction between analyst and analysand will or may be represented. The analyst must be affectively present, involved, and willing. His or her feeling state is of critical importance here. Often the analyst cannot or will not let himself or herself be so used. The analyst does not love the analysand and does not understand the meaning of the converged play modes, displacement and enactment; the match is not good. I have often wondered if the representational world can only be entered if the match between analyst and analysand is "good enough." Is there a protective shield available to the inscape so that it is sealed against intrusion unless the overlap is appropriate? Is the result of a mismatch simply a stalemate in the analysis, with no remodeling but also no injury occurring—or do catastrophes of enormous significance regularly occur when mimetic openness is achieved in the absence of facilitating overlap? Certainly, in actual development we analysts are familiar with a broad range of ways in which goodness of fit, presence of overlap, and shifting aliquots of love and hatred are managed and metabolized within the infant–caregiver dyad and triad. Multiple pathways of self-development; defensive, adaptive, and restitutive constriction; sequestration and elaboration are clinically encountered and in a certain sense constitute the diagnostic nosology of self-development and disorder.

In *Beyond the Pleasure Principle* (1920), Freud pondered the capacity of the mental apparatus to both record and remain continuously responsive to new experience. This led to his famous statement "Consciousness arises instead of a memory trace." In the spirit of the earlier Freud of *Project for a Scientific Psychology* (1895), as well as the later theoretician, I would now like to suggest an extension of this thought. Often in relational dialogue, the external and the interactive are primarily recapitulated in terms of memory and representation. It is an example from the terminology of our age of CD-ROM, read-only memory. The role of the repetition compulsion in this arrangement is particularly germane, and the concept of transference fully applicable. It is, however, possible in intimate relationships to achieve circumstances in which the reprogramming mode is utilizable. Such openness to mimetic mobility necessitates a series of conditions that developmentally might be labeled "primary maternal preoccupation" (Winnicott), love as it is felt from analyst to analysand and vice-versa), overlap of agendae with a trusted other, an asymmetry in the relationship so that the needs of one party are placed in conspicuous prominence while the needs of the other are not disregarded (S. Cooper, personal communication, 1992).

In the analytic playroom, the reprogramming mode can be activated. Often such an opportunity is signaled by the convergence of the displacement and the interactive enactment modes. The openness of the analysand must be matched by the availability of the analyst. The analyst must feel, speak, and play. The interaction is then represented. Once admitted to the relational inscape, the effect of the representation is determined at least in part by what else is there, by the company it keeps. With children, development is our ally, and we analysts are temporally closer to the last "open period" of programming, of representational ground laying. It often seems that new representations, specifically of the analyst–analysand dialogue, are more easily and expectably introduced into a "less cluttered" space. With older analysands, the repetitions and iterations may be, usually are considerably more formidable—but the opportunity still exists, and with this opportunity a reemergence of hope, a respite from despair.

To return to the hypothetical, it seems likely that the representational world—and its attendant affective history and repertoire—is encoded in the genome as a result of the analysand's initial endowment and subsequent transactional experience (Herzog, 1991). The opening and reopening of the programming mode must, therefore, mean the establishing of conditions in which and by which the genome can be altered. Processes such as phosphorylation, secondary messenger induction, protein activation, and ultimately an alteration in base pair sequence in messenger RNA must occur. This certainly happens in drug intervention, and it must also happen in mimetic remodeling as it occurs in self–self conversation in the analytic process. To restate this in a perhaps outrageous paraphrase of Freud: Memory and perception are different and the same depending on the operational mode selected. Consciousness and structural recording and alteration likewise can be differentiatable or superimposed, depending on the way in which the intimate dialogue is operating.

Analysis offers the chance for new play as well as replay. The ego's capacity for play—even when deformed, as in the case of trauma (Herzog, 1992)—features the capacity for recovery in the presence of certain delineable kinds of interplay. Something happens when a particular form or particular forms of overlap occur. Analysand and analyst together create a new poem (see chapter epigraph). Aporia replaces certainty. The repetition compulsion is challenged. Mimetic openness is possible and new representations are facilitated. A self seeking an encounter with another self finds someone home. There is an encounter: the representational door reopens and intrasychic change is possible.

I'm five. The petals of my timeless play
can unfurl while Mother hoes out other gardens.
The next-door child and I, alone with my toys,
confine to the dining room our discreet noise.
From the doorway: *"Betty, come here!"* The uprooted flower
falls dead with no warning. What had my friend done,
rolled a dime-store car over the tabletop,
stood on a chair to wave the little dust mop?
I will never know. She is tethered to Mother's hand
and Mother's voice begins the long scolding.
I start a soldier's march around and around
the table, stomping each foot to stomp out her sound.
Faster around I stomp until it is over,
Betty is gone and Mother takes hold of me.
"What's the *matter* with you? Why is your face so red?
Why, you're *crying,* your whole face is dripping wet!
Well, if that isn't silly I'd like to know what is!
I wasn't scolding *you,* I was scolding *Betty."*
She laughs. "Go wash your face." The room blears.
My hand wipes and finds all the unfelt tears.

Soon it is supper time. In the kitchen they feed
and talk, while I, invisible as I was
in high-chair days, silently sit on Sears,
wearing the weight of my big and bigger ears.
"Well, you'll never guess what your crazy kid did today—
if that wasn't the limit!" The story swells
into ache in my stomach, then Dad's laughter and hers
slice and tear like knives and forks and a worse
hurt is opening in my middle; in familiar
smells and muddle of voices, mashed potatoes,
dimming light, hamburger, thick creamed corn,
the milk-white chill, a self is being born.

And is swept away through seething clots of minnow
in the nearly hidden creek that weeps through the meadow,
smeared with mud from its suckling roots of willow,
to tributary, to river, deep and slow,
whose soblike surges quietly lift her and carry
her unjudged freight clear to the mourning sea.
And there they are, all of the heavy others
(even Mother and Father), the foundering, floating, or sinking
human herd, whose arm strokes, frail, awry,
frantic, hold up their heads to inhale the sky,
which gilds the tongues of water or soothes them to stillness
with white silk covers strewn with onyx and pearl.

She is with them, inept dog-paddler that she is.
The heavens whirl and drift their weightless riches
through streaky splendors of joy, or bare unending
lodes of blazing or ice-blue clarity.
With them all, she is scraped by crusted rock,
wrenched by tides untrue to heart or to clock,
fighting the undertow to shapelessness
in smothering deeps, to what is insufferable.
If those she can reach go under she cannot save them—
how could she save them? Omnipotent dark has seized them.
She can only sink with each one as far as light
can enter, meeting drowning eyes and flesh still spangled
with tiny gems from above (a sign of the rare
her watered eyes never need), pointing to where,
up, in the passionate strain, lives everything fair
before she flails back to the loved, the illumined air.

> —Mona Van Duyn (1993)
> "The Delivery"

REFERENCES

Freud, S. (1895), Project for a scientific psychology. *Standard Edition,* 1:295–397. London: Hogarth Press, 1966.

—— (1920), Beyond the pleasure principle. *Standard Edition,* 18:7–64. London: Hogarth Press, 1955.

Herzog, J. M. (1982), On father hunger: The father's role in the modulation of aggressive drive and fantasy. In: *Father and Child,* ed. S. H. Cath, A. K. Gurwitt & J. M. Ross. Boston: Little, Brown, pp. 301–315.

—— (1984), Fathers and young children: Fathering daughters and fathering sons. In: *Frontiers of Infant Psychiatry, Vol. 2,* ed. J. D. Call, E. Galenson & R. L. Tyson. New York: Basic Books, pp. 335–343.

—— (1991), Temperament and transaction: Constitutional, maturational and experiential components in character formation. *Bull. Anna Freud Centre,* 14:184–197.

—— (1993), Play modes in child analysis. In: *The Many Meanings of Play in Child Analysis.* New Haven, CT: Yale University Press, pp. 252–266.

—— & Ross, J. M. (1985), The sins of the fathers: Notes on fathers, aggression, and pathogenesis. In: *Paternal Influences in Health and Disease,* ed. E. J. Anthony & G. H. Pollack. Boston: Little, Brown, pp. 477–511.

Sandler, J. (1960), The background of safety. *Internat. J. Psychoanal.,* 41:352–356.

Stevens, W. (1982), *The Collected Poems of Wallace Stevens.* New York: Vintage Books, pp. 239–240.

Van Duyn, M. (1993), *Firefall: Poems by Mona Van Duyn.* New York: Knopf, pp. 79–80.

Weil, A. P. (1985), Thoughts about early pathology. *J. Amer. Psychoanal.* Assn., 33:335–352.

Winnicott, D. W. (1968), Communication between infant and mother, mother and infant, compared and contrasted. In: *What Is Psychoanalysis?* London: Balliere, Tindall and Cassell, pp. 1–30.

—— (1974), Fear of breakdown. *Internat. Rev. Psychoanal.,* 1:103–107.

12

Process with Involvement

The Interpretation of Affect

Paul L. Russell

T here are a number of amusing stories, which make the rounds, of people awakening in the morning from cosmic, revelatory dreams in which the meaning of life has been revealed to the dreamer. The dreamer wakes, dimly remembering the dream, dimly remembering having woken in the night just barely enough to jot the revelation down. In the punch line the dreamer reaches over the next morning and reads the scribbled message.

I had my own revelatory dream, although I don't have the scribbled note to corroborate it, let alone anything that sheds light on it. I have only a computer notation that says that on May 18, 1987, I dreamt that "structure is the passage of process with involvement."

I don't think that I had then the foggiest notion what it meant, although something made me enter it in my computer. I must have thought it meant something or other, and that maybe I would be able to make more sense of it later on. More recently, I found myself thinking that the most important, and the most difficult, part of therapy is the *involvement* that the process requires. I vaguely remembered the computer note, retrieved it, and was disappointed that there was nothing more. Nonetheless, that brief statement felt correct, as though it knew something. This chapter consists, for the most part, of belated associations to my dream, and an attempt to say what it is that the dream may have been inviting me to know.

The key word seems to be "involvement." For therapy to work, the therapist must be involved. Whatever therapy is, it is not something that can be done alone; but a lot hangs on the nature of the involvement. The word has connotations that begin to wander quite a distance away from the therapeutic. I could, at this point, scuttle "involvement" and settle, as Freud did, for something like "evenly hovering attention."

But if I did that, I think I would lose what my dream was trying to tell me. Let me follow the idea of involvement, with all its problems. There are three possible perspectives on the nature of the involvement that might help. Even if they help, we will still have to accept their transitional or interim nature until we can understand what "process with involvement" might be in its own right.

The first perspective would be to say that the therapist is involved with the patient *and his or her therapy*. The involvement is with a person and that person's process. I will have to leave open for the moment exactly what that process is: something along the lines of a growth process; a developmental process; a healing, self-realizing process that by its very nature cannot be programmed or predicted. It is almost, but not quite, circular to say at this point that the process requires precisely the kind of involvement I am attempting to define.

The second perspective is that the therapist attempts to keep his or her needs to a minimum. Is it possible for one to have an involvement in which one expresses no needs? The probability is overwhelming that one simply cannot. Can it perhaps then be said that the needs of therapist and patient are reciprocal? In exchange for a fee, a workable schedule, and a minimum of violence, the therapist contracts to contain his or her other needs to a usable minimum. The fee allows the therapist to deflect and defer an important segment of his or her needs away from the patient. The two others (a workable schedule and a minimum of violence) are included among what the therapist needs in order to *do* the work. The 50-minute hour is a real need. One needs to be able to say to a patient, in a way that is unimaginable with one's spouse, "Our time is up!" Patients (understandably) will object to these constraints, but it is important that the therapist experience and know them as real needs. The arrival of the next patient is not the real reason a therapist needs the hour to end.

We therapists probably must, as well, give over any need we might have for the patient to get better. We might wish this, perhaps, or hope for it. But not need it. The process depends on the patient's being able to discover that need to be his or her own.

The third perspective on the involvement of the therapist is that this involvement is, in contrast to most other kinds of involvement, in a context or a psychological space where the patient heretofore has been *alone* and *incompetent*. I am making the assumption that these tend to coincide. I will need the rest of my chapter to explain this.

Before I begin, however, let me say one or two things more about the nature of the therapist's involvement. Freud said that psychoanalysis (let us say any psychotherapy relationship) has no model in real life. This may be the safest assumption, because anything we might invoke— parent, teacher, mentor, pastor, and so on—contains elements that in some crucial context our patient will need us *not* to be. Nonetheless, let us say that the fact of the human need for parenting comes closest to whatever it is that allows for the possibility of the treatment relationship.

I am also going to assume that (good) therapies are more similar than different. The need to distinguish between therapeutic modalities is much more the need of the therapist and the third party[1] than the need of the patient. For the patient, therapy is therapy. It is always in a relationship. A patient relates to a therapist, not a modality. Chances are that if therapy takes place at all, it will be risky, costly,[2] painful, and will take time and work. I refer to all of this as the "unitary theory of the treatment process." All therapies comprise (to varying degrees) the elements of *each* of the modalities: they are all too short; they are all too long; they all terminate somehow or other; they all involve individuals, couples, groups, and families; they are all analytic, cognitive, affective, and behavioral; they all involve the forgetting and remembering of history; and they all focus on the present. Theory, technique, and modality are transitional objects of the therapist and serve, more than anything else, the function of allowing the therapist, in whatever way he or she can, to be *in* the relationship.

One final thing that probably ought to be said at the outset is that the treatment process has, as one of its fundamental organizers, *crisis.* This can be seen at two separate, but related, points. The first is whatever crisis it might be that originally brings the patient into treatment. The second is the crisis of the treatment process itself. I am using the term "crisis" in the largest possible sense. The original crisis might be between two people, for example, a couple; or it might be privately experienced by one person; or it could be between an individual and a larger group, for example, mandated by a court. The motivation for therapy need not come from the patient. What is more reliable is the existence of some kind of crisis, however hard it may be, initially, to locate. The treatment process attempts to gather in the crisis, wherever, however, and whenever it may have taken place. The crises may be multiple, may be confluent, and will of necessity retreat, reemerge, and reform. It is, however, some kind of crisis that makes possible, defines, and organizes the treatment process.

[1]HMOs and insurance companies need, more than anything else, brevity.
[2]The emotional cost is more important than the financial cost.

It is also quite reliable that the treatment process itself will experience crises. The viability of therapy itself will be seriously at stake at some point, usually more than once, from the patient, from the family, from the therapist, or from contingencies of whatever sort. There is no such thing as leisurely therapy. A leisurely therapy amounts to its own crisis. Here again, the therapy *needs* the crisis to organize, define, and understand itself. The negotiation of the crisis *is* the therapy. But we need to learn this all over again each time it happens.

At this point, to bring these themes together, I need to outline some assumptions about the nature, structure, and function of *affect*. This is because what the therapist does, to the extent that he or she does anything (over and above being involved), is to interpret affect. It would be very easy to lay too much emphasis on this; the most important speaker, the crucial interpreter of affect, is the patient. The therapist's interpretation of affect serves the function of a useful error for the patient, much as the mother's (mis)interpretation (by smiling or talking) of something from the baby that was to begin with not a smile, but then makes possible the real smile. I do not mean that we, as therapists, don't at times make lucky guesses, important lucky guesses. I mean more that (thankfully) the process does not totally depend on our being right.

I think I need to begin by assuming, by asserting, the absolute centrality of affect. The work of psychotherapy amounts to the problem of affect. The moment there are more than two neurons between receptor and effector, the moment there is a delay between stimulus and response, the moment when choice might be possible, one is presented with the problem of affect. "Knee-jerk" is the name we give to instinctive, atavistic, unconsidered, boilerplate responses. We contrast the (stimulus → response) instinct of, say, an insect,[3] with the enormous complexities of everything inside the "black box[4]" of the human being. Presumably the (Darwinian) trade-off for investing in all this hardware and software is the capacity to perceive, discriminate, expand, evaluate, and effectuate *choice*. The most important thing inside the black box, the "CPU[5]" of the mind, is *affect*. All the agencies of the mind report to affect.

---

[3]It turns out that insects, especially the social ones, are far more intelligent and complex than we give them credit for being.

[4]It would be impossible to make a linear diagram of the box, but it would have to include complex interconnections between (at very least) sensation, memory, perception, imagination (of what is potential), attachment, intentionality, creativity, affection, cognition, and the capacity to act.

[5]The C(entral) P(rocessing) U(nit) of a computer. The computer analogy is a peculiarly poor one; affect resists programming.

Putting things this way runs counter to the more customary ways (dating back to the ancient Greeks) of putting things. Rationality (located in the brain and mind) is separate from the passions: noble passions (in the chest and heart) and base passions (in the stomach and below). Even today common parlance distinguishes "emotional" from "rational," "subjective" from "objective." Freud's theory of the mind draws heavily on this split. His psychology was a psychology of conflict. The part of the mind entrusted with "preserving the traces of reality" (ego and secondary process) is distinct and separate from the part of the mind that experiences urgency (id and primary process). The ego's job is not an easy one. Frequently finding itself the helpless rider on a runaway horse, the ego has to wage ceaseless warfare against the untrammeled peremptory demands of the id (except when sleeping and dreaming). Wishing and reality-testing are always at odds with one another. Conflict is the only evidence we have of wishes of which we are not aware. Neurosis is the price we pay for the incompatible demands of our inner and outer worlds.

The component of Freud's system that suffered most from lack of attention and failure of development was affect. For Freud, early on, affect was a derivative by-product of drive discharge into the interior of the body. The major quotient of the drive energy went toward the thought and muscular activity required to make things happen. The drive energy channeled into affect performed an ancillary, auxiliary function. The preparatory function of sexual excitement, for example, or tears, or the various effects of adrenaline, were manifestations of affect. It served several purposes: it prepared the body for the activity at hand; it served to discharge excess or overload energy;[6,7] and it also served a kind of signal alert function, focusing mental energy on the task at hand.

Much later in his writing (Freud, 1926), the signal function of affect took a quantum leap forward. Anxiety, for Freud, was the prototypic affect in this regard, alerting the ego to danger. Other writers have extended and developed the signal concept for other affects. The crucial point is that affect comes much closer to ego than was previously thought. It performs a signal, that is, a recognition and processing, function, an ego function. From this point forward, reality testing is as inextricably linked with affect as it is with ego. Ego is affect. Signal and

---

[6]There was a limit, here. Beyond a certain point the excess energy was subject to repression because it was experienced as unpleasurable—the so-called wine-vinegar theory.

[7]This normal capability of channeling energy into the body interior served as a prototype or model for Freud of the pathological mechanism of conversion.

preparation connect with, and require, everything that we think of as ego. I am going to call this the "cognitive function of affect."

Affect performs many functions, seamlessly, smoothly, and for the most part nonconflictually. To break down affect into its functional components does violence to the organic, integrated nature of affective functioning, but I know of no other way of laying out the material. There is modest justification for this in its contribution to understanding the task of therapy. Therapy attempts to understand affect. We try to make sense of what we and our patients are feeling. The amazing part is that doing so makes possible the development, the evolution, of feeling—the capacity to in fact change, and to choose somewhat more, what we feel.

THE BASIC COMPONENTS OF AFFECT

What follows are perspectives on, dimensions of, and ways of approaching and understanding affect. Human feeling is a highly complex, organic, integrated phenomenon, and to minutely examine it is inevitably to risk losing it. Nonetheless, it has helped me to think of feeling as incorporating each (at least) of the components explored below. It is important to remember that none of the components is fully developed at any given point. Each has its own developmental spectrum, and the treatment process can be thought of in terms of the evolution of each of the components.

In what follows, I will try to hint at ways each of these perspectives plays an ongoing role in the treatment process. Each plays a necessary role in the nature of the therapeutic involvement. Each lends itself to interpretation.

Wish

Affect necessarily includes intention. Every feeling contains a wish. Some feelings more obviously contain intention (e.g., rage or sexual desire) than do others (e.g., contentment or boredom). Nonetheless, I think it helps to assume that every affect, however understated or in the background, contains at least a slight tendency in one direction rather than another. Another way of saying it would be to say that feeling something makes that particular something that much more likely to happen.

Even if it does not turn out to be the basic drive, sexuality is a magnificent paradigm of the power, the depth, the capacity for metaphor and disguise, of every affect. The sense of agency must develop. One of the major places that trauma takes its toll is in the development of capacity to wish.

Psychoanalysis, in its first 20 years, was an instinct psychology. Interpretations were of intention.[8] Intention remains possibly the most powerful organizer of affect. It is never irrelevant to ask, "What is it I really want?"

Memory

Perceptions, events, and memories are categorized, are organized, affectively. The prototype of this is trauma. Trauma can be measured by the extent to which future events are understood as repetitions or variants of a traumatic event. However, every memory is affectively tinged. Without affect, memory would be pointless. Without memory, affect would have no referent.

An enormous amount of what one can (or cannot) remember depends on what one can (or cannot) afford to feel. Trauma is repressed, it falls into amnesia, because it is unbearable to feel. The treatment process depends on some things becoming more capable of being felt with someone than they are when one is alone. What one can remember has a great deal to do with who one is with.

Cognition

Affects inform. Learning to trust what one feels is learning to use feeling as information. Every feeling is trying to tell us something. The signal theory of affect (namely that affect signaled something, performed a reality-discriminating function) was first elaborated in terms of a few prototypic affects, such as anxiety and depression. It took a little while to realize that the same principle applies to every affect. The cognitive function of affect is made necessary by the fact that affect must embrace event as well as intention.

An enormous amount of the treatment process includes rendering feelings comprehensible. Knowing that a certain feeling makes sense in a certain context makes it possible to use the feeling as signal of the context. Everyone knows (by feeling) more than they realize. Feeling is always interpretable as information.

Communication

Affects are inherently communicative, contagious, infectious. Again, sexuality is a magnificent paradigm. Competent sexuality is inherently communicative.

[8]Albeit of a very few intentions. Sexuality at first, then sexuality and aggression.

Having a feeling includes an invitation, an exhortation, to whomever one is with. The invitation can be one of simple participation or to be a specific actor in a highly complex scenario. The extent of the invitation is complicated and uncertain but nonetheless always there. It does not help for the therapist to be unimpacted, uninfluenced. Genuine immunity for either party probably can occur only after exposure to the infection. Interpretation includes the interpretation of communication, its risks and its inevitability.

Negotiation

Given all of the above, affect is necessarily and inherently negotiative. Feeling something impacts on whomever one is with, and necessitates a negotiation around the management of that particular feeling. All of this goes on constantly, usually seamlessly. What is usually thought of as negotiation is what happens when the more usual background affective negotiation fails.

An enormous amount of the treatment relationship consists of negotiation. I would like to suggest that within the treatment process affective *negotiation* is far more important than interpretation. Interpretation, to whatever extent it works, works as negotiation more than anything else. One of the most crucial negotiations consists of whether things have to happen now, feel now, the same way they always have. One of the major purposes of this paper is to replace the concept of interpretation with the concept of negotiation. Nevertheless, one of the most potent negotiations is an interpretation. The job of the therapist is to feel the ways in which interpretation and negotiation increasingly come together.

Ownership

An essential element of affect is ownership. This is not necessarily given, and in fact depends on emotional development. There are moments in very early life, as well as moments of crisis, when it is not at all clear who owns a given feeling. Ownership, however embarrassing, conflictual, or painful, is in the long run far more efficient than anything else.

The ownership of affect is one of the most powerful, crucial parts of the treatment process. There are inevitably aspects of any treatment relationship that the therapist must take "on loan." Ownership of affect is distributed among whomever is available. This is a necessary consequence of our being a social species. Ownership of affect is a relatively late acquisition, but its capacity for empowerment cannot be overestimated. Ownership of affect (to the extent it occurs) is necessarily negotiated.

Attachment

Every affect performs some attachment function. This includes even the negative, destructive affects: hate, disengagement, the attempt at detachment. The only successful detachment is death but it is successful only for the dead person. The living remain attached, each in their own way, to everyone they have known or imagined. The involvement of the treatment process follows necessarily and inevitably from the attachment function of affect.

One of the most powerful interpretations it is possible for a therapist to make is that of attachment. The question, How connected are we? (given this new event, given this painful memory, given the awareness of a context in which the patient has always been alone) is necessarily a new event. It helps enormously to interpret the need and dependency of the patient on the therapist as appropriate, entirely appropriate, given the work of the treatment process. The task is not to create some bootstrap operation out of the dependency but to discover the exact place where the patient once needed someone and then discovered that they were alone.

Another way of framing the issue of attachment is to say that technique includes helping the patient ask or say the thing you as therapist most dread hearing. It is an act of attachment.

Development

The living of life changes—sometimes dramatically, sometimes hardly at all—how one feels. Life stages influence how one feels what one feels. Again, psychosexual development is a paradigm. In one sense this is obvious; what is not so obvious are the countless ways in which agency, contingency, ownership, and choice all influence how one develops, how one grows into what one feels. Every day is a life stage.

It also helps enormously to be able to interpret what is going on, however intense, however bizarre, however shameful, conflictual, and extremely uncomfortable, as an extremely skillful rendering of what needs to be discovered with the therapist. It is not so easy for the therapist to remember that every affect has a vital developmental potential.

Competence

Affect is, in a fundamental sense, task oriented. Competence consists of the capacity to feel that which in fact you need to do. The most difficult concept to explicate, but essentially the most important part of what I wish to convey, is affective competence. One knows what is, what is not, what one wants, what one needs, what can be, and what cannot be, by feeling it. The notion of affective competence walks a knife-edge; on one side is the tendency to understand it in terms of what one should feel (which never works[9]), and on the other side is the tendency to understand it in terms of what one cannot feel, that is, to understand incompetence as deficit. It is true that the treatment process inevitably includes grief. Memory is an act of grief (Loewald, 1976). But it is also true that competence is a discovery, which is by definition a surprise. Grief is necessary but not sufficient.

It may be that competence is not, in the long run, interpretable. It is simply to be used, enjoyed, and (perhaps, by a therapist) seen.

THE COMPULSION TO REPEAT

One of the clearest ways in which one can see the development of affect, the growth of affective competence, and the architecture of the treatment process is in the repetition compulsion (and its rendering) as it takes place in treatment. The material quoted here is taken from my paper "Trauma Repetition and Affect" (Russell, 1990).

> What follows is a composite representation of a number of classical writers [see also Laplanche and Pontalis, 1973; Loewald, 1976].

> The confusion of memory with perception. Something experienced as occurring in and totally determined by the present situation, but which, in the last resort, we can only understand as determined by the past. In short, a memory which masquerades as a present-day event. The repetition compulsion operates functionally as a resistance to affect, to remembering with feeling

> Strictly speaking, therefore, the compulsion to repeat is discernible at the time only by an outside observer; anyone undergoing a compulsive repetition is unaware that it is a repetition and experiences it instead, indeed insists upon it, as a new event, however vaguely familiar. This is one of the reasons why psychotherapy cannot take place alone; it represents one of the basic limits of introspection. This makes it hard to define the repetition compulsion experientially, unless one also includes those moments, often long after the fact, when one begins to wonder whether more is going on than a series of unpleasant fortuitous recurrences.

> Let me suggest, then, as an experiential definition, something a bit further along on the spectrum of what we might call ego awareness,

---

[9]The superego is by definition, and demonstrably, incompetent.

namely: The repetition of that which, so far as we know, we would far rather not repeat.

This covers a lot of ground. It can be a very simple affair, or extraordinarily complex. It can be of such complexity and power that one has the impression that it is the act of an intelligence that is more than a match for one's own. It can at times operate like a doom, a nemesis, a curse. The same thing will happen, again and again, despite one's best efforts at avoidance, prevention, or control. In fact, it gets its name precisely on this account; that despite the apparent wish to avoid the pain, the cost, the injury of the repetition, one finds oneself repeating nonetheless, as if drawn to some fatal flame, as if governed by some malignant attraction which one does not know and cannot comprehend or control. It has, in other words, all of the external earmarks of a volitional act, and yet the person is unaware of wishing any such thing. In fact, quite the contrary; he or she would wish to avoid it.

The repetition compulsion can be observed, experienced, and understood in three ways:

(1) As a subject, as someone who is in the midst of repeating

(2) As an observer, possibly a participant observer

(3) As a theoretician of the repetition compulsion

The person who is repeating is the least likely to describe what is happening as compulsive repetition, although what is happening may well feel all too familiar. The subjective experience is most often one of overload; of pain; of externality, with the situation being determined by external persons and events in the present; and of helplessness, that is, the inability to do very much to alter the situation. The subjective experience is traumatic, even if the trauma has happened before.

Observers, depending on how close they are to the subject, and how much they participate, may notice a discrepancy between the inner experience of the subject and the way in which they themselves would experience and assess what is going on. The outside observer tends to be able to think of, imagine, and suggest ways in which the experience might be different. Observers are aware of possible stances, attitudes, strategies, ways of feeling, and so on that would, in their opinion, make a very great positive difference to the sense of overload, pain, externality, helplessness, and trauma felt by the subject. The observer is loath to describe what is going on as trauma.

If the observer in any way attempts to push any of this on the subject, he or she uncannily becomes (for the subject) a powerful part of the externality that is problematic and acutely painful. The subject may actually attempt at this point to embrace some of the observer's sense of effectiveness, but it tends to be artificial and premature, and requires some degree of enforced psychological distance (repression? dissociation?) from the intensity of the sense of trauma. In any event, the liability remains for a repetition, at some triggering point, of the situation of overload.

At a further degree of remove, in trying to understand the repetition compulsion what do we make of the above? Let us say, in a somewhat global and not altogether helpful way, that the repetition compulsion is defined by the inability to experience, to *feel,* the event in any other way than the way in which he or she experiences it. It repeats because it doesn't feel any different. It is a psychological black hole from which the subject can see or feel no way out.

The description above hints at some earlier event in the subject's life, which the observer (and anyone else) might well describe as genuinely traumatic, and which the subject might be said to be repeating. This is of course an assumption, even though some fairly strong evidence exists that something traumatic must have happened. The main reason this is all still an assumption, false memories aside, is that the subject—let us now call him or her a patient—does not remember it; not, at least, in any way that makes a difference. Every patient belongs to the False Memory Society. *The patient was unable to experience then, and is unable to remember now, the traumatic event in the way that he or she needs to in order to be able to locate the event in the past and to feel differently enough that the present and the past can be distinguished.* The rather clumsy visual metaphor I have used before is that it is like the camera trying to take a picture of injury to itself, while it is being built. In this context, time has stopped.

The point about whether the trauma is real or not, is this: Whether or not we can know what did happen, we must assume that some injury occurred, from which the person needs to heal. The only thing that works is the healing process. And the healing process includes the *rendering* of the repetition compulsion into the treatment.

I can make a few more comments from the stance of the theoretician. It should also be said now that the treatment process provides the eventual opportunity to combine and integrate all three points of observation: Both therapist and patient will be participant observers, both will attempt to understand as subject, object, and observer.

The components of affect listed above become increasingly confusing, disorienting, and paradoxical, the closer one approaches the repetition compulsion. Like a Geiger counter approaching a lode of radioactive material, each of the components becomes increasingly loud, and increasingly, paradoxically, impossible to locate.

Wish: The repetition compulsion is a paradox of intentionality. Did I do this or was it done to me? On one hand the experience is of something happening from the outside, the agency is external; on the other hand, there are hundreds of ways in which it becomes obvious, even to the person involved, that the repetition compulsion is motivated. It could happen in no other way.

Memory: The repetition compulsion is a paradox of time. Is this now or was it then? Despite the uncanny déjà vu, in the midst of the repetition there is no nonparadoxical solution as to when this is happening now/happened then.

Cognition: Is this real? Can I trust what I seem to know about what is happening?

Communication: Do I want you to feel this? Are you wanting me to feel this?

Negotiation: I do not believe that I am negotiating any of this; and yet I must be. Am I making all of this happen?

Ownership: Ownership is paradoxical in the midst of compulsive repetition. The question "Is this me or is this you?" becomes intensely unanswerable.

Attachment: I do not feel attached to you or to anyone in the midst of this; and yet it is also true that the only way I can feel attached to anyone at all is through this happening in this way. *Who are you?*

Development: There must be, I must find, some way to feel about all of this that I cannot, that I do not have, now. What is it that I am looking for, that I need?

Competence/Effectiveness: Can I choose what I feel?

Whether the repetition compulsion originally happened this way or not, it is *experienced* by the patient as the loss of someone the person needed to have had there, but who was not there.[10] And the repetition will occur until that someone is found. It is also true that the repetition compulsion operates as a safety device, as a preventive against the injury happening again. It includes the entire collection of methods the person made use of *at the time* in order to survive. The devices are almost exclusively lonely devices. Devices such as trust, safe dependence, or competent negotiation were not available then, and are irrelevant, even dangerous, now. The reason I say almost and not totally lonely is that people do repeat with real live other people. It is the one remarkable piece of competence in the repetition. It is capable, therefore, of being

---

[10]This can be, but does not need to be, an actual helpful, caring person whom the person once had in his or her life but then was lost. It can also be the loss of someone who might have been there but was not. This kind of loss is harder to grieve. (This point was often made by Elvin Semrad.)

repeated with a therapist. This is both the danger and the safety of the treatment process.

I mentioned previously that a crisis is delivered into the treatment process, an inevitable crisis, and, potentially, a mutative one. This crisis amounts to a crisis of repetition. The crisis is delivered into the treatment process in broad schematic strokes and consists of the patient's delivering something which begins as his or her personal, compulsive repetition, something very similar to the repetitive destructive patterns that have occurred before in the patient's life, and which becomes, in the process of the negotiation of the treatment process, a crisis of attachment involving *both* patient and therapist. I refer to this process as the *rendering* of the repetition.

The repetition compulsion, in the emotional context in which it takes place, is inversely related to intimacy. It functions, very much as does an addiction, *in lieu of* intimacy. It is a contrivance to control risk, a search for safety—the safety of not involving anyone else. Genuine intimacy makes the repetition compulsion unnecessary. However, the individual tests every potential intimacy through the repertoire of his or her repetitions to the extent that the intimacy survives. If this process continues, the repetition becomes, very gradually, less a repetition and more a genuine negotiation. This is the rendering of the repetition. As the repetition compulsion is rendered, the meaning of the phrase "search for safety" begins to change. The safety of aloneness is gradually, very slowly, relinquished in favor of an utterly new event in this particular context: safety within a relationship. The repetition compulsion can yield to nothing other than attachment and involvement. It can yield only to a relationship that is prepared to undertake at least as much risk and pain as occurred when the repetition began. The fully rendered repetition will deliver a situation that replicates the potential terror, damage, and destruction that made the person give up on the possibility of human connection being of any use to him or her.

There are at least two very real risks in this process as it unfolds. The first is that the disaster that happened once will indeed happen again. One can almost define the rendering of the repetition as a process that will *make* the disaster happen, will coerce it, if there is the slightest, remotest chance that it could. There is a perverse intelligence to this arrangement. It is as if the person is saying, "I cannot trust you until I know for sure that this will not happen again. If it is going to happen, let us have done with it, get it over with, while I still have some coping strategies, some life and energy left, before we do anything else."

Anyone undertaking the therapeutic process has to be prepared for the patient being at times far more able to make happen with us some variant of his or her repetition than we are able to prevent it from happening. A lot rides, however, on what that variant in fact is. The problem with trying to script emotionally corrective experiences for the patient (as with Franz Alexander's or similar techniques) is that there is no way of knowing, until it is dangerously about to happen, what it is the patient needs you not to be. The safest technique is honesty. The therapist does not need to be, and cannot be, a better parent. The therapist can be someone the patient might have *wished* to have as his or her parent, but the therapist cannot *be* that parent. We can only be the therapist. The most corrective experience possible for the patient is to be with who-the-therapist-in-fact-is, provided he or she is in fact safe. The unsafe therapist is the therapist who wants to be anything other than a therapist. The skill in the treatment enterprise consists of remaining a therapist, no matter how immersed we may become in the patient's repetitions, and our own, as well. The treatment consists of the patient's being able to discover and rediscover who the therapist is, as often as this is needed. The rendering of the repetition will powerfully deliver to the therapist every conceivable invitation to be someone other than a therapist. The treatment process consists of, in addition to the therapist's attempt to understand the patient, the patient's discovery of who the therapist is.

It is the patient's discovery of who the therapist is, *as therapist,* that connects directly with the second great risk of the treatment process. It is precisely that discovery that gives words, gives feeling to all of the ways in which this experience was not there before, the ways in which what happened before was different. The repetition compulsion is an attempt to coerce identity. The technique of therapy consists of the therapist's being able to survive the attempt to coerce identity and to emerge as different. He or she does this not so much by doing as by being—by being a therapist and attempting to understand the patient's emotional experience. Good therapy is a profound stress and will inevitably put the patient in touch with a pain that he or she has not felt before. It is this pain, however, which will enable the patient to remember as memory as opposed to repetition.

What I have tried to arrive at in this chapter, is a place where the word "involvement" describes, better than any other word I can think of, what it is the therapist *does*. The therapist is involved with who the patient is, with who he is with the patient, and with what is now *happening,* most especially between them. The therapist is involved with the constant, unending negotiation of the possibility and conditions of the treatment to take place and to continue. It takes work. It is hard. The hardest part is the pain. The pain of memory. The technique I have found, if I can call it that, is to try to know the time and the place where I become uninvolved. The most dangerous part of the treatment process is when both parties wish for, invite, noninvolvement. That is the most dangerous repetition. Memory, feeling, and desire are in this context all new structures. Structure is the passage of process with involvement.

REFERENCES

Freud, S. (1926), Inhibitions, symptoms and anxiety. *Standard Edition,* 20:87–172. London: Hogarth Press, 1959.

Laplanche, J. & Pontalis, J.-B. (1973), *The Language of Psychoanalysis*. New York: Norton, pp. 78–80.

Loewald, H. (1976), Perspectives on memory. In: *Papers on Psycho-Analysis*. New Haven, CT: Yale University Press, 1980, pp. 148–173.

Russell, P. (1990), Trauma Repetition and Affect. Unpublished manuscript.

13

Listening to Affect

Interpersonal Aspects of Affective Resonance in Psychoanalytic Treatment

George G. Fishman

P sychoanalysis has acquired a robust vocabulary with which to describe the desirable endpoints of treatment. These include: greater self-understanding, changes in self-concept, enhanced ability to feel inwardly "held," improved capacity for closeness, shifts in the inner representations of relationships, and achievement of a new integration or a new object experience. All of these abstract terms refer to types of potential within the patient that are realized through the very grounding medium of affect.

I offer five preliminary considerations concerning the role of affect. First, Paul Russell (1993) described the way that the core transferences come to the foreground as repeated "crises of attachment" that make clear how past trauma has affected the patient's capacity to feel. The corollary is that for every patient, help will ultimately involve combinations of the understanding, containment, metabolism, and expansion, of various affects.

Second, there follows a caveat. Affects, as developmentalists[1] have pointed out (Demos, 1984; Stern, 1985; Beebe, Jaffe, and Lachmann, 1992), are essentially communicative. As soon as we therapists closely attend to the role of the emotions, we are automatically pulled into the interpersonal domain of the patient–therapist relationship, with all its attendant hazards. It is the specific purpose of this chapter to explore

The author wishes to acknowledge the help of Drs. Grantley Taylor, Paul Russell, and Ginger Chappell in clarifying the ideas presented in this chapter.

[1]Many theoretical and research studies have been devoted to the communicative function of affects. I also refer to Bion (1977), Emde (1991), and Tomkins (1991).

through clinical examples the joys and woes of what I will term this "affect's eye view" of the treatment process.

I will call attention to how, in the interest of safety, therapists have maintained prescribed rules for visiting this domain. We have locked a therapist's attunement to the primary task of observation and understanding with prescriptive terms like "trial identification." However, whenever a therapist lingers in this attunement, a bevy of conceptual warning sirens concerning potential countertransference enactment caution her not to let the pull of a gut feeling cause the therapist to lose her head. Until recently, we therapists may have conceded here and there that the therapeutic relationship needed a minimum of relational oxygen to survive, but we were unwavering in our belief that transference grows and thrives in a mainly anaerobic environment.

Third, I want to note that psychoanalysis now stands at a unique turning point in its ambivalence toward the interpersonal implications of a focus on affects. It might be fair to say that many therapists are enthusiastically diving into this awareness. We are no longer trying to quarantine the benefits and liabilities of interaction within artificial conceptual boundaries, like the "real relationship." The body of intersubjective (Stolorow, Brandchaft, and Atwood, 1987; Trop and Stolorow, 1992) and interpersonal (Gill, 1982; Mitchell, 1987; Greenberg, 1991) perspectives I will loosely designate as "relational" has accepted that the attachment between patient and therapist, when all goes well, is asymmetric (Cooper, 1993), but nonetheless real, whole, and affective.

Fourth, the relational framework is based on a familiar sine qua non of all our theories, namely, the continued acknowledgment that safety and therapeutic effect are assured as long as both therapist and patient are committed to reflecting on all that goes on between them. However, it has provided us with a new grasp of the dynamics of linkage between feeling and understanding and of interpersonal versus intrapersonal process. The relational viewpoints and the writings on countertransference enactment (Jacobs, 1986; McLaughlin, 1991; Renik, 1993a, b) support the idea that patient and therapist must repeatedly find themselves letting go and falling into the relationship if they are ever to reach real understanding. The idea of therapeutic abstinence has been altered even within modern ego psychology. For example, Boesky (1990) recently wrote: "If the analyst does not get emotionally involved sooner or later in a manner that he had not intended, the analysis will not proceed to a successful conclusion" (p. 573).

Fifth, I hope to reinforce certain implications of developmental research as the potential anchor for our anxious embrace within the interpersonal dimension of the concept of joint participation. Specifically, contemporary infancy research is based on a fundamental awareness that rhythms of affective interchange are essential to all human relatedness. Even though adult interactions have evolved way beyond the nonverbal orchestrations of mother and infant (Stern, 1985) so evident in infant research data, it is nevertheless clear that every adult dyad similarly engages in unique mutually achieved patterns of affective communication that simultaneously echo, evoke, and repair earlier patterns.

THE CRISIS OF THE MOMENT—
THE INSIDE AND OUTSIDE OF EXPERIENCE

In order to lay the groundwork for how I will focus on affect in the interpersonal sphere, I must allude briefly to certain observations about therapists' current emphasis on the difference between what I am calling the "inside" and the "outside" of experience. In an earlier essay, entitled "The Crisis of the Moment" (Fishman, 1993), I suggested that although the word "moment"[2] has always been used to refer to points of affective impact in a treatment hour (Strachey, 1934), therapists were beginning to give it a new signification. I will now present a sketch of my conclusions.

Through the works of Paul Gray (1973, 1990), Anton Kris (1982), and Donald Spence (1982, 1987), we have improved on our "rules of evidence"—our definition of data. In particular, therapists have realized that the best way to decode the meaning of any affective moment is to stay within the immediate surround of the patient's associations. However, all three authors have supported the conventional wisdom of regarding the patient's manifest content, including the affects, as important mainly for its resonance with deeper, intrapsychic meanings.

Schwaber (1990, 1992a,b) has repeatedly challenged that wisdom by advocating that the therapist restrain the urge to plunge quickly beneath the surface, and, instead, carefully listen to what is on the patient's conscious mind. She inadvertently discovered that when a patient's affect is taken at face value, as I noted earlier, its communicative function stands out. Schwaber's rich clinical examples have repeatedly

---

[2]For example, Gray (1990) writes: "I characterize the kind of phenomena that alert my analytic listening as those *moments* when I observe that point of intrapsychic stress which forces the ego to interfere with the emerging material. . . . At such *moments,* there is invariably a "change of voice" (p. 1087).

Schwaber (1990) notes: "Some years back, I tried to illustrate a mode of listening to clinical material which would sharpen the focus on *moment to moment* verbal and non-verbal cues and on their relationship to the analyst's silent or stated interventions" (p. 230).

and unwittingly demonstrated that a patient, in any heated moment, is trying to relate a sense of the therapist's participation that the therapist may not be aware of. Schwaber herself has consistently addressed the patient's wish for a response from a neutral, interpretive position.

But, to say it in a way that conveys the urgency, in the treatment of adults, when either patient or therapist pays attention to the immediacy of what they feel in a given moment, they cannot help but sense that their affect is an informing response to the other and needs, in turn, to be responded to, not interpreted. Thus, in the context of a relationship, affect, on a first pass, tends to find its origins inside, in the interaction, not outside, in reference points beyond immediate experience. The infancy literature indicates that from the very beginning this is the natural state of affairs. For instance, Beebe and colleagues (1992) write: "There is a dynamic interplay between mother and infant, and each affects the other's actions perception, affect, and proprioceptions to create a great variety of mutual regulatory patterns" (p. 65).

Here lies the danger I have called the "crisis of the moment." It is the *fear* that affirmation of what the patient feels in the moment will pull the therapist into blind enactment rather than understanding of the transference. In other words, the patient will convince, coerce, and manipulate the therapist into believing that what he or she feels so urgently to be on account of the therapist's action or inaction requires a direct, not an interpretive, response. If the therapist complies, it is hard not to believe that the enduring, intrapsychic origins of transference, the very signature of the patient's psyche, will be submerged rather than uncovered.

Many of us have relied on self psychology as one of the most theoretically appealing compromise formations for this intrapsychic versus interpersonal dilemma. Kohut (1984) boldly and brilliantly recognized how often every patient, regardless of diagnosis or level of functioning, pleads for recognition of what he or she feels with immediacy. However, ironically, Kohut disregarded the affective specificity that shapes a patient's need for validation. Instead, he believed that all individual instances belong to the abstracted category of selfobject need. By this belief, he hoped to give the patient's peremptory desire for give-and-take a proper intrapsychic basis. From the technical side, Kohut proposed empathic immersion as a legitimized form of participation that stayed shy of gratification and would yield to interpretation. Analysis, in terms of formal therapeutic role and action, would remain "analytic."

However, Kohut unwittingly fueled the crisis of the moment from the depths of his own insight. In his last book, *How Does Analysis Cure?* (1984), he began the chapter on the role of empathy with a clinical vignette. The patient was a fragile man who had had several unsuccessful therapies. This patient was adamant that his suffering was a response to the actions of others and that he needed them to admit that they had caused his pain. Needless to say, after a honeymoon period and an interruption in the treatment, the patient began to blame Kohut for his pain as well. Kohut desperately attempted to reach the patient, who was undergoing a dangerous decompensation. He responded to his patient from the depths of what he felt was his empathic immersion in the patient's selfobject needs. Kohut poignantly noted:

> And as we finally came to see . . . the content of all my various interpretations had been cognitively correct but incomplete in a decisive direction. . . . What I had not seen, however, was that the patient had felt additionally traumatized by feeling that all these explanations on my part came only from the *outside:* that I did not fully feel what he felt, that I gave him words but not real understanding, and that I thereby repeated the essential trauma of his early life [p. 182; italics added].

This is the point. Most interpretations, of any theoretical persuasion, in moments of this kind, invariably feel like too many words spoken too far away from the patient's immediate, conscious sense of the relationship—as Kohut says, from the *outside.* Conventional attempts at understanding, even empathic immersion within selfobject need, when offered in the moment, can serve as a defense against the possibility of what comes more naturally, namely, meaningful affective participation. In other words, in the moment, in the immediacy of experiencing any affect, the patient desires a response from the therapist that feels like it comes from *inside*[3] their mutual attachment.

The relational, intersubjective, and constructivist perspectives, by recognizing the importance of mutual participation, offer better reasons and guideposts for staying within the relationship. They each advocate a therapeutic form of noblesse oblige—if the therapist can forgo the belief that he knows better in order to learn the evolving terms of the relationship, the patient eventually will construct a responsible version of his intrapsychic contributions. Mitchell (1987) illustrated an alternate way of being inside the narcissistic patient's experience when he wrote:

> Analysands manifesting narcissistic transferences generally need to be joined in their self-admiration or idealization in order to feel involved,

[3]Atwood and Stolorow (1984) state that "Psychoanalysis is . . . a science of the *intersubjective,* focused on the interplay between the differently organized subjective worlds of the observer and the observed. The observational stance is always one within, rather than outside, the intersubjective field . . . being observed" (p. 41).

to feel that something important is happening. The analyst cannot feign this participation. . . . What is called for is not a forced assumption of some prescribed "analytic" demeanor, either "neutral" or "empathic," but a willingness to meet and engage the analysand on his own terms [p. 211].

I call attention to the phrase "meet and engage." Mitchell (1987) recognizes that: (1) the dictates of any technique are likely to inhibit the therapist, and (2) what the patient needs can only be defined ostensively—it has to stem from the therapist's genuine affects in the moment. I maintain that "meeting" and "engaging" imply, are signifiers of, a quality of affective resonance that is gradually created between patient and therapist during a succession of painful false starts.

CASE ILLUSTRATION

Some of the terms I am using, like "crisis of the moment," may inadvertently throw us off the track. The phenomena I am describing are so much a part of everyday work and, usually, so subtle, that their importance is often missed. A case example will help to further specify the nature and meaning of affective resonance.

Mr. Y, a young professional man, sought treatment to overcome, among other things, certain blocks to sustained intimacy. The patient possessed an unusual gift of expression. His associations were rich. His own reflections on his associations were brilliant and lucid. Mr. Y was intellectual, but he could hardly be called obsessional. He related warmly and everything he articulated was mindful of the possible existence, meaning, and consequences of his affects, both manifest and hidden. Despite this attunement to himself, the problem was, by his own account, that the edges of Mr. Y's experience with me and others were too clean and dry. He and I often sensed that he was affectively outside of our relationship.

During the early hours of the treatment, he was speaking of a central trauma, the loss of his mother to the ravages of a chronic illness. The precipitate of this painful experience was a pattern with women that involved jarring oscillations between passion and anger or anger and disengagement. He could feel deeply, but such intensity was a signal that the attachment would not last. Mr. Y was, as usual, fully, almost vigilantly aware that the pattern persisted on account of something he could not let go of. He needed to grieve. We were both hyperaware of the resonance of all these matters in the developing transference.

It was at a certain point in one hour that a summary of a short story[4] came to his mind. A group of Native Americans approached a rancher and asked to buy a bison. The rancher initially refused the offer because he viewed them as hungry savages pining for the kill. The tribesmen persisted and finally bought the animal.

Then came the surprising denoument of the story and the hour. Mr. Y related that, instead of doing what the rancher had predicted, the tribesmen dressed in ceremonial costume and staged a ritual hunt. They had become all too aware that their land would soon be taken, and more importantly, that life as they had known it would be forever gone. It became clear that they were trying to retrieve not just a bison but a waning sense of pride in and attachment to who they had been meant to be.

Mr. Y and I had been following these thoughts as was our custom, trying out the resonance of key words, putting things together, scanning for whispers of feeling. Both of us, I realize in retrospect, had been slanted toward "observant participation." However, as soon as the story was finished, there was a dramatic and uneasy silence. I was overcome by something that resisted an immediate label. In the next moment, my eyes filled up and I felt I was not just going to cry—I was about to lose it. Needless to say, I did not think this would be very good for either of us. At the same time, I was as sure as I could be that Mr. Y was feeling something akin to this and that he knew I had been very moved by what he had said. I just held on and so did Mr. Y. We somehow felt our way in silence together to a landing place. I was composed enough to acknowledge that he had touched on his need to grieve something that was very hard to lose. At the time, I sensed that something else was going on between us that was captured by the content of neither my words nor his. Mr. Y's sadness was an immediate response that asked to be addressed. I hoped that my words at least indicated that I could be inside the relationship, with him, as he tried to deal with his racking grief. I wanted to convey that I would try to avoid what the rancher did, to make erroneous assumptions or turn my back. More importantly, I realize that in speaking to him I was also urging myself to persist in the difficult task of challenging my resistances to my own sources of grief.

Mr. Y and I have had many occasions to review this moment. My silent participation in that painful instant, without immediate comment or interpretation, seems to both of us to have been a crucial event. This

---

[4]Spence (1982) has covered the liabilities of narrative smoothing. In this instance, I want to make clear that I am reporting my memory of my hearing of the summary. I have no idea at this point what layers of "distortion" I have added to what Mr. Y actually said.

moment became a major signature of the treatment as many more similar moments have evolved.

AFFECTIVE RESONANCE—LINGERING, MALINGERING, AND EMERGENCE

I will attempt to discuss the implications of this case example so as to expand our understanding of the nature of affective participation from inside the patient's experience. I will divide the discussion into two categories: lingering versus malingering, and emergence.

Lingering versus Malingering

It is uncanny that McLaughlin (1987) himself, an author of the term "enactment," could have spoken about my mindset as well as his own when he described a similar confrontation with a patient's unresolved grief. He wrote: "[I] . . . could understand better how certain early losses of my own, and the necessity to hover near the grieving ones around me, were contributing to my more than trial identification . . ." (p. 562).

It is apparent that "trial identification" was not an apt description for the emotional immersion I felt in relation to Mr. Y. I want to distinguish between two ways of understanding my having fallen inside the patient's experience of the relationship. The first I term "malingering," and is the view from the moderate perspectives within modern ego and self psychology. In accord with this view, my lapsing into sadness was a countertransference enactment of one or another of the transference themes echoed in the content. For instance, the sadness could be construed as my yielding to Mr. Y's latent wish that we, too, would become bonded tribesmen, upholding his pride in the face of loss. Or, did we cry as fellow hunters and typical males over the loss of a totem, a cherished sport, in order to not feel the wish to kill each other? Or, was the hunt turning the passive into the active—had he once felt like the bison, prey for the restitution of a parent's fading pride? Or, to conjecture in the spirit of Hoffman (1979), was he aware of my potential reaction to him in my actuality as a psychoanalyst? After all, I was another kind of tribesman whose land was also in jeopardy, and maybe my sadness confirmed that I did need him for the narcissistic restitution involved in being able to do my ritual hunt, namely psychoanalytic treatment.

In other words, within this first framework, my enactment, my feeling from the inside of the relationship, must be reexternalized. Crying with one's patient may be meaningful, gratifying, and "aerobic," but it is not therapy. The therapeutic moment, according to Gray (1990), occurs when affect[5] is registered as a "change of voice" in the patient. This is a point at which a drive derivative is struggling to break through. It is an opportunity to help the patient *observe* the moment and the defense used to contain and ward off unconscious desire or aggression. As I noted in the Kohut example, even empathic immersion in Mr. Y's selfobject needs, in traditional self psychology, has to be translated into outside observation. In answer to these admonishments, I say that I worried plenty and believe that, needless to say, every therapist should when her affect speaks loudly.

In summary, the first framework for understanding affective participation advocates for clean experiential edges. Affect within the bounds of trial identification is enabling for the therapist. However, when a therapist's affect goes beyond these bounds, it is countertransference-induced malingering. This may be necessary, as expressed by the term "necessary evil." Jacobs (1986), McLaughlin (1991), and Renik (1993a,b) all unwittingly continue the pejorative implications of enactment so that we might never forget that its informing function is limned by the constant danger that it will derail the very process it is supposed to illumine. I, of course, totally agree that therapists need to heed this danger, but this labeling still leaves the subject of affective participation in the mudroom of psychoanalysis.

The second perspective, relatively speaking, highlights the values of lingering, of affectively participating with, interacting with, and engaging the patient. This view starts with Hoffman's (1979, 1992) assumption that Mr. Y already has an anticipation of what my experience of his story will be. He has been alive quite a while and has an impressive store of expectations and experiences of how others react to him. Specifically, the critical moment of sadness was surrounded by, among other things, associations to how intolerant the women in his life had been of his doing his thing, namely, weaving his pattern of passion, anger, and disengagement. His hope was that if some woman could bear these emotional waves, he would be enabled to grieve. But he expected, from experience, that he inevitably exceeded everyone's limits.

It became clearer, as we worked together, how this expectation might have begun in his dealings with mother. She was a woman who we believed had suffered early trauma. She herself had never been able to let go and grieve. Instead, it appeared that she looked for restitution through passionate union and, when disappointed, spent her rage

---

[5]Gray conspicuously avoided discussions of countertransference enactment. It seems that his guidelines for listening to the patient are rooted in the more cognitive, secondary process, reaches of the "third ear."

in distancing, blaming attacks. Through numerous events and inter-actions, she had become a major source of the patient's grief. Most important, within the context of this second perspective, is that, at the same time, the legacy of identifications inherited by Mr. Y could not guide him in grieving. Like all of us, Mr. Y used the wisdom of this legacy to limit his expectations of what an *interaction* with another could deliver. Please note: I say wisdom, not distortion, and interaction, not wish or need.

From the vantage point of the second perspective, the critical moment could be understood as a subliminal "invitation" for me to reveal my potential as a mentor in grief. I believe that my unwitting participation had a facilitating function beyond what is implied by our usual definition of "enactment." To see this, let us imagine that I had been able to turn the flood of my grief into a more contained signal. I feel that the very act of framing an interpretation of any potential latent content at that critical moment would have been no less an interfering enactment. The subtext of any interpretive intervention, at that time, would have subtly enjoined the patient to reflect on what he felt. Throughout Mr. Y's life, reflecting had been a form of "bucking up" in the face of emotional pain. It was a style woven from his experience with both parents. Lastly, it closely matched my own defensive proclivities in the face of similar pain. If I had not palpably struggled with "losing it," I easily could have been absorbed into the ranks of his problematic introjects and forsworn entry into a "new object" realm.

Emergence

The discovery that I made in this instance is akin to what many others have been observing. What often needs to be interpreted first is the patient's sense of the therapist having found or missed the opportunity to helpfully participate in the affective moment. Unwittingly, the inter-pretation serves as more than transmitted knowledge from therapist to patient. It functions also as a signifier, or a potential mobilizer, of a new affective integration of the relationship. Both patient and therapist, in fits and starts familiar to each of them, confront the effects of their inescapable "fall" into affective mutuality. I am certainly not recom-mending that we abandon the subtle, self-reflective, cautious way in which therapists usually work. Every act of lingering, of necessity, has an aspect of malingering. However, I join with many others in the aware-ness that a religious belief in "good technique" and "therapeutic neu-trality" are ways to stay blind to observing and guiding one's repeated and necessary daily plunges into the "within" of relating.

One way to make the fact of this subtle participation more acceptable is to examine another fault line in both classical defense analysis
and mainstream self psychology. This problematic assumption is that Mr.
Y's sadness reflects, depending on the theoretical lens being used,
the presence of other, deeper, unconscious feelings, conflicts, or self
states. All of these are assumed to be formed structures lying deep in
the unconscious, which fuel his unyielding desire for the lost object.
Unfortunately, when we fix our gaze on these latent structures, we often
end up staring at a virtual reality and miss the fact that something is
emerging that has never been even unconscious before. Manifest affect,
if it is helped to evolve, will fulfill a potential for meaning that was not
preordained. Margulies (1993) offered an example of his work with a
patient discovering his grief in order to illustrate the quality of emergence. He writes:

> It was almost as if now, as an adult, he might go back and feel what he, as a
> child, could not directly experience. As a child, he had no way to gain
> access to the feelings, they remained unelaborated affects. It was not that
> for him the memories and affects were *first in consciousness* and then
> repressed, or even that they were in unconscious, developed form and split
> off from consciousness. For this man these feelings and memories remained
> undeveloped, like a crowded and pale seedling that has never seen light.
> Now he has access to a newly developing state of mind [p. 196].

Modell (1990) has incorporated Edelman's (1986) neuronal group
selection theory to explain this same phenomenon of emergence. A
central idea is that memory is composed not of fixed representations
but of fluid categories of experience ready to "find" a similarity in
the present.

My addendum to Margulies and Modell is to stress that the emergence
within the patient of crucial affective meaning requires that the therapist
be more than an attuned "receiver." The emergence is the result of the
comingling of two separate minds. The patient's potential mindset is
elaborated by the mixing, matching, and clashing of the therapist's and
patient's affects. In this process, the patient's subjectivity is "embodied"
in an existence it has never had before. Mr. Y's racking grief and its threat
to overwhelm could only exist inside a mutual participation. In other
words, if I had failed to linger, if I had blocked my full participation, I
would have apprehended sadness, but it would have been sadness of
another, paler color. My patient, Mr. Y, learned in the crucial moment
that it is necessary to yield to his hopes that I could enactively help him
develop and bear his sadness in order not to uncover, but rather to
create, an understanding.

To summarize this discussion of emergence, I must state that the paradox of the repetition compulsion (Russell, 1993) is that it refers to something that has never exactly happened before but feels very familiar. The paradox is predicated on emergence. To say it another way, if therapist and patient do not reach a new object experience, they will not stand a chance of effectively dealing with old object experience.

I will cite another example, a case of Balint's (1968), in order to consolidate our understanding of how critical the emergence of a particular affective mutuality is to the effort at understanding and working through. I rediscovered this vignette in the midst of Mitchell's (1987) discussion and critique of the concept of regression. It made me realize how much Michael Balint had subliminally influenced my own views on affective participation, so I went back and reviewed this case. The patient was a woman in her late twenties who despite her liveliness complained of "an inability to achieve anything." Balint (1968) eventually tied her social and academic constrictions to her submission to a father introject. This internal voice enjoined her to

keep her head safely up, with both feet firmly planted on the ground. In response, she mentioned that ever since her earliest childhood she could never do a somersault; although at various periods she tried desperately to do one. I then said: "what about it now?"—whereupon she got up from the couch and, to her great amazement, did a perfect somersault without any difficulty [pp. 128–129].

This moment proved to be an important breakthrough. However, Balint, in trying to understand this critical moment, was uncomfortable with an explanation based on the return of the repressed. He stated: "One can only repeat something that one has done at least once before; and perhaps equally, one can regress to something that has existed at least once before. But, as the case history shows, my patient had never been able to do a somersault" (p. 129). He began to use the term "new beginning" to describe this emergent order of change.

I thoroughly agree with Mitchell (1987) when he links the success of the intervention to Balint's ability to become a new object. Mitchell wrote: "Perhaps the crucial event was not the patient's somersault at all, but the analyst's invitation, through which he stepped out of the transferential integration in which he was participating and thereby transformed the relationship" (p. 155). In the main, I agree. However, I would prefer to tone down even further the way the words "stepped out" resonate conscious deliberation. I believe, or would like to believe, that things just happened. I would prefer to say that the patient and therapist had managed to successfully mix it up, to fall into a long affective interchange that continually challenged and reworked the compromises between safe restraint and creative letting go. But let us be clear that although the somersault appears to define the apogee of the interaction, the "crucial event" was related to how we understand the analyst's "invitation." Balint (1968) himself emphasized the work that preceded the somersault and said: "The incident itself, though impressive, was insignificant" (p. 132). Similarly, my own spin is *not* on the inviting per se, that is, the action as a corrective technique, provocative suggestion, deliberate support, or gratification. Rather, I would like to think that Balint's action, his invitation, came as a result of a very undeliberate process, a shift in the range of his affective responses to his patient. His nodal question—"what about it now?"—was a signifier of that shift for both patient and therapist.

I also would like to believe, based on similar experiences of my own, that Balint had to overcome many personal sources of restraint that had become rationalized as proper technique. The breakthrough was equally perhaps his own access to spontaneous excitement, which then became the necessary precursor to the patient's somersault. In other words, as Jacobs has demonstrated in his work (Jacobs, 1986), therapeutic restraint had itself become part, in this instance, of an enactment of a daughter's submission to a father's excessive caution. Note that the choice is not between enactment and neutrality. There is only a forced choice between modes of enactment or what I prefer to call "affective participation."

The crucial events in these clinical examples are important not just as breakthroughs but also as the visible, punctate markers of what is more typically a long, stumbling, partly invisible process. First, in each instance, patient and therapist resonated within and metabolized a critical dimension of affective experience, which allowed the emergence of yet another affective dimension. Second, the empirical evidence from these case examples does not support the premise that these are simple instances of transference gratification. Rather than stabilizing the therapeutic process at some surface level, the participation by all three therapists was critical to its deepening and progression. Third, as Renik (1993a,b) has stated, as a result of these releasing interactions, the patient digested an embodied understanding rather than compliantly incorporated the therapist's "ideas." All of this awareness critically informs our current understanding of transference analysis.

A THEORETICAL HOME FOR AFFECTIVE PARTICIPATION

A theoretical home for therapists' accumulated observations on the facilitative role of affective interaction can be derived from the findings of developmental research. Infancy data have overwhelmingly supported the importance of the patterns of mother–infant interaction for the development and regulation of the child's affects (Beebe & Sloate, 1982; Stern, 1985; Tronick, Cohn, and Shea, 1986; Solyom, 1987; Lichtenberg et al., 1992). However, infants are preverbal, their affect shifts are pronounced, and their self-regulatory strategies are easily overwhelmed. There clearly are problems with any wholesale assimilation of these findings into our work with adults. Nevertheless, this body of research convincingly supports what we are now appreciating from clinical observation—that affect regulation is never a fully internalized process.

To reiterate, throughout the life cycle important aspects of the expression, expansion, metabolism, and containment of affect are still best described as intersubjective process. To quote Beebe and colleagues (1992):

> Our overview of the research documenting the negotiation of mother–infant interaction suggests two consequences for our understanding of the analytic dyad. First, the "rules" that the patient has internalized through the experiences of joint constructions between patient and analyst will contribute to the organizing principles in the transference. Second, the manner in which the relatedness is constructed will bear the stamp of both participants [p. 76].

I will translate this statement with some poetic license. What makes the subject of affective resonance so important is that it is a form of joint construction that establishes basic rules, like the rules governing self and agency. For example, the joint construction of tolerance limits for sadness reworked many of Mr. Y's internal rules of attachment. To be able to grieve a relationship within a relationship was to be able to commit to one. Similarly, Balint and his patient jointly constructed acrobatic metaphors that could be "introjected" to loosen up the firm grip of "father rules" in order to permit the patient an expanded sense of what she could intend.

However, construction is a word with edges that are too clean for describing how the process works. Let me suggest a little more of its essence in adult communication by making a comparison with a game of catch.[6] Both the passing back and forth of a baseball and an emotional resonance are interpretive actions. In the two instances, each partner's reactions instill particular attributions of agency into the other. For

---

[6]Demos (1984) describes the engagement of a 15-month-old girl in a game of catch that becomes the medium for a critical affective exchange with her mother.

example, one person may signal to the other that the ball, or the anger or love, has been thrown too softly or too hard by returning it with a corrected spin. Dropping the ball, failing to return it at all, like the still face experiments done with infants, is a sure means of destroying a partner's sense of potential effectiveness in the relationship. In the days of classical abstinence, patients too often spent their hours masking their pleas for a genuine response, and, receiving none, withdrawing into empty compliance.

The major internalizations of childhood, the introjects, are abstracted records of these reciprocal interactions between parent and child (Sandler, 1978). Let me say this another way. Embedded within the concept of projective identification (Bion, 1977; Ogden, 1982, 1986; Kernberg, 1993) is the sense of critical emotional "catch." In other words, the concept is not just the name for a primitive defense mechanism, but also a way of referring to a group of functions vital to a back-and-forth within any relationship, which ultimately either establishes or precludes a firm sense of agency. This is well known to couples and family therapists (Dicks, 1967).

We have been progressively realizing that mutual projective identification is the process that informs and supports the critical affective resonance within both the parent–child and therapist–patient relationship. For example, Demos (1984) stated that her formulation of a parent–child interaction "requires that the adult not only join the child by producing a response that is somewhat similar in intensity and duration to the child's response, but also lead the child on to the next step by helping the child to fashion a response to his affective experience" (p. 15). The therapist, like the parent, unconsciously engages with his or her projective identifications in order to locate a helpful, complementary response to what the patient is feeling. It is understandable that the more familiar defensive, "good riddance" aspect of projective identification is the essential cost for its adaptive metabolizing and shaping functions (Sandler, 1976; Ogden, 1986; Tansey and Burke, 1989).

In terms of this defensive side, therapists know too well that a parent's accurate unconscious recognition of a child's problematic affect state may not lead to helpful or loving actions. The parent must ultimately consult with her introjects in order to find a resonance that matches that of the child. The same holds true for a therapist. For all of us, as therapists and parents, on many occasions our own internalized parents are unreliable guides. In turn, no child or patient wants to own a problematic feeling that is being unconsciously handed over by a parent or therapist from his or her own storehouse of troublesome introjects. In cases where the affect is labeled by either patient or therapist as "toxic," the game of catch has high stakes. Eventual integration and ownership either emerges from a bilateral process or does not happen at all. To quote Ferro (1993): "it is not only the right interpretation but also our internal transformational labours that will enable us to metabolise the projective identifications which paralyse us. This may be a slow, laborious and often painful task" (p. 926). These brief thoughts give us a glimpse of the potential theoretical home and functional centrality of mutual affective resonance.

CONCLUSION

The affect's-eye or relational view of treatment I have presented invites many caveats and counterarguments that must be taken seriously. Make no mistake, says the voice of the devil's advocate, how much precipitates of the individual unconscious—our internalized wishes, schemas, and unconscious self-criticism (Kris, 1990)—run our lives: one person's deepest internal phantasy can easily dictate the interactional menu for two (Boesky, 1990). I respond with qualified agreement. It is the intent of this chapter not to contradict this wisdom but to point out how therapists are restructuring it in the face of what we are learning about the interpersonal dimension.

In conclusion, I wish to focus on two points. First, affective participation is important not just in the treatments where the patient clamors for recognition but in every treatment. This state of affairs cannot be helped, but it can be and often is overlooked. Second, there is no "guide" to this participation. It happens for better or worse, spontaneously and genuinely. The only "decision" to be made is whether to loosen our grip so that we may more readily experience the falls to the within.

All of this is captured in a personal parable of mine. I have always regarded affects as very much like pigments. This similarity was validated for me when I took a watercolor class. I soon discovered that this unruly medium seemed to have a mind utterly of its own. I unwittingly began to tame it by the painter's rule of abstinence—I gave it as little water as I could. I had become attached to the so-called "dry brush" technique. As a result, my rendering of the still life had clean edges—as it turned out, too clean. At the table I later realized was reserved for the advanced students, I was awed by the work of a woman who seemed to splatter paint everywhere on her paper. There were runs and sprays of color constantly surprising each other and eroding any sense of clear boundary. The artist herself seemed to barely look at the unrestrained signatures of her brush while she talked animatedly to various members of the class. The image that emerged on her pad was vibrant, beautiful, and coherent. I came to learn the definition of the technique she had mastered. It is called "wet on wet" painting.

This example allows me to narrow my thesis: I have come to believe that good treatment is a balance of dry brush and wet on wet techniques. An excess of either can lead to a less than satisfactory skew in the results. In every successful treatment, the patient and therapist create via wet brush a unique orchestration, whether we call it a better mutual integration (Mitchell, 1987), a new beginning (Ornstein, 1974), or a new object experience. Only by the patient and therapist's recognizing their mutual engagement will the dry brush efforts to frame and interpret have embodied meaning. If I might add a codicil to the legacy of Fairbairn: the ego is interaction seeking. In terms of the affects, I quote Baranger, Baranger, and Mom (1983): "He who doesn't cry doesn't get cured and he who doesn't cry doesn't cure" (p. 10).

REFERENCES

Atwood, G. & Stolorow, R. D. (1984), *Structures of Subjectivity.* Hillsdale, NJ: The Analytic Press.

Balint, M. (1968), *The Basic Fault.* London: Tavistock.

Baranger, M., Baranger, W. & Mom, J. (1983), Process and non process in analytic work. *Internat. J. Psycho-Anal., 64*:1–16.

Basch, M. (1976), The concept of affect: A re-examination. *J. Amer. Psychoanal. Assn., 24*:759–777.

Beebe, B., Jaffe, J. & Lachmann, F. M. (1992), A dyadic systems view of communication. In: *Relational Perspectives in Psychoanalysis,* ed. N. J. Skolnick & S. C. Warshaw. Hillsdale, NJ: The Analytic Press, pp. 61–82.

—— & Sloate, P. (1982), Assessment and treatment of difficulties in mother–infant attunement in the first three years of life: A case history. *Psychoanal. Inq., 1*:601–624.

Bion, W. R. (1977), Learning from experience. In: *Seven Servants.* New York: Aronson, pp. 1–111.

Boesky, D. (1990), The psychoanalytic process and its components. *Psychoanal. Quart., 59*:550–584.

Cooper, S. H. (1993), Interpretive fallibility and the psychoanalytic dialogue. *J. Amer. Psychoanal. Assn., 41*:95–126.

Demos, V. (1982), Affect in early infancy: Physiology or psychology? *Psychoanal. Inq., 1*:533–574.

—— (1984), Empathy and affect: Reflections on infant experience. In: *Empathy II,* ed. J. Lichtenberg, M. Bornstein & D. Silver. Hillsdale, NJ: The Analytic Press, pp. 9–34.

Dicks, H. V. (1967), *Marital Tensions.* New York: Basic Books.

Edelman, G. (1987), *Neural Darwinism.* New York: Basic Books.

Emde, R. N. (1991), Positive emotions for psychoanalytic theory: Surprises from infancy research and new directions. *J. Amer. Psychoanal. Assn. (Supplement), 39*:5–44.

Ferro, A. (1993), The impasse within a theory of the analytic field: Possible vertices of observation. *Internat. J. Psycho-Anal., 74*:917–930.

Fishman, G. (1993), Crisis of the moment. Unpublished manuscript.

Gill, M. (1982), *Analysis of the Transference, Vol 1.* New York: International Universities Press.

—— (1988), The interpersonal paradigm and the degree of the therapist's involvement. In: *Essential Papers on Countertransference,* ed. B. Wolstein. New York: New York University Press, pp. 304–338.

Gray, P. (1973), Psychoanalytic technique and the ego's capacity for viewing intrapsychic activity. *J. Amer. Psychoanal. Assn.,* 21:474–494.

—— (1990), The nature of therapeutic action in psychoanalysis. *J. Amer. Psychoanal. Assn.,* 38:1083–1097.

Greenberg, J., (1991), *Oedipus and Beyond: A Clinical Theory.* Cambridge, MA: Harvard University Press.

Hoffman, I. Z. (1979), The patient as interpreter of the analyst's experience. *Contemp. Psychoanal.,* 19:389–422.

—— (1992), Some practical implications of a social constructivist view of the psychoanalytic situation. *Psychoanal. Dial.,* 2:287–304.

Jacobs, T. (1986), On countertransference enactments. *J. Amer. Psychoanal. Assn.,* 34:289–307.

Kernberg, O. F. (1993), Convergences and divergences in contemporary psychoanalytic technique. *Internat. J. Psycho-Anal.,* 74:659–674.

Kohut, H. (1984), *How Does Analysis Cure?* Chicago: University of Chicago Press.

Kris, A. (1982), *Free Association.* New Haven, CT: Yale University Press.

—— (1990), Helping patients by analyzing self-criticism. *J. Amer. Psychoanal. Assn.,* 38:605–636.

Lichtenberg, J., Lachmann, F. M. & Fosshage, J. L. (1992), *Self and Motivational Systems: Toward a Theory of Psychoanalytic Technique.* Hillsdale, NJ: The Analytic Press.

Margulies, A. (1993), Empathy, virtuality, and the birth of complex emotional states. In: *Human Feelings,* ed. S. L. Ablon, D. Brown, E. J. Khantzian & J. E. Mack. Hillsdale, NJ: The Analytic Press.

McLaughlin, J. T. (1987), The play of transference: Some reflections on enactment in the psychoanalytic situation. *J. Amer. Psychoanal. Assn.,* 35:557–582.

—— (1991), Clinical and theoretical aspects of enactment. *J. Amer. Psychoanal. Assn.,* 39:595–614.

Mitchell, S. A. (1987), *Relational Concepts in Psychoanalysis.* Cambridge, MA: Harvard University Press.

Modell, A. H. (1990), *Other Times and Other Realities.* Cambridge, MA: Harvard University Press.

Ogden, T. J. (1982), *Projective Identification and Psychotherapeutic Technique.* New York: Aronson.

—— (1986), *The Matrix of the Mind.* Northvale, NJ: Aronson.

Ornstein, A. (1974), The dread to repeat and the new beginning. *The Annual of Psychoanalysis,* 2:231–248, New York: International Universities Press.

Renik, O. (1993a), Analytic interaction: Conceptualizing technique in the light of the analyst's irreducible subjectivity. *Psychoanal. Quart.,* 62:553–571.

—— (1993b), Countertransference enactment and the psychoanalytic process. In: *Psychic Structure and Psychic Change, Essays in Honor of Robert S. Wallerstein, M.D.,* ed. M. J. Horowitz, O. F. Kernberg & E. M. Weinshel. Madison, CT: International Universities Press, pp. 135–158.

Russell, P. (1993), Crises of attachment. Unpublished manuscript.

Sandler, J. (1976), Countertransference and role responsiveness. *Internat. Rev. Psycho-Anal.,* 3:43–47.

——— & Sandler, A. M. (1978), On the development of object relationships and affects. *Internat. J. Psycho-Anal.*, 59:285–296.

Schwaber, E. A. (1990), Interpretation and the therapeutic action of psychoanalysis. *Internat. J. Psycho-Anal.*, 71:229–240.

——— (1992a), Psychoanalytic theory and its relation to clinical work. *J. Amer. Psychoanal. Assn.*, 40:1039–1058.

——— (1992b), Countertransference: The analyst's retreat from the patient's vantage point. *Internat. J. Psycho-Anal.*, 73:349–362.

Solyom, A. E. (1987), New research on affect regulation: Developmental, clinical, and theoretical considerations. *Psychoanal. Inq.*, 7:331–347.

Spence, D. P. (1982), *Narrative Truth and Historical Truth*. New York: Norton.

——— (1987), *The Freudian Metaphor.* New York: Norton.

Stern, D. (1985), *The Interpersonal World of the Infant.* New York: Basic Books.

Stolorow, R. D., Brandchaft, B. & Atwood, G. (1987), *Psychoanalytic Treatment: An Intersubjective Approach.* Hillsdale, NJ: The Analytic Press.

Strachey, J. (1934), The nature of the therapeutic action of psychoanalysis. *Internat. J. Psycho-Anal.*, 15:127–159.

Tansey, M. J. & Burke, W. F. (1989), *Understanding Countertransference.* Hillsdale, NJ: The Analytic Press.

Tomkins, S. S. (1991), *Affect, Imagery, Consciousness, Vol. 3: The Negative Affects: Anger and Fear.* New York: Springer.

Tronick, E., Cohn, J. & Shea, E. (1986), The transfer of affect between mothers and infants. In: *Affective Development in Infancy,* ed. T. B. Brazelton & M. W. Yogman. Norwood, NJ: Ablex, pp. 11–26.

Trop, J. L. & Stolorow, R. D. (1992), Defense analysis in self psychology: A developmental view. *Psychoanal. Dial.*, 2:427–442.

14

From Structural Conflict to Relational Conflict

A Contemporary Model of Therapeutic Action

Martha Stark

N umerous papers have been written about the therapeutic action of psychodynamic psychotherapy, and numerous authors have addressed the issue of what it is about the therapeutic process that is actually curative. I think Stephen Mitchell (1988) offers one of the most clinically useful ways to categorize the different theories of therapeutic action. He delineates three: the drive-conflict model, the deficiency-compensation model, and the relational-conflict model. The first is a theory about structural conflict, the second is a theory about structural deficit, and the third is a theory about relational conflict.

Mitchell suggests that although clinicians work in a complex combination of ways, most of them either consciously or unconsciously conceive of the therapeutic action of psychodynamic psychotherapy as involving primarily the resolution of structural conflict, the filling in of structural deficit, or the resolution of relational conflict.

In what follows, for the sake of clarity I will be using the pronoun "he" instead of the more cumbersome "he/she."

I will begin by highlighting some of the essential features of each of these three different theories of therapeutic action.

THE DRIVE-CONFLICT MODEL OF THERAPEUTIC ACTION

First is the drive-conflict model of classical psychoanalysis, in which patients are said to suffer from structural conflict—conflict between id impulse pressing "yes" and ego defense countering "no" (with the superego coming down usually on the side of the ego). The therapeutic action involves resolution of such conflict by way of interpretation, particularly interpretation of the transference.

Paula Heimann (1956) once suggested that the therapist must repeatedly ask himself the following question: "Why is the patient now doing what to whom?" (p. 307). The answer to this question constitutes the transference interpretation. And as the patient comes to understand, deeply, why he is now doing what to whom, he gains insight into the internal workings of his mind.

As the ego gains insight by way of such interpretations, the ego becomes stronger. The increased ego strength enables the ego to experience less anxiety in relation to the id. The ego's defenses therefore become less necessary, the tension between id and ego is eased, the patient becomes less conflicted, and we speak of the patient's conflict as having been resolved.

It was, of course, Freud who put forth this theory of therapeutic action. He believed that if the therapist could but unearth the secrets of the patient's unconscious, making the patient conscious of what had once been unconscious, then the expanded knowledge and increased ego strength would facilitate resolution of the patient's structural conflict. Freud believed that the "truth" (buried within the patient) would set the patient free. Jacques Lacan (cited in Levenson, 1991) has said, "To end therapy successfully, we must know what he [the therapist] knows, which is, in essence, nothing we didn't already know" (p. 8).

Ultimately, it is a one-person theory of therapeutic action, relying as it does upon interpretation and insight—not upon relationship and experience.

This first model, then, is a drive-conflict (or conflict-resolution) model of therapeutic action.

THE DEFICIENCY-COMPENSATION MODEL OF THERAPEUTIC ACTION

Second is the deficiency-compensation (or developmental-arrest) model. No longer is insight thought to be the curative factor; rather, a "corrective experience" is thought to be what heals.

Morris Eagle (1984) has captured well the essence of such a position with the following: "If . . . one conceptualizes pathology in terms of developmental defects, then the therapeutic aim is some sort of repair of this defect—usually via the therapeutic relationship" (p. 134). The second model is thus a two-person theory of therapeutic action, with the therapist no longer just an observer but a participant as well.

In a deficiency-compensation model the patient is seen as suffering not from conflict but from deficit. The deficit is thought to arise in the context of failure in the early-on environmental provision, failure in the early-on relationship between infant and caregiver (or "mothering person"). Now the therapeutic aim is the provision of that which was not provided by the mother early on. It is in the context of this new relationship between patient and therapist that the opportunity exists for reparation—the new relationship a corrective for the old one.

Making good a deficiency is at the heart of what heals. The healing involves, then, a real experience in the present with a new object, a relationship in the here-and-now that is compensatory for damage sustained early on at the hands of the infantile object.

Those who embrace the first theory, the drive-conflict theory of therapeutic action, conceive of the therapist as an objective observer positioned outside the therapeutic field, the therapist a more or less neutral screen onto which the patient casts shadows that are then interpreted by the therapist. Those who embrace this second theory, the deficiency-compensation theory of therapeutic action, conceive of the therapist as also a participant—a new good object able to provide a corrective experience.

Self psychologists are major proponents of the deficiency-compensation theory. Some of them believe that it is the experience of gratification itself that is compensatory and ultimately healing. Most of them, however, believe that it is the experience of working through frustration against a backdrop of gratification that promotes structural growth. In other words, most of them believe that if there is no frustration of need, no thwarting of desire, then there will be nothing that needs to be mastered and therefore no impetus for internalization and the laying down of psychic structure. Growing up (the task of the child) and getting better (the task of the patient) have to do with learning to master the disenchantment that comes with the recognition of just how imperfect the world really is—optimal disillusionment.

I am here reminded of a *New Yorker* cartoon in which a gentleman, seated at a table in a restaurant by the name of The Disillusionment Cafe, is awaiting the arrival of his order. The waiter returns to his table and announces, "Your order is not ready, nor will it ever be."

According to self psychology, when the selfobject therapist has been experienced as gratifying (or "good") and is then experienced as frustrating (or "bad"), the patient deals with his disappointment by taking in the good that had been there prior to the introduction of the bad—which enables him to preserve internally a piece of the original experience of external goodness. These transmuting internalizations are part of the grieving process and are the way the patient masters his disappointment.

As the patient grieves, he must feel, to the very depths of his soul, his anguish and his outrage that his infantile objects were as they were, the transference object is as it is, and his contemporary objects are as they are. The patient must come to accept the fact that he is ultimately powerless to do anything to make his objects, both past and present, different. He may be able to change himself, but he will never be able to change his objects.

Within the context of the safety provided by the relationship with his therapist, the patient will be able to feel, at last, the pain against which he has spent a lifetime defending himself. Such is the work of grieving— and surviving the experience of having had and then lost.

Until the patient can confront the reality that his objects are as they are, then he will be destined to feel helplessly unhappy. As long as the patient locates the responsibility for change within others and experiences the locus of control as external, he will be consigning himself to a lifetime of chronic frustration and angry dissatisfaction. Only as the patient confronts the pain of his disappointment, doing now what he could not possibly do as a child, will he get better.

As Sheldon Kopp (1969) has written, "Genuine grief is the sobbing and wailing which express the acceptance of our helplessness to do anything about losses" (p. 30). Later he remarks, "By no longer refusing to mourn the loss of the parents whom he wished for but never had, [the patient] can get to keep whatever was really there for him" (p. 33).

Self psychology is ultimately a theory about grieving—grieving the loss of illusions about the perfection (or the perfectibility) of the object. It is about paradise lost—having illusions, losing them, and then recovering from their loss. It is about transformation of infantile need into mature capacity, that is, transformation of the infantile need for one's objects to be other than, better than, who they are into the capacity to accept them as they are.

Self psychology is about optimal disillusionment, transmuting internalization, accretion of internal structure—in other words, working through disruptions of the selfobject (or positive) transference. Internalized selfobject functions become psychic structures that enable the person to have capacity—where once he had need.

To this point, then, we have addressed ourselves to the first and second models of therapeutic action. The first model of therapeutic action, the drive-conflict model, speaks to the importance of insight and the rendering conscious of what had once been unconscious. The second model of therapeutic action, the deficiency-compensation model, speaks to how important it is that the patient have a corrective experience with a new good object.

THE RELATIONAL-CONFLICT MODEL OF THERAPEUTIC ACTION

As we shift now to a consideration of the third model of therapeutic action, I would like to make the rather bold claim that there are times when the patient needs the therapist to participate not as a good object but as a bad object, the old bad object, and exerts pressure on the therapist to become that object. It is the patient's need to be in relationship with the old bad object that is addressed by the third model of therapeutic action, the relational-conflict model espoused by a number of contemporary psychoanalytic theorists, including Joseph Sandler (1976), Merton Gill (1982), Irwin Hoffman (1983), Patrick Casement (1985), Jay Greenberg (1986), Christopher Bollas (1987), Stephen Mitchell (1988), and Lewis Aron (1990).

Whereas most of those who embrace the deficiency-compensation model of therapeutic action emphasize the patient's lack of conflict about being in relationship with a new good object, most of those who embrace the relational-conflict model believe that the patient is conflicted about being in relationship with new good objects. This third model emphasizes, therefore, not structural conflict but relational conflict.

In order to help us understand this third model, let us consider the following: In the psychoanalytic literature, reference is repeatedly made to the idea that the therapeutic setting recreates symbolically the early-on relationship between mother and child. What exactly does this mean? Does it mean the creation of a new good relationship unlike anything this patient has ever before experienced? Or does it mean a recreation of the old bad relationship that this patient actually had?

In fact, it means sometimes the creation of something new and good (which is addressed by the deficiency-compensation model) and sometimes a recreation of something old and bad (which is addressed by the relational-conflict model).

When the patient has had the experience of "not enough good" early on and, as a result, now has a deficit or an impaired capacity, then the patient must have the opportunity to experience "new good" in the relationship with his therapist in order to fill in the structural deficit.

The relational-conflict theorist, however, is interested not only in the experience of not enough good early on but also in the experience of "too much bad," as happens when the patient has been traumatized— whether emotionally, physically, or sexually. When the patient has had the experience of too much bad early on, it is internally recorded in the form of pathogenic introjects or internal bad objects. At any time, these pathogenic structures can be activated and delivered (by way of projection) into the treatment situation, thereby contaminating the patient's relationship with his therapist. As a result, the patient will have difficulty experiencing the therapist as, simply, a new good object—which is why the traumatized patient is said to suffer from conflict about being in relationship with new good objects.

The relational-conflict theorist contends, therefore, that when the patient has had the experience of too much bad early on, then—in order to resolve his relational conflict—he must have the opportunity to rework the internalized trauma by experiencing first old bad in the relationship with his therapist and then "bad-become-good."

Jay Greenberg (1986) writes, "If the analyst cannot be experienced as a new object, the analysis never gets under way; if he cannot be experienced as an old one, it never ends" (p. 98)—which captures exquisitely the delicate balance between the therapist's participation as a new good object (so that there can be a "starting over" or a "new beginning") and the therapist's participation as the old bad object (so that there can be a reworking of the internalized trauma).

In the relational-conflict model, therefore, the therapeutic setting is thought to offer the patient an opportunity to recreate in the here-and-now the original environmental failure situation, an opportunity to relive, to reexperience, indeed, to reenact, within the patient–therapist relationship, the original trauma.

This time, however, because the therapist is not in fact as bad as the parent had been, there can be a different outcome. Ultimately, the therapist must challenge the patient's projections by lending aspects of his otherness (or, as Winnicott (1965) would say, his "externality") to the interaction, so that the patient will be able to have the experience of something that is "other-than-me" and can take that in. What he internalizes will be an amalgam, part contributed by the patient (the original projection) and part contributed by the therapist, part old and part new. There is repetition of the original trauma but with a much healthier resolution this time—the repetition leading to modification of the patient's internal world and integration on a higher level. I am suggesting, therefore, that the patient has, often simultaneously, both a need for the therapist to be the good parent he never had (which is addressed by the deficiency-compensation model) and a need for the therapist to be the bad parent he did have (which is addressed by the relational-conflict model).

And so it is that the patient brings to the relationship with his therapist a need for the old bad object—in other words, a need to be failed. The need is to be now failed (as he was once failed) but to have the opportunity, this time, to accuse the wrongdoer (or perpetrator) and to encounter a response different from, and better than, the original response. Repeated experiences of bad-become-good will, over time, transform the patient's need for bad into a capacity to tolerate good—thereby resolving the patient's conflict about being in relationship with new good objects.

If the therapist never allows himself to be drawn into participating with the patient in his reenactments, we speak of a failure of empathy. If, however, the therapist allows himself to be drawn into the patient's internal dramas but then gets lost in the reenactment, then we speak of a failure of containment.

It is such a fine line that the therapist must tread. On the one hand, the therapist must have the capacity to respond empathically to the patient's need to be failed, the patient's need to have the therapist be the old bad object. On the other hand, the therapist must also have the capacity to step back from his participation in the reenactment in order to provide containment.

Relational-conflict theorists believe that the patient will draw the therapist into his dramatic reenactments just as he has drawn everyone else in. The therapist is not expected to avoid this unwitting participation, but what is expected of him is that he be able to recognize such participation once it is in process and that he have the capacity to do something about it.

With respect to the countertransference, whereas both the drive-conflict theorist and the deficiency-compensation theorist conceive of the therapist's countertransference as avoidable and, when it does occur, as undesirable, the relational-conflict theorist conceives of the therapist's countertransferential participation in the patient's transferential reenactments as inevitable and even desirable.

If the therapist has the wisdom to recognize and the integrity to acknowledge his countertransferential participation, then patient and therapist can go on to look at the patient's transferential need to be failed in old, familiar ways. The patient will have the opportunity to understand his investment in getting his objects to fail him, that is, his compulsive need to recreate with his contemporary objects the early-on traumatic failure situation. Patient and therapist together will be able to observe the power of the patient's repetition compulsion—namely, that here too the patient has succeeded in recapitulating the past in the present, repeating in the transference that which the patient cannot remember and has not yet resolved (but needs to remember and must eventually resolve).

If the therapist has both the capacity to respond empathically to the patient's need to be failed and the capacity to provide, ultimately, containment, then the patient will be able to have the powerfully healing experience of bad-become-good.

This model is clearly a two-person theory of therapeutic action—but whereas the deficiency-compensation model involves the therapist's participation as a new good object, the relational-conflict model involves the therapist's participation first as the old bad object and then as a new good object.

CLINICAL VIGNETTE

To demonstrate the relational-conflict model in action, I will present a clinical vignette that speaks to the patient's need to be failed by her therapist. It is a story about a patient of mine, Ann, with whom I worked for many years.

Periodically Ann would fault me for being unempathic. I would take seriously her claim that I was being unempathic and would ask, specifically, about what I might have done or said that was unempathic. Ann, however, was never quite able to come up with any real evidence of empathic failure on my part. So it would be clear to us both that it was a case of "mistaken identity"—that she was inaccurately perceiving me as her bad, unempathic mother. Once she understood that we were talking about distortion, not reality, that the "real" object of her anger was her mother, not I, then she would dutifully rail against her mother.

Over the course of the first few years of our work together, Ann frequently faulted me for lacking empathy but never was she able to provide any real proof to support this. Repeatedly I would offer her my genetic interpretation of her transference distortion, namely, that her misperception of me—as unempathic—must speak to how unresolved she still was about her mother.

I was failing to recognize that the negative transference kept emerging because I was not doing something quite right. Whenever a patient complains again and again about a specific something with respect to the therapist, then the therapist is probably doing something wrong—if not the specific something about which the patient is complaining, then something else.

In this particular situation, I was not fully appreciating Ann's investment in getting me to be her unempathic mother. I was not fully appreciating her need to have me fail her. Over and over again, Ann was delivering her need to be failed into the treatment situation; over and over again, I was thwarting it. By being so unflinchingly "empathic," I was actually being unempathic.

As long as I refused to accept her projections, as long as I refused to participate with her in her reenactments, I could not really be available to her as an effective transference object. I had my own need—to be empathic no matter what!—and so, unwittingly, was not really letting Ann use the transference to work through the unresolved relationship with her toxic mother.

As Paul Wachtel (1986) has observed, "[I]t is in the very act of participating that the analyst learns what it is most important to know about the patient" (p. 63). By remaining more observer than participant, I was, in effect, denying myself access to important information about just how attached my patient was to her unavailable mother.

And so things continued in this way for several years. In the meantime, of course, we were getting other kinds of work done, but we were not making any real headway in terms of the patient's repeated experience of the objects in her world as "not understanding."

At the end of our third year, however, there came a session in which something different happened. Ann, as usual, faulted me for being unempathic; also, as usual, we looked at what I might have done or said that would be making her experience me in this way. In fact, this time she did have evidence—which I shall recount in a moment. Let me first say, however, that as soon as Ann protested my lack of empathy, I realized that indeed I had been incredibly unempathic. Furthermore, as I thought about it, I recognized that I felt strangely elated, even glad that I had said what I had.

Ann had been talking about how upset she was about her parents' sudden announcement that they were getting a divorce. Not only was I not with her in her obvious upset, but I was absolutely delighted that her parents were finally getting out of what had been an absolutely horrid, mutually destructive relationship.

And so instead of "Oh, that's terrible," I blurted out something to the effect of "Wow, that's great!"

Now what was really happening?

First, I was probably carrying, on Ann's behalf, the pleasure she felt but could not acknowledge about the fact that her parents were at last getting the long-awaited divorce; she could not let herself experience pleasure about that because it made her feel too guilty, too disloyal. Second, and more important, I was finally willing to let myself be drawn into Ann's internal drama, willing to let myself become a player on her stage.

And so she had finally succeeded in getting me to become her bad, unempathic mother, thereby recreating with me—in fact and not just in fantasy—the early-on relationship with her mother.

I am, of course, speaking of projective identification, in which the patient exerts pressure on the therapist to accept her projections and to participate as the old bad object.

But now there was opportunity, where before there was not—opportunity for the patient to have, ultimately, the experience of bad-become-good.

I immediately apologized to Ann for having been so outrageously unsympathetic at a time when I knew that a part of her desperately wanted my support. In acknowledging my error and apologizing for it, which is something her mother had never done, I was introducing something new. Ann had never before had the experience of being wronged and then of having that wrong acknowledged and an apology offered.

In short, by allowing myself to be made bad, I was accepting Ann's projection. But, by demonstrating my willingness to own my unempathic behavior and by offering her an apology for having been so unsupportive, I was showing her that I was not, in fact, as bad as she had feared I might be. I was providing a form of ''corrective feedback.''

To repeat what I said earlier: When there is the internal absence of good (in the form of deficit or impaired capacity), the patient must be given the opportunity to deliver his need for good into the relationship with his therapist. Gradual internalization of the good encountered there is the process by which the internal absence of good is corrected for.

But when there is the internal presence of bad (in the form of pathogenic introjects that are the internal records of early-on traumas), the patient may not be able to experience the object as good because of the patient's conflict about being in relationship with new good objects. When the patient's traumatic history has been internally recorded and structuralized in the form of internal bad objects, the patient must be given the opportunity to detoxify these pathogenic structures before he will be able to experience new good.

This can be done when the patient is able to recreate with the therapist the interactional dynamic that had characterized the original relationship with the toxic parent. A negative transference will emerge in which the therapist is either experienced as the old bad parent (if projection is involved) or made to become the old bad parent (if projective identification is involved).

It is by working through the negative transference that the patient's relational conflict will be resolved and the patient's need to experience his therapist as the old bad object will gradually become transformed into the capacity to experience him as a new good object. It is this working-through process that will enable the patient to master the original trauma and to transform it into healthy structure and capacity.

As for Ann, after we worked through my failure of her she was able, finally, to separate from her mother and, at last, to relinquish her investment in being failed. As her conflict about being in relationship with good objects was resolved, her need to be misunderstood became transformed into a capacity to tolerate having someone really be there for her.

Interestingly, never again has Ann mistakenly experienced me as unempathic.

To summarize, the second model (the deficiency-compensation model) stresses the therapist's participation as a new good object, whereas this third model (the relational-conflict model) stresses the therapist's participation as first the old bad object and then a new good object.

The second model conceives of the therapeutic action of psychodynamic psychotherapy as involving correction for the internal absence of good by way of working through disruptions of the positive transference, whereas the third model conceives of the therapeutic action as involving correction for the internal presence of bad by way of working through the negative transference—that is, working with the positive transference in order to fill in structural deficit in the one instance and working with the negative transference in order to resolve relational conflict in the other instance.

Incidentally, the deficiency-compensation model pays little attention to the internal presence of bad; in fact, self psychologists have no place in their theory for pathogenic introjects. Reinforced need, increased vulnerability, and impaired capacity, yes—but no pathogenic introjects or internal bad objects. It is to the third model that we must look in order to understand the patient's intense attachments to his internal bad objects and his compelling need to recreate with the therapist the interactional dynamic that had characterized the early-on relationship with the traumatizing parent.

A SECOND CLINICAL VIGNETTE

To demonstrate another instance of the relational-conflict model in action, let me offer the following vignette from Patrick Casement's 1985 book *On Learning from the Patient.*

A female therapist was seeing a patient in three-times-a-week psychotherapy. The patient, Ms. G, had been traumatized as a child by her mother's repeated absences. The mother had had cancer, was hospitalized on several occasions, and died when the patient was 4 years old.

In therapy the patient was able to recognize that she had felt responsible for her mother's death, that she had linked her intense need for her mother to the mother's repeated absences and eventual disappearance.

Ms. G frequently failed to show up for sessions; and, when she did come, she was usually late. The therapist began to recognize that Ms. G was making her feel as abandoned and uncertain as Ms. G (in the face of her mother's repeated disappearances and eventual death) must have felt when she was a little girl.

The therapist was then able to interpret to Ms. G her awareness of how unbearable it must have been when she (the patient) was so often left in the state of not knowing what was happening to her mother.

Meanwhile, the therapist never lost sight of how important it was to Ms. G that she (the therapist) always be there for the sessions, whether the patient came or not. The therapist knew that her own reliability and ongoing constancy were crucial.

But one morning the therapist overslept. Ms. G arrived at her therapist's office for her early morning session, only to find herself shut out. She remained outside the locked door until the cleaner arrived. For the duration of what would have been her appointment, she was looked after by this cleaner, who expressed particular concern about the therapist's absence because it was so unusual for her not to be there.

Ms. G was of course terribly frightened that something really serious had happened to her therapist. Perhaps there had been an accident, or her therapist had been hospitalized, or she had even died.

How are we to understand this sequence of events?

We remember that Ms. G had long been concerned that it was her dependence on her mother and the intensity of her need that had proved too much for her mother and ultimately killed her.

"It is uncanny," writes Casement, "how this therapist unconsciously reproduced a real failure in the therapy which was so close to the experience of her patient's own childhood trauma" (p. 90). It is uncanny that there was such a dramatic repetition in the transference of the early-on traumatic failure situation.

Casement goes on to say that "when a patient is confronted by a real issue like this, about which he or she can be genuinely angry with the therapist in the present, it can . . . become a pivotal experience in the therapy" (pp. 90–91).

And Winnicott (1963) elaborates on this with the following:

> [C]orrective provision is never enough. . . . In the end the patient uses the analyst's failures, often quite small ones, perhaps manoeuvred by the patient. . . . The operative factor is that the patient now hates the analyst for the failure that originally came as an environmental factor, outside the infant's area of omnipotent control, but that is *now* staged in the transference. So in the end we succeed by failing—failing the patient's way. This is a long distance from the simple theory of cure by corrective experience [p. 258].

In the relational-conflict model, which involves a staging in the transference of the early-on traumatic failure situation, this is exactly what happens.

We have all been trained to understand that we, as therapists, will often fail our patients because of our own unresolved issues—in Winnicott's words, our subjective countertransference. The relational-conflict model, however, enables us to understand that some of our failures are staged by the patient and are therefore instances of objective countertransference. In response to the patient's need to be failed, we may well end up failing the patient in the ways that his parent had failed him.

The patient gets us to fail him in ways specifically determined by his past—and we must be able to let the patient make us fail him in such ways. It is how we then deal with our failure of the patient, that is, the capacity we bring to the working-through process, that will determine whether the patient is retraumatized or helped to achieve belated mastery.

EMPATHIC FAILURES DETERMINED BY THE PATIENT'S HISTORY

Only in the past several years have I come to understand an important relationship between the deficiency-compensation model and the relational-conflict model. It has to do with the empathic failures of self psychology (self psychology, as we have seen, is a deficiency-compensation model).

I knew that selfobject transferences were inevitably disrupted by the therapist's empathic failures. And I knew that therapists were thought to have failed the patient empathically when they had failed to perform the selfobject function assigned them by the patient.

In fact, therapists will fail their patients repeatedly and will make many mistakes. I had assumed that such failures were more or less random events, but that the mistakes the patient picked up on (and experienced as devastatingly unempathic) would be those to which the patient was particularly sensitized because of his early-on history. For example, a hitherto punctual therapist might happen one day to be late, which would be very upsetting for a patient whose parent was unreliable. Or a therapist who was not ordinarily critical might happen one day to say something that either seemed to the patient to be critical or was actually critical, which would be very painful for a patient whose parent was judgmental.

I am now coming to understand, however, that in fact many of the therapist's so-called inevitable empathic failures are not random events that just happen, but rather specific events that are very much determined by the patient's history. The therapist, ever responsive to the patient's need to be failed and to the pressure exerted on him by the patient to become the old bad object, may well allow himself, unwittingly, to be drawn into failing the patient in ways specifically determined by the patient's traumatic history.

In other words, it is not just that the therapist has a profound impact on the patient but that the patient has a profound impact on the therapist and that the therapist's empathic failures are indeed sometimes "manoeuvred" by the patient, as Winnicott so astutely observed. In fact, one might even say that some of the therapist's failures of the patient arise from the therapist's empathic attunement to what the patient most needs in order to achieve belated mastery.

I am talking, of course, about the connection between the deficiency-compensation model of self psychology that highlights the therapist's inevitable empathic failures and the relational-conflict model of contemporary psychoanalytic theory that involves the patient's recreation in the here-and-now of the early-on traumatic failure situation. In essence, I am talking about the relationship between empathic failure and projective identification.

In the example Casement (1985) offers, Ms. G had unconsciously prompted her therapist to fail her in ways specifically determined by her traumatic history. Casement writes, "The nature of this failure had a terrifying similarity for the patient to her own childhood trauma. She consequently experienced, in the present with her therapist, her own obliterating anger that belonged to the original trauma" (p. 91).

Casement continues, "The patient was able to find in this experience a real opportunity to *use* her therapist to represent the mother who had 'failed' her, who had inexplicably shut her out by not being there. She could now begin to attack her therapist with her own strongest feelings about that earlier (and this present) failure, with her therapist surviving these attacks of rage upon her" (pp. 91–92).

Winnicott (1969) writes about how important it is that the therapist survive the patient's attempts to destroy him, how important it is that the therapist demonstrate indestructibility in the face of the patient's outrage. The key to this survival is to be found in the patient's discovery that the therapist has a strength that is not created by the patient, a strength that is outside the sphere of the patient's omnipotence, something new and good that derives from the therapist and that can then be taken in by the patient.

In the example above, when the therapist, by surviving the patient's rage about being abandoned, is able to demonstrate that she is not the old, bad, abandoning object but a new, good, resilient object with internal resources, someone who does not collapse, does not retaliate, and does not withdraw in the face of the patient's intense feelings, it is a powerfully corrective experience for the patient—the experience of bad-become-good.

The case of Ms. G is a dramatic illustration of the relational-conflict model in action.

SUMMARY

How does contemporary psychoanalysis conceive of the therapeutic action of psychodynamic psychotherapy?

Where once the focus was on the patient's attaining insight by way of interpretation, now it is thought that a "corrective experience" by way of the relationship itself between patient and therapist may sometimes be necessary to supplement the interpretive work.

Where once structural conflict was in the limelight, now structural deficit and relational conflict have assumed center stage.

Where once psychoanalysis was conceptualized as a one-person theory of therapeutic action with the important relationships being those that existed among id, ego, and superego, now psychoanalysis is also conceptualized as a two-person theory with the important relationships being those that exist between the patient and his objects.

Where once the therapist was thought to be an observer, for the most part neutral but periodically misperceived by the patient as someone he was not, now it is believed that an important part of what makes the therapist an effective transference object is his actual participation as either a new good object or the old bad object.

Where once countertransference was thought to be avoidable and, if it did occur, undesirable, now countertransference is seen as inevitable and as offering the therapist one of the most effective ways to understand the internal workings of the patient's mind.

From structural conflict to structural deficit to relational conflict, we have come a long way in terms of our understanding of the therapeutic action of psychodynamic psychotherapy.

REFERENCES

Aron, L. (1990), One person and two person psychologies and the method of psychoanalysis. *Psychoanal. Psychol.,* 7:475–485.

Bollas, C. (1987), Expressive uses of the countertransference: Notes to the patient from oneself. In: *The Shadow of the Object.* New York: Columbia University Press, pp. 200–235.

Casement, P. (1985), Forms of interactive communication. In: *On Learning from the Patient*. London: Tavistock, pp. 72–101.

Eagle, M. (1984), *Recent Developments in Psychoanalysis*. New York: McGraw-Hill.

Gill, M. (1982), The interpersonal paradigm and the degree of the therapist's involvement. *Contemp. Psychoanal.*, 19:200–237.

Greenberg, J. (1986), Theoretical models and the analyst's neutrality. *Contemp. Psychoanal.*, 22:87–106.

Heimann, P. (1956), Dynamics of transference interpretations. *Internat. J. Psycho-Anal.*, 37:303–310.

Hoffman, I. (1983), The patient as interpreter of the analyst's experience. *Contemp. Psychoanal.*, 19:389–422.

Kopp, S. (1969), The refusal to mourn. *Voices*, Spring, pp. 30–35.

Levenson, E. A. (1991), *The Purloined Self*. New York: Contemporary Psychoanalysis Books—William Alanson White Institute.

Mitchell, S. A. (1988), Penelope's loom: Psychopathology and the analytic process. In: *Relational Concepts in Psychoanalysis*. Cambridge, MA: Harvard University Press, pp. 271–306.

Sandler, J. (1976), Countertransference and role-responsiveness. *Internat. Rev. Psycho-Anal.*, 3:43–47.

Wachtel, P. L. (1986), From neutrality to personal revelation: Patterns of influence in the analytic relationship. *Contemp. Psychoanal.*, 22:60–70.

Winnicott, D. W. (1963), Dependence in infant-care, in child-care, and in the psycho-analytic setting. In: *The Maturational Processes and the Facilitating Environment*. New York: International Universities Press, 1965, pp. 249–259.

—— (1965), *The Maturational Processes and the Facilitating Environment*. New York: International Universities Press.

—— (1969), The use of an object. *Internat. J. Psycho-Anal.*, 50:711–716.

Index

253